M000312426

013195

The
Committed
Word

James Engell

The Committed Word

Literature and Public Values

The Pennsylvania State University Press
University Park, Pennsylvania

Library of Congress Cataloging-in-Publication Data

Engell, James, 1951–
    The committed word : literature and public values / James Engell.
        p.   cm.
    Includes bibliographical references and index.
    ISBN 0-271-01890-9 (cloth : alk. paper)
        1. English literature—18th century—History and criticism.
    2. English language—18th century—Rhetoric.   3. Rhetoric—Political
    aspects.   4. Literature and society.   5. Public interest.
    I. Title.
    PR442.E47   1999
    808—dc21   98-43336
                                                                              CIP

Copyright © 1999 The Pennsylvania State University
All rights reserved
Printed in the United States of America
Published by The Pennsylvania State University Press,
University Park, PA 16802-1003

It is the policy of The Pennsylvania State University Press to use acid-free paper for the first
printing of all clothbound books. Publications on uncoated stock satisfy the minimum
requirements of American National Standard for Information Sciences—Permanence of
Paper for Printed Library Materials, ANSI Z39.48–1992.

To
John Engell

If literature is not everything, it is worth nothing. This is what I mean by "commitment." It wilts if it is reduced to innocence or to songs. If a written sentence does not reverberate at every level of man and society, then it makes no sense. What is the literature of an epoch but the epoch appropriated by its literature?

—Jean-Paul Sartre, *The Purpose of Writing*

Culture's worth huge, huge risks. Without culture we're all totalitarian beasts. After all, what technology promises is that . . . the world is ours to dominate. The only thing that stands up against that is culture. And culture is more than just being able to get it on CD-ROM. Culture is going into the library, and finding an old book on an old shelf, and opening it, and it has the patina of the past and maybe hasn't been taken out in five years, and that's part of its virtue at this point. There's a small communion that takes place between the book and yourself, and that's what's disappearing.

—Norman Mailer, in *New Left Review*

Contents

List of Illustrations   viii
Preface and Acknowledgments   ix

1   The Committed Word   1
2   Burke's Poetry and Prophecy   15
3   Pope's American Constitution   33
4   Swift Considers Words, Intelligence, and the Academy   51
5   Hume's Cultural Critique   63
6   Vico Tells the Story of Stories   81
7   The Politics of Greed   99
8   Robert Lowth, Unacknowledged Legislator   119
9   Lincoln's Language, and Ours   141
10   Recommitment   163

Notes   175
Index   193

List of Illustrations

Frederick Douglass, attributed to Elisha Hammond	11
Caleb Bingham, *The Columbian Orator,* title page	12
Caricature of Burke by James Gillray	28
Shays's Rebellion, pardon by Governor James Bowdoin	37
The mechanical frame of signifiers, *Gulliver's Travels*	55
David Hume by Allan Ramsay	72
Giambattista Vico, *La Scienza nuova,* frontispiece	96
"the King" scratched out: autograph lines, Pope's *To Bathurst*	117
Robert Lowth	127
Autograph fragment of Lincoln's "House Divided" speech	144
Lincoln and son Tad, photograph by Anthony Berger	159

Preface and Acknowledgments

The Committed Word attempts to augment the ways we have come to regard literature, and to reawaken literary qualities of language in our deliberations over public values and expressions of cultural life. I also hope to suggest how education in rhetoric, now often misunderstood or neglected, can serve the common good without becoming mired in either partisan squabbles or academic pedantry. I have tried to employ an accessible style open to the reader who is not a specialist. Each essay in this book reveals how an individual, often now not known primarily as an author or writer, masters language in the hope of imparting pleasure but also of changing society and commenting on the human condition. Together, these profiles explore how committed individuals, despite different purposes and professions, and despite the varied tenor of governments familiar to them, resort to heightened language in order to secure knowledge, test beliefs, deliberate policy, and promote action.

This book benefited from the observations and insights of numerous colleagues and critics. Their suggestions have sharpened each essay, and my debts are many. My sincere appreciation goes to Hugh Amory, James Basker, Lawrence Buell, Gerald Chapman, Kevin Cope, Anthony Dangerfield, Viscountess Eccles, John Engell, John Faulkner, Christopher Fox, A. C. Goodson, Alan Heimert, Gwin Kolb, Beth Kowaleski-Wallace, James Kugel, Samuel Longmire, Gregory Maertz, Irwin Primer, Ruben Quintero, Bruce Redford, Edward Rosenheim, John Staines, Albrecht Strauss, Giorgio Tagliacozzo, Janice Thaddeus, Kevin Van Anglen, and Donald Phillip Verene. I am particularly grateful for the shrewd and learned advice of Andrew Delbanco and Howard Weinbrot. The only things for which I can claim full credit are errors of fact and errors of judgment.

For the opportunity to test these chapters in their first forms, I thank the American Society of Eighteenth-Century Studies (ASECS), the California State University at Los Angeles, the Columbia Faculty Seminars, the Harvard Center for Literary and Cultural Studies, the Johnson Societies of the Central Region and of Evansville, the Modern Language Association, the Notre Dame Conference on Swift, the South Central ASECS, and the Whitney Center for the Humanities at Yale. Only Chapter 7 and parts of Chapter 6 have been published previously: an earlier version of "The Politics of Greed" appeared as "Wealth and Words" in *Modern Philology* and is copyrighted by the University of Chicago Press. *New Vico Studies* published sections of "Vico Tells the Story of Stories."

Illustration credits appear on appropriate pages.

The librarians and staff of the Harvard College libraries, especially of Widener and the Houghton, aided enormously in my research. These professionals are not only the collectors and custodians of a superb library, they are expert teachers and scholars. I am grateful to Philip Winsor and the Pennsylvania State University Press for their helpful, exemplary roles as editor and publisher. In a difficult environment, it seems to me that this press maintains the integrity of its mission and exercises the highest editorial standards. I thank Ann Donahue, who helped prepare the final text for printing. Publication of *The Committed Word* is supported by a grant from the Fred Robinson and Hyder E. Rollins Funds in English and American Literature and Language at Harvard.

After examining this volume the reader will, I hope, entertain a somewhat changed idea of what constitutes literature. It is my conviction that cultivating a full range of literary and rhetorical achievement fosters aesthetic and intellectual pleasure but something more as well: a heightened sense of shared social experience, an awareness of dissent and diverse views, a love of language in practical as well as artistic contexts, and a more powerful ability to express the values we debate and the values we enshrine. We cannot have one kind without the other.

1

The Committed Word

This book explores how dedicated individuals use literary means to frame political, cultural, and educational convictions. The strength of their thought, the force of their arguments, cannot be separated from the literary qualities of their writing.

Public discourse, political debate, educational policy, and cultural practices, as well as the spiritual life of a nation: these depend on intricate, powerful relations between language and human motivation, between words and values. A linguistically resourceful exercise of writing or speaking aimed to persuade a reader or listener to believe or to act thus links the power of words to social and political realities. Despite the dominance of visual images in television, computers, and other media, the difficult problems facing society most fully disclose themselves and are successfully resolved, or not, through language. It is ultimately with words that we debate, legislate, make treaties, teach, define, and discover values other than our own. Commenting on Tom Moore's *Life of Byron*, Macaulay remarks, "The deeper and more complex parts of human nature can be exhibited by means of words alone." It is ironic that as society and the world grow more pluralistic and complex—and hence need the diversity, pluralism, and complexity of language even more—we often resort to the potential reductionism and inadequate simplicity of the visual, to what Coleridge and Wordsworth call, aware of its political overtones, "the despotism" or "the tyranny of the eye." This essay and the ones that follow argue against those thinkers who contend that literature is no different than other cultural "texts," or who imply that literature has no special power to break out of its own prison house of cultural construction. Such liberating power is, in fact, a signal mark of literary achievement. *The Committed Word* argues that the literature produced by writers between Swift and Lincoln deals with political, cultural, religious, and educational issues in ways directly relevant to us.

This book examines writing that offers relevance not simply because it provides historical clues, say, to the origins of modern financial scandal and national debt, the British subjugation of India, the American Constitutional Convention, or the education of the individual soul in a mass culture driven by technology and analytical disciplines. The writers profiled here retain relevance, too, because they demonstrate that literature need not enclose itself in a self-referential, mandarin world but can and does engage—with enormous impact—political contests and cultural debates. These writers offer us models of such engagement. Not that we should imitate Edmund Burke's style, his prophetic grandiloquence, for example, or write op-ed pieces in Pope's heroic couplets. The models they provide are intellectual templates of a deeper, less mechanical type. They afford imaginative ways to apply literary techniques to a changed and changing present.

Two hundred years ago, these authors look to classical writers almost two millennia old. Yet they are able to follow—to emulate—those earlier writers with fresh spirit, reinvigorated technique, and contemporary *application,* a word Burke prefers to *imitation.* However varied in genre, temperament, and conviction, their words transform past models into new verbal arsenals and encourage us to do the same. While diverse in political convictions and literary taste, the thinkers in this volume share a conviction that the art of politics and the values of society must include the study of human motives and passions linked inextricably to the study of their written and oral expressions. Armed with this understanding, we find the boundaries between political science, psychology, literature, economics, religion, biography, and aesthetics fruitfully indistinct. We recapture a sense that writers such as Shakespeare and Milton are gifted not only in beauty of phrase and new combinations of words, but also in their grasp of affairs, governments, morality, and general knowledge domesticated into wisdom. The original name in ancient Greece for such a writer was not *poet* but *sophist*: someone who expresses wisdom. A later group we now call the Sophists appropriated this title and tried to discredit the poets. With the possible exception of Lincoln, the figures treated here were regarded in their own day, though perhaps not now, as *literary* talents. We need to recall, as Raymond Williams and others have pointed out, that "literature" and "literary" then had broad connotations; like "letters" or "lettered," they signified the expression of all knowledge, experience, and belief, not just fiction or belles lettres.

Literature can be considered an aesthetic end in itself, as in the doctrine of "pure poetry," which originates with Joseph Warton in the 1750s. But literature can be conceived, too, as Lincoln understood it, as that great instrumentality, that medium or vehicle, which not only permits but constitutes the deepest expression of all knowledge not purely technical or quantitative. But because the modern study of literature, especially since World War II, has centered around poems, plays, and novels—in other words, around fictional works—or around literary theory explicitly, though not exclusively, applied to fictive works, the study of literature as rhetoric, as the mode for the persuasive power of resourceful, often figurative language, has lost ground. This bias is even one reason that some have criticized professors of literature for being out of touch with "the real world." Moreover, the study of rhetoric, communication, and public speaking in our schools has become increasingly separated from the study of what we usually call literary texts. Suspicion and distrust have even developed between these two areas that both deal with language. The divorce is unproductive.

Many earlier thinkers and writers, whether of poetry, fiction, or intellectual prose, value rhetoric, oratory, and literary analysis as fundamental disciplines. Regarding them as foundational to all theories and forms of knowledge and value, as well as to every practical, interested call to action, they study these disciplines energetically. Their precursors extend back to Aristotle's *Rhetoric* and earlier, though the writers examined in this book are often suspicious of tradition, especially when venerated blindly. Commitment to the study of language and composition as a prerequisite and continuing condition of social and political acts, as well as of aesthetic creations, traces its roots to the oral formulaic poets, whom Vico calls "the founders of civil society." Adam Smith and Joseph Priestley, now known chiefly in economics and science, produce key works of literary criticism. Smith begins his career by delivering university lectures on rhetoric. Burke's Parliamentary speeches, Wollstonecraft's *Vindication of the Rights of Woman,* Pope's ironic satires against George II, Robert Lowth's *Lectures on the Sacred Poetry of the Hebrews,* Hume's *Essays,* Swift's critique of academies and politics, Vico's *New Science,* the Lincoln-Douglas Debates, and the Gettysburg Address—these all exemplify committed literature. Here, some of these writings, and others, form profiles and case studies spanning almost a century and a half (1726–1865), from the publication of *Gulliver's Travels* to the death of Lincoln. This time represents, in many ways, a golden age of Anglo-American public rhetoric. Chapters essay different examples of literary commitment, each presenting its own application, with each application changing over time. This book addresses both British and American literature and elaborates on their intimate connections.

I hope to bring alive writers who have fallen under a spell of remoteness where they lie dormant, seemingly far from the concerns of most present-minded academics and public commentators. Because these authors possess a latent power we can tap, this book aims to break the enchantment by which they have often been alienated from contemporary intellectuals and left to the antiquarians.

Sartre coins the phrase "engaged literature," *la littérature engagé,* but excludes poetry from his category. Here I use committed literature to mean all talented writing or writing of genius—not crude or clumsy propaganda, but writing that aims to persuade, to carry one point of view, or to explore contested intellectual terrain. This terrain covers politics, ethics, government, beliefs, law, education, national culture, and the spiritual life of the community.

2

The essays take up varied but interrelated issues. "Burke's Poetry and Prophecy" reexamines the categories, largely limited and simplistic, under which he has fallen and recognizes at the core of his major writings a prophetic power at once literary, political, and intellectual. Casually placed in the conservative fold, where some admirers are glad to welcome him and many enemies pleased to relegate him, he nevertheless furnishes as devastating a critique of imperialist greed as of revolutionary excess. The essay reassesses Burke at large, stressing his ability—attained through a combination of principles, detailed knowledge, and understanding of human motivation—to foresee the consequences of actions in politics and society.

The "brief epic," to use Milton's phrase, of the Connecticut Wits, *The Anarchiad*, figures in the ratification of the U.S. Constitution at the 1787 Philadelphia convention. Arguably, this poem has more immediate political influence in the United States than any other in our history, and perhaps as much as any work of literature, including Stowe's *Uncle Tom's Cabin*, Sinclair's *Jungle*, or Carson's *Silent Spring. The Anarchiad* takes its inspiration from Alexander Pope's *Dunciad*, a poem that thus has unforeseen resonances with the oldest viable written constitution in the world.

The third voyage of Swift's *Gulliver's Travels* is traditionally assumed to be about science, but the longest episodes concern semiotics, codes, politics, and the academy, a series of links extended to a meditation on the overlap between the intelligence and the academic communities. Swift has interesting things to say about the excesses and misuses of codes and theorizing: how, succumbing to those excesses, academic communities build political pretensions, and how political communities attack others while covering their own sins.

Hume's essays on culture, criticism, morals, and taste, and his *History of England*—distinct from, but related to his writings on epistemology and technical matters of philosophy—counter many debates in the so-called Culture Wars. He posits, in his own words, a "mitigated skepticism," what one commentator calls "skeptical realism," a rare attitude that refuses polemics, polarizations, and simplifications. He at once avoids defending absolute or eternal truths yet rejects relativism vigorously.

Vico argues that culture ultimately depends on the operation of the human mind as it creates and reshapes culture through narratives and myths. The relationship we have to cultural values and their history is thus *essentially* one of a literary or rhetorical nature, a series of interconnected stories, topoi, and characters. This conviction shares important ground with work of recent psychologists such as Jerome Bruner, and even with work in the mind and brain sciences. Vico argues that any education lacking this literary dimension forfeits something absolutely fundamental. A corollary follows: any person without this literary sense of narrative will be unable to construct a full personal identity, and will be unable to contribute to or to criticize the larger narratives and myths of collective culture.

Chapter 7 traces Pope's critique of scandals in public finance and politics.

Remarkable parallels with the savings and loan fiasco and other modern fiscal corruptions surface. As Pope faced a new economic system increasingly dominated by paper money rather than specie, we enter a world of digital transactions. His critique of wealth and words casts bright light on the predicaments of money, language, credit, and credibility.

Studying Robert Lowth's lectures on the poetry of the Hebrew Bible, and putting that together with scholarship on Hebrew poetry, aesthetic criticism, and modern literary commentary, I conclude that Lowth's work provides a firm foundation for theories of the sublime and of the symbol crucial to later generations in which Burke, Kant, and Coleridge win greater, though perhaps not more deserved, fame. Lowth's failure to wrest Hebrew poetry into any metrical pattern—yet the high premium he puts on its composition as *poetry*—encourages Blake and Whitman to produce poetry in English (Whitman's "new Bible") that does not scan regularly. Lowth's efforts help found the modern practices of irregular and free verse. His emphasis on poetry and prophecy fuses the aesthetic with the visionary, and both with a sense of history, in this case the history of a particular people and culture. Lowth is a hugely underrated figure.

Perhaps the most unexpected surprise in these essays may be the discovery that no matter how colloquial and homespun Lincoln's conversational remarks, stories, or ex tempore oral comments may be, his more formal written prose has origins not only in Shakespeare and the King James Bible, long recognized, but primarily and more directly in his youthful reading of exactly the kind of committed literature examined by the other essays in this volume. I trace these origins directly to Addison and Steele, Hume, Johnson, Defoe, Gibbon, Robertson, Hugh Blair, and others. As a boy, Lincoln first encounters all these writers in his copy of Lindley Murray's *English Reader*. When Lincoln's own often stated admiration for those who signed and ratified the Declaration of Independence and the Constitution is added to what we know of his early and later reading, and when his own writing is studied, it becomes evident that his prose is not the product of a folksy or distinctively American plain speech. His written style owes its power and eloquence to the committed literature, American and British, produced in the century before his birth.

3

It is not my contention that English and American letters during the years covered in this book enjoy more—or less—political and cultural involvement than before or since. Such a generalization falls beyond my scope, perhaps beyond anyone's. A companion set of profiles might move through figures such as Frederick Douglass, Winston Churchill, George Orwell, Wilfred Owen, Eleanor Roosevelt, Martin Luther King, Jr., and Learned Hand. But many people during the century and a half spanned by this volume view public discourse, politics, culture, and religion as fit subjects for an explicitly literary treatment. Politicians and cultural commentators apply themselves to the study of language and rhetoric, because they believe those disciplines form the cornerstone of political education, public presentation, social morality, and pulpit delivery. They do not commit themselves to its study in the cozy self-deception that literature provides allusions known only to a ruling clique as some passport to privilege, though that attitude exists for a few and always will. They act in the belief that literature not only *expresses* thought and feeling but *is* the most nuanced and powerful form of thought and feeling, one uniquely fundamental to a full articulation of individual and social existence.

The following chapters, then, essay different examples of such literary commitment. Each presents its own application, and each application itself must change in time. Milton, who uses learning to defend free, even revolutionary, speech—including speech that would deny his own learning and conviction—remarks in *Areopagitica* what every writer in this volume, with the possible exception of Lincoln, reads: "Truth is compared in scripture to a streaming fountain; if her waters flow not in a perpetual progression, they sicken into a muddy pool of conformity and tradition." That's one mark of a classic: to revitalize, for the here and now, truths, forms, and experiences from the past, yet to combine familiarity with novelty in a perdurable compound. It escapes univocal interpretation, transcends propaganda, and exceeds fixed meanings anchored to one time and place. It attains that multivalent state where, as Justice William Brennan, speaking at Georgetown University in 1987, said of the Constitution: its "genius . . . rests not in any static meaning it might have had in a world that is dead and gone, but in the adaptability of its great principles to cope with current problems and current needs." This statement shares in the best spirit of statecraft and public discourse drawn from the time of Burke and Jefferson—the Constitution of the American republic a supreme product of foresight sharpened by the past—where writers apply the works of older authors to their own, often massively changed, realities. This awareness forms part of the enterprise from the start. In Jefferson's words, "no society can make a perpetual constitution. . . . The earth belongs always to the living generation."

In this spirit, if connections with more contemporary issues surface, I have elected not to suppress them. This involves some leaps, for example, from Roman bribes to the English South Sea Bubble scandal to the American savings and loan bailout, or from Vico's theories of education to debates over modern curricula. Yet these essays do not support one preconceived idea or current ideology. I am not proposing a strict method or "-ism" for applying the literature at hand. It remains magnetic and alive because it possesses intelligence and genius. It defies formulation and resists rigid ideological appropriation.

The chapters do not stitch together a unified sense of literary-political progression or evolution from Pope through Lincoln, nor do they imply an across-the-board cultural critique. They are not arranged chronologically. Least of all do I want to imply some "progress" or linear development occurring through these case studies. Writers avail themselves of possibilities currently open and attempt to create or exploit new ones as the old crumble or give them leverage. But I do contend that politicians, educators, lawyers, historians, economists, journalists, and philosophers of that time do not see literature as a separate preserve. Literature they habitually regard as a source of knowledge both essential and instrumental to society and culture, one permitting an architectonic vision of public policy and discourse as well as of private aesthetic pleasure. In 1859, Abraham Lincoln delivers his "Lecture on Discoveries," devoting most of it to "*signs* to represent *things*," not only to speech, but especially to writing and printing. "Writing," he concludes, has many benefits, but was of "greatest help, to all other inventions."[1] This is Lincoln's cogent way of refuting the argument, already being made, that writing is simply another coequal text in the mix of all cultural representations.

The forms of committed literature may change. We too often reduce such literature to sound bites, labels, slogans, and thirty-second spots. But there is nothing new in this. In the English-speaking world of the eighteenth and nineteenth centuries, political nicknames and cartoon sketches are common. The drive to avoid ornate language, to be pithy and short, does not begin with television or the bumper sticker. The prizing of "plain speech" is not especially American either, but develops in the seventeenth century and flourishes in the new rhetorics produced by Adam Smith, Hugh Blair, James Beattie, Robert Lowth, and George Campbell. Their textbooks, or versions of them, such as the one by John Quincy Adams, are required in British and American schools for more than a century. In mass media, such as newspapers—Andrew Jackson rarely read books but devoured newspapers and bound them as library volumes in his Tennessee home, the Hermitage—America turns to a more popular and, in some ways, to a less nuanced vehicle for public discourse.[2] This has the advantage of reaching more people but can result in the sacrifice of intelligence for quick, mass intelligibility. Nevertheless, many of Jackson's bound newspapers, tightly printed without pictures or blank spaces, contain more words than many current books.

As so often is true, the great exception that proves the rule is Lincoln. He brilliantly combines the older virtues of the written Enlightenment—whose literature, along with Shakespeare and the Bible, he diligently studies and applies from his youth—with the spoken virtue of the common, tersely phrased anecdote that hits home. Little more than a month after Union victories at Gettysburg and Vicksburg, Lincoln writes to James H. Hackett, "Some of Shakespeare's plays . . . I have gone over perhaps as frequently as any unprofessional reader . . . Lear, Richard Third, Henry Eighth, Hamlet, and especially Macbeth." Yet, a few months later in November, seconds after he delivers the Gettysburg Address, he reportedly tells the man sitting next to him (Edward Everett or Ward Lamon, reports vary) that the speech "wouldn't scour," referring to a plow blade where the turned soil sticks instead of dropping.[3] Lincoln's "unprofessional reader" raises the ghost of Johnson's "common reader," pursued by Virginia Woolf and Queenie Leavis, a vital idea that still provokes debate and whose importance is indicated by our quarrels over such a reader's continued actual, or merely mythical, existence.

In Britain, her colonies, and the fledgling American republic, forms of political and linguistic reductionism and fragmentation already rear their heads. New journals and newspapers multiply; readerships grow; some periodicals develop party or cultural allegiances and square off against each other; authors such as Pope and Johnson tailor different editions of their published works for different socioeconomic markets; figures such as Edwards, Wesley, and Coleridge engage in crusades or lecture tours; artists such as Hogarth and Rowlandson produce literate political and cultural cartoons. To trace these developments would require separate studies. They might provide materials for a large, encompassing theory. I have restricted myself to individual cases and specific inferences, leaving others to paint a comprehensive historical canvas depicting in minute detail the relation of committed literature to culture at large, or to discover a single theory explaining that relation. Yet, as R. S. Crane pointed out years ago,[4] theory cannot and should not be avoided. The bond between literature and public values can be viewed from the vantage of theoretical models, and these are employed when they seem illuminating. My principle has been to preserve and to investi-

gate the historical contingencies of the writing discussed, to respect its arguments, conditions, and genres—paying attention to each of these as seems
apposite—but not to freeze this writing as a series of specimens. I hope to
suggest what qualities of thought transcend the historical moment even while
addressing it, and what techniques remain useful as well as aesthetically pleasing.
I've tried to avoid one dogmatic theory or polemic linking all these studies.
Seeing them under the lens of a monolithic view violates their integrity and
complexity.

The primary aim, then, is to reestablish a deeper, more useful, concrete
awareness of connections between literature and political and cultural values.
This is a bond between language and power, a bond established through case
studies, not through one abstract theory about power and language. To see this
bond in sharpest contrasts of freedom and injustice, there is perhaps no stronger
case in the records of the Anglo-American world than that of Frederick Douglass. In his *Narrative* (1845), he relates how, "soon after I went to live with Mr.
and Mrs. Auld," while still a slave, "[Mrs. Auld] very kindly commenced to
teach me the A,B,C. After I had learned this, she assisted me in learning to spell
words of three or four letters." Then Mr. Auld "forbade Mrs. Auld to instruct
me further, telling her . . . that it was unlawful, as well as unsafe, to teach a slave
to read." The vehemence of his master's alarm reveals to Douglass how important those lessons are, so he sets out "with high hope, and a fixed purpose, at
whatever cost of trouble, to learn how to read." It is clear to Douglass that,
regarding his master, "What he most loved, that I most hated. That which to
him was a great evil, to be carefully shunned, was to me a great good, to be
diligently sought." The sentences here are classically balanced, the thought,
logic, and phrasing a model of crisp rhetoric and public discourse that Douglass
soon masters.

Where then does Douglass learn to achieve more than "the A,B,C" and
"words of three or four letters"? After all, the *Narrative* is purposely subtitled,
"Written by Himself." In the next chapter, he tells how, at "about twelve years
old . . . I got hold of a book entitled 'The Columbian Orator.' Every opportunity I got, I used to read this book. . . . I found in it a dialogue between a master
and his slave" in which "the whole argument in behalf of slavery was brought
forward by the master, all of which was disposed of by the slave." And this
resulted "in the voluntary emancipation of the slave on the part of the master."
Douglass makes the point that, "In the same book, I met with one of Sheridan's
mighty speeches on and in behalf of Catholic emancipation. These were choice

Frederick Douglass, attributed to Elisha Hammond. Painted about the time Douglass's *Narrative* was first published in 1845. Reproduced by permission of the National Portrait Gallery, Smithsonian Institution, Washington, D.C.

THE

COLUMBIAN ORATOR:

CONTAINING A VARIETY OF

ORIGINAL AND SELECTED PIECES;

TOGETHER WITH

RULES,

CALCULATED TO

IMPROVE YOUTH AND OTHERS IN THE ORNAMENTAL
AND USEFUL

ART OF ELOQUENCE.

⸻

BY CALEB BINGHAM, A. M.

Author of The American Preceptor, Young Lady's Accidence, &c.

⸻

" CATO cultivated Eloquence, as a necessary mean for defending
the Rights of the People, and for enforcing good Counsels."
ROLLIN.

FIFTH TROY EDITION.

PUBLISHED ACCORDING TO ACT OF CONGRESS.

⸻

TROY:

PRINTED AND SOLD BY PARKER AND BLISS,
AT THE TROY BOOK-STORE, SIGN OF THE BIBLE.

1811.

Title page of *The Columbian Orator* by Caleb Bingham, a book that inspired
Frederick Douglass. The collection enjoyed dozens of editions. Reproduced
by permission of the Houghton Library, Harvard University, Cambridge,
Massachusetts.

documents to me. I read them over and over. . . . What I got from Sheridan was a bold denunciation of slavery, and a powerful vindication of human rights. The reading of these documents enabled me to utter my thoughts, and to meet the arguments brought forward to sustain slavery."[5] Douglass had purchased *The Columbian Orator* at a local Baltimore bookshop for fifty cents, a large sum then. Here is a clear instance of the force of committed literature. Douglass is led by a previous model, in this case a British one written by Richard Brinsley Sheridan, playwright, member of Parliament, and son of Thomas Sheridan, himself author of the famous text *Elocution* (1762) used for decades in Great Britain and North America. Douglass, like Lincoln and Sheridan, sees the value of committed literature. He will change a nation, and his own writing will become a model for succeeding generations.

In Chapter 10, I suggest ways in which we might recapture the instruction and education needed to maintain the strong link that binds liberty to eloquent language. Most importantly, I seek to provoke new applications and to suggest fresh models for the writing, educating, and believing that occupy us as citizens who must choose and act.

2

Burke's Poetry and Prophecy

This essay attacks the prevailing view that Burke is a champion of conservative or neoconservative thought. That attitude, fostered even in advanced institutes of public policy—and accepted in government, insofar as any government stops to consider the history of empires—that root assumption, watered or rather watered down by a selective, misleading focus on the *Reflections on the Revolution in France,* distorts and misserves the strength and branching of Burke's thought. Two or three one-volume selections of Burke's writings are in print, though for several years none was, and the Clarendon Press is publishing a new standard edition of his speeches and writings. But while Burke emphasizes that he valued his writings on India most, and wished most to be remembered by them, in a cultural and historical myopia our school texts and paperback trade books virtually exclude these writings and remain dominated by reprints of the *Reflections* assigned in government or history courses, a trend reinforced by every commem-

oration and significant anniversary of that revolution. Yet the only fair selection
of his works, remarked Hazlitt—a political liberal—is all of them. Students of
literature rarely study this innovator and master of intellectual and affective
discourse, except to read the *Reflections* and parts of the *Inquiry into . . . the
Sublime and Beautiful*. Yet in his texts, human realities and facts are transformed
by imaginative power and vision. We might say Burke combines, to use De
Quincey's distinction, the Literature of Knowledge *with* the Literature of Power.
That, at least, was the opinion many Romantics held of Burke, even many
with radical convictions; his peculiar genius kept him immune from the usual
downward reevaluation placed on the Augustans. When Coleridge supposed no
one would set Johnson before Burke, he was not only echoing Johnson's own
statement that "Burke is the first man everywhere"—and the only man, incidentally, whom Johnson declined to debate—Coleridge was also voicing the opinion of his generation.[1]

Critics who see Burke as a darling bastion of monarchical or imperial concerns, or venerate him as a patron saint of privileged institutions and inherited
titles—Burke declined the peerage offered him by George III—have not only
misread him in the fundamental and intellectually perilous sense of misreading,
they likely have not read him much at all. In prefacing his *Burke, Disraeli, and
Churchill: The Politics of Perseverance*, Stephen Graubard remarks that, "Several
generations of Conservatives, old as well as 'new,' have succeeded so well in
advertising their particular hero's virtue that the term 'Burkean' . . . is a word
of opprobrium among many who hear his praise but neglect to read his works."[2]
During the past generation, despite much talk about the politicizing of literary
studies and the pervasive presence of ideology, literary and political studies have
often continued to specialize respectively and to separate themselves in the academy. We run the risk of forgetting that the best exercise of responsible power
must commingle with—it is not possible without—both an articulate analysis
and expression of power in evocative, persuasive language. If this interpenetration of language and power ceases, then literature grows solipsistic and power
becomes enfeebled in a reign of error that "misspeaks" or, worse, deceives with
cynical malice. The latter happens in Orwell's *1984* and Huxley's *Brave New
World*, where powerful forces use language to pervert human dignity, where
peace becomes war and love is hate.[3] But it also happens everyday and shapes
ethical decisions. An example of some years ago involves President Reagan engaged in dialogue over his visits to death camps and German war cemeteries,
the kind of situation Burke grasped well, where time, suffering, pained memory,

and the irony of medals and awards are all played out, half following a careless script written by those in power, a script that exacerbates suffering and widens rather than closes wounds. Finally, all innocent parties become embittered, and what should never be forgotten becomes obscured in the defensiveness and self-justification of decisions too embarrassingly calculated to revoke, too stubbornly held for apology. As readers of literature examine texts, often without directly confronting the moral and political nature of much poetry and intellectual prose, and as officials in government are increasingly given evidence to consider serious literature as a preserve of balkanized readers incapable of administering collective, practical human effort in "the real world," Burke slips further from view.

Scandalously, the *Norton Anthology of English Literature,* the most widely used and prestigious literary textbook of the past three decades, at present contains not one word by Burke. He has been cut. The only fair selection is apparently nothing at all. Especially at a time when broad claims are asserted about interdisciplinary study and the relations between politics and literature—that all literature has a political dimension or that literature and politics both share in a larger discourse of power—it seems strange to drop a figure who so obviously fuses the two areas. Perhaps for some, taking politics and literature together really means promoting a specific political agenda or current ideology rather than a broad inquiry into the art of politics, verbal expression, and literary art. If so, that might explain why Burke, perceived to violate such a specific agenda, would be ignored.

The reason I begin this way, in a brief effort to place Burke at a crossroads of literature and prophecy, is that I assume prophecy and poetry, taken together, are, in fact, inextricably bound up with power. And by power I do not necessarily mean day-to-day politics (though that enters in), but power considered as what shapes and controls human destiny; what affects our lives and our pursuit of happiness; what endows and protects our inalienable rights and human dignity; and what, conversely, erodes or attacks moral law. For this essay, the hope is that we can accept as a postulate what longer examination would verify: Burke is a statesman and writer beyond simple ideologies and categories. Least of all is he susceptible to rubrics of our impoverished political labels—whatever unimaginative variations stem from the threadbare use of "liberal" and "conservative," "left" and "right."[4] If there are still prophets in our secular age, Burke may be considered one. In power of language and vision he is a poet in the capacious sense of that word, a poet as Plato and Isaiah and Ezekiel are poets.[5]

2

It might help to instance what Coleridge calls Burke's "surview of mind," his foresight—how he grasped issues and events. This surview characterizes Burke's wisdom, and in its operative mode permeates and forms the powerfully qualified cadences and clauses of his writing. And such a surview permits him to call on many levels of style and diction, from the periodic and ornate to the tersely colloquial and sharply imperative, from epic height to the street vendor's "truck and huckster"—as Burke phrases it in his *Speech on Conciliation with the Colonies* (March 22, 1775); and then to amass this nuanced linguistic variety not for rhetorical amazement and professional self-enhancement, but for nuanced, practical goals.

For Burke, "the case of America was a new case; it was a nation *sui generis*." In the way it came into being historically, it was, and so it has remained.[6] (Burke knew the North American colonies well; as a young man he seriously considered emigrating to them.) He is convinced that after the events of 1789, in France, "revolution" would henceforth mean "to make a new world, throw out the past and start the world over" again, as one would in a second creation myth. His prescience leads him to regard "this strange thing, called a revolution in France," in contrast to "our revolution (as it is called)" of 1688, which was "in truth and substance, and in a constitutional light, a revolution, not made, but prevented."[7] To us this new sense of revolution seems commonplace. But Burke—along with Blake—are among the first to see its significance, to realize a fundamental change in the nature of nations and nation making.

When full-scale war with the American colonists seems probable, Burke offers the Duke of Richmond concrete proposals "towards preventing the ruin of your Country; which if I am not quite Visionary, is approaching with greatest rapidity." He appends that "a Speculative despair is unpardonable where it is our duty to Act."[8] Burke is a prophet who would act, not just look on—though despite his profound efforts on behalf of peace and conciliation, despite his various secret diplomacies and eloquent correspondences with Americans such as Franklin, Britain enters her eighteenth-century Vietnam with disastrous consequences fiscally and politically.

On July 4, 1776, unaware his timing is ironical, Burke writes, "What will become of this People," the Americans, and asks "to what Providence has destined them and us?"[9] In one speech remaining in manuscript, an "Address to the British Colonists in North America," he wishes their new union success but warns them not to turn their back on that liberty first made known to them by Commons: "It may not even be impossible that a long course of war with the administration of this country may be but a prelude to a series of wars and contentions among yourselves, to end at length . . . in a species of humiliating repose, which nothing but the preceding calamities would reconcile to the dispirited few, who survived them" (6: 192). A terrible breakup of all colonies in endless internecine, armed struggles never occurred, but one might think of Shays's Rebellion, the deadly Whiskey Rebellion, Aaron Burr's new republic, the Missouri Compromise, the Compromise of 1850, bloody Kansas, and ultimately the Civil War, whose casualties for North and South still exceed those for all other wars fought by the United States combined.

Trying to stem the tide of war, Burke in 1777 warns his electors in a *Letter to the Sheriffs of Bristol,* "For be fully assured, that, of all the phantoms that ever deluded the fond hopes of a credulous world, a Parliamentary revenue in the colonies is the most perfectly chimerical. Your breaking them to any subjection, far from relieving your burdens, (the pretext for this war,) will never pay that military force which will be kept up to the destruction of their liberties and yours. *I risk nothing in this prophecy*" (2: 237; emphasis added). And he could not have been more right in it. Later, Burke continues to wonder about the future United States. In 1785, expressing a fear he had held at least eight years, "He said that he would not be surprised at the defection of some of the colonies from the Union—I believe," reports Thomas Somerville, writing in the second decade of the nineteenth century, "I believe he mentioned the southern states."[10]

Burke generally fears what might happen in the aftermath of any revolution of the new style. About America he says, "For once I confess"—and the "once" is not false modesty but true bafflement of an otherwise vatic statesman—"I apprehend more from the madness of the people than from any other cause."[11] This foreshadows his attitude to the French Revolution, but his anxiety about the course of "the madness of the people" would apply to purges after most new-style revolutions, whether in the Soviet Union, Idi Amin's Central African Empire, Pol Pot's Cambodia, China with the Red Guards spearheading a Cultural Revolution, Ceauşescu's Romania of the 1970s and 1980s, or Bosnia and Herzegovina in the 1990s. "[A]midst all these turbulent means of security to their system," says Burke about the newly established revolutionaries in his *Thoughts on French Affairs* (December 1791), "very great discontents everywhere prevail. But they only produce misery to those who nurse them at home, or exile, beggary, and in the end confiscation, to those who are so impatient as to remove from them. Each municipal republic has a *Committee*. . . . In these petty republics the tyranny is so near its object that it becomes instantly acquainted with every act of every man. It stifles conspiracy in its very first movements. Their power is absolute and uncontrollable. No stand can be made against it" (4: 352). This is political correctness with a vengeance.

Or we have this prescient remark, applicable to Vietnam, Lebanon, Northern Ireland, El Salvador, the former Yugoslavia, Rwanda, or to the mentality of nuclear proliferation: "War is much more likely to follow war in any Country than originally to break out in one that is long composed. The first breach is terrible to the quiet. Nothing is dreadful to a man which is habitual to him. The massacres that have been made in civil Wars, the proscriptions that have followed in other times & Countries have often begot the very War they were intended to prevent."[12]

We might say, without exaggeration, too, that twenty years before the revolution from which Burke so violently recoils, he foresees it, already resonant with alarm for its European repercussions. In *Observations on . . . the Present State of the Nation* (1769), he warns ominously, "Indeed, under such extreme straitness and distraction labors the whole body of their [French] finances, so far does their charge outrun their supply in every particular, that no man . . . who has considered their affairs with any degree of attention or information, but must hourly look for some extraordinary convulsion in that whole system: the effect of which on France, and even on all Europe, it is difficult to conjecture" (1: 331).

And then again, twenty years later, at the end of the *Reflections,* itself written five years before Napoleon orders his artillery to rake the Tuileries, and nine years before Napoleon takes charge on the eighteenth day of Brumaire, 1799, Burke unhesitatingly predicts that, "In the weakness of one kind of authority, and in the fluctuation of all, the officers of an army will remain for some time mutinous and full of faction, *until some popular general,* who understands the art of conciliating the soldiery, and *who possesses the true spirit of command, shall draw the eyes of all men upon himself.* Armies will obey him on his personal account. There is no other way of securing military obedience in this state of things. But the moment in which that event shall happen, *the person who really commands the army is your master*—the master (that is little) of your king, the master of your Assembly, the master of your whole republic" (3: 524–25; emphasis added). This principle, which ends in military dictatorship, has been acted out ad nauseam in many countries caught in struggles of overthrowing an imperial or oligarchical power and replacing it with one espousing the people's welfare. To adduce the list of nations taxes general knowledge, and more will be added.

Less well known than Burke's pronouncements on France is his shuddering appraisal of the political upheavals that would eventually shake Germany. They will, he says, upset the European balance of power and eventuate in a crisis or series of crises more serious and far-reaching than those even of the French convulsions. In *Thoughts on French Affairs,* Burke broods over this possibility: "A great revolution is preparing in Germany, and a revolution, in my opinion, likely to be more decisive upon the general fate of nations than that of France itself. . . . If Europe does not conceive the independence and equilibrium of the Empire [the German Electorates] to be in the very essence of the system of balanced power in Europe, and if the scheme of public law, or mass of laws, upon which that independence and equilibrium are founded, be of no leading consequence as they are preserved or destroyed, all the politics of Europe for more than two centuries have been miserably erroneous" (4: 330). Earlier, Hume, traveling there, observed, too: "Germany is undoubtedly a very fine Country, full of industrious honest People, & were it united it wou[l]d be the greatest Power that ever was in the World."[13]

The "revolution" to which Burke refers may be taken as the rise of German nationalism and its idea of a unified German state, one that dominated European diplomacy and war from Bismarck through the fall of the Third Reich—the legacy now continuing with a reunified Germany facing West and East, and Europe pivoting around it.

Yet, remarkable as they are, it is not chiefly by specific "predictions" that Burke is prophetic; he can make these because he grasps moral and historical principles that govern different peoples and nations differently. He then envisions the results of these operative principles upon the complex realities of a given national or social situation though time. As Blake avows in his marginal comment to the bishop of Llandaff's *Apology for the Bible,* a statement applicable to Blake's own prophetic books, "Prophets in the modern sense of the word have never existed. . . . Every honest man is a Prophet[;] he utters his opinion both of private & public matters Thus If you go on So the result is So[.] He never says such a thing Shall happen let you do what you will. a Prophet is a Seer not an Arbitrary Dictator." This form of prophecy, which Blake identifies with the ancient prophets—influenced by Robert Lowth's work on Hebrew poetry and prophecy (see Chapter 8)—this form Burke uses to exercise his surview. It is also how Winston Churchill later foresees, in a 1910 memorandum, that if things were to go on so, Germany would wage war, invade France through Belgium, and the ensuing conflict would last not a year or two, as "experts" assumed, but four or five. Churchill's later prophecies in the mid-1930s concerning Nazi rearmament and their virulent doctrine of racial purity went virtually unheeded while England slept.

Coleridge even ventures that, "In Mr. Burke's writings . . . the germs of almost all political truths may be found."[13] Earlier in the *Biographia,* Coleridge remarks on Burke with a characterization worth giving at length. In it Coleridge makes a distinction between opinion and knowledge, a distinction Washington invokes in his Farewell Address (1796), and one that, running back to Aristotle, is found in many figures who write about political and social issues in literary language, including Swift, Johnson, and Wollstonecraft:

> If then unanimity grounded on moral feelings has been among the least equivocal sources of our national glory, that man deserves the esteem of his countrymen . . . who devotes his life and the utmost efforts of his intellect to the preservation and continuance of that unanimity by the disclosure and establishment of *principles.* For by these [principles] all *opinions* must be ultimately tried; and (as the feelings of men are worthy of regard only as far as they are the representatives of their fixed opinions) on the knowledge of these all unanimity, not accidental and fleeting, must be grounded. Let the scholar, who doubts this assertion, refer only to the speeches and writings of EDMUND BURKE at the commencement of the American war and compare them with his speeches and writings at the commencement of the French revolution. He will find the *principles* exactly the same and the deductions the same; but the practical inferences almost opposite in the one case from those drawn in the other; yet in both equally legitimate and in both equally confirmed by the results.

At this point, Coleridge specifically credits Burke with a prophetic power:

> Whence gained he this superiority of foresight? Whence arose the striking *difference,* and in most instances even, the discrepancy between the grounds assigned by *him,* and by those who voted *with* him, on the same questions? How are we to explain the notorious fact, that the

speeches and writings of EDMUND BURKE are more interesting at the present day, than they were found at the time of their first publication; while those of his illustrious confederates are either forgotten, or exist only to furnish proofs, that the same conclusion, which one man had deduced scientifically, *may* be brought out by another in consequence of errors that luckily chanced to neutralize each other. . . . The satisfactory solution is, that Edmund Burke possessed and had sedulously sharpened that eye, which sees all things, actions, and events, in relation to the *laws* that determine their existence and circumscribe their possibility. He referred habitually to *principles.* He was a *scientific* statesman; and therefore a *seer.* For every *principle* contains in itself the germs of a prophecy; and as the prophetic power is the essential privilege of science, so the fulfilment of its oracles supplies the outward and, (to men in general), the *only* test of its claim to the title.[14]

It is thus explicitly to Burke, and not to the child in Wordsworth's "Intimations" ode that Coleridge applies the title of *seer* or *mighty prophet.*[15] By "scientific," Coleridge does not mean modern experimental science but systematic knowledge. Furthermore, "that eye, which sees all things" probably alludes to the mysterious and providential all-seeing eye venerated by the Freemasons. It appears, not coincidentally, in the frontispiece Vico selects for *The New Science* (see Chapter 6), and on the Great Seal of the United States. (Coleridge was an avid reader of Vico.) "Providence" derives, after all, from *pro-videre,* to see ahead or through. Elements of this symbolism, a providential eye associated with a pyramid, bear further resemblance to Coleridge's own personal seal or logo, which he uses as a signet to seal his letters sent from Malta in 1805. Here logo is taken not in its present, but in its profound sense, connected for Coleridge with an intellectual and spiritual Logos.[16]

3

Burke is prophetic not merely in political surview and acumen, but also in inspired speech. When foreseeing and warning of tragedy, his voice is strikingly similar to John of Gaunt's deathbed prophecies in *Richard II* (2.1) about the fate of England and its monarch: "Methinks I am a prophet new inspir'd / And

thus expiring do foretell of him: / His rash fierce blaze of riot cannot last."
Burke's voice resounds in form, too, with the Hebrew prophets who speak in
impassioned declamation, and on whom Burke draws in his *Inquiry.* He appeals
to a prophetic spirit in submerged quotations. For instance, in the *Reflections,*
speaking of the English Declaration of Right, he states its "penetrating style has
engraved in our ordinances, and in our hearts, the words and spirit of that
immortal law" (3: 257). He is echoing Jeremiah 31:33: "I will put my law in
their inward parts, and write it in their hearts."[17] Just a few years before Burke
publishes the *Inquiry,* Robert Lowth sees in the Hebrew Bible a sublime poetry
based more on stress, rhythm, and parallelism than regular meter or rhyme (see
Chapter 8). As Lowth does in his popular lectures, so Burke in the *Inquiry*
probes the sources of sublime poetry in its combination of suggestive obscurity
and sharply etched, minute specificity.[18] It is to this sense of poetry, to language
powerfully elevated, to the cadenced, feeling, imaginative use of words in the
service of moral power—not to poetry as "metrical composition"—that Burke
belongs.

Burke uses poets and writers in ways that add resonance and rescue older
meaning into new relevance and application. Literature for him is available for
new contexts—without violating its original spirit—to afford mythic, prophetic
power. In his many allusions to Greek history and drama, Milton, Shakespeare,
and Pope, we do not hear a shallow habit of show learning, but an active,
applied use of archetypal power and reference. He brings the present and future
into relief together through an imaginative comparison with events and moral
dilemmas of the past expressed in the passionate speech of poets.[19] Readings of
literature are to be put to use, constantly reinterpreted for human situations at
hand—not to alter facts of composition or to scrutinize authorial intention, but
to see poetry as a living power and way of addressing changes in time, to give
texts life through new readings and applications. Burke's use of literature makes
it relevant; in his learning of ancient and modern authors, the last thing he
becomes is a narrow antiquarian or pedant.

Seeing statecraft and literature, poetry and liberty, as inextricably fused,
Burke turns to and constantly draws upon those who speak about the destiny of
a people: Virgil, Juvenal, Isaiah, St. Paul, Milton. Others, of course, admire such
power: Gray, for example, though in his prophetic poems he applies more to
the past. "The Bard" and "The Progress of Poesy" are largely historical in
nature, no matter how much Gray hopes they might provide inspiration for
future achievement. In Burke's writings there is as much direct knowledge and

imaginative application of Milton's poetry as in Blake or Wordsworth. This is not, of course, a question of stylistic imitation, for then Keats's first "Hyperion," Edward Young's *Night Thoughts,* and a raft of blank versifiers would come more readily to mind. This is a wider grasp and use of Milton's poetic and prophetic expression of power and politics as they are turned to problems of the here and now. Although Blake regards Burke in some sense as a false prophet, Burke has affinities with him. While in the case of the French Revolution Blake inverts and opposes Burke's prophetic stance, as prophets against empire they are curiously parallel.[20]

In the frequent, faulty labeling of Burke as a status quo conservative or traditionalist, we are urged to forget—if the labelers ever knew—that he deeply questioned the British presence in India, that he desired parliamentary reform but was afraid to take it up for fear of opening a Pandora's box, and that he vigorously denounced the slave trade before Wilberforce did. Burke spoke in favor of the abolition of slavery: in his words, "a trade begun with savage war, prosecuted with unheard of cruelty, continued during the mid passage with the most loathsome imprisonment and ending in perpetual exile and unremitting slavery, was a trade so horrid in all its circumstances, that it was impossible a single argument could be adduced in its favour." This son of a mixed Catholic and Protestant marriage, educated by a Quaker schoolmaster in Dublin and married to the daughter of an Irish Catholic doctor, felt that the Irish situation was intolerable, and that England must address the needs of the Irish people by ending the "unjust, impolitic" Penal Laws governing property and religion. He fought for broad, expanded religious toleration for Catholics and Dissenters even while supporting the establishment of a national church, a liberal view at that time, but one that has received scant attention.[21] We also tend to forget that the *Reflections* is not a parliamentary instrument and—unlike Burke's hundreds of speeches—has no direct connection to any legislation or policy voted by Commons.

We find Burke using poetic imagery as a kind of typology: With loss imminent in the American War, he turns to a kind of domino theory, though elegantly phrased in his quoting of *The Dunciad*: "Thus one star, and that the brightest ornament of our orrery, having suffered to be lost [America], those who were accustomed to inspect and watch our political heaven, ought not to wonder that it should be followed by the loss of another:

> So star would follow star, and light, light,
> Till all was darkness and eternal night."[22]

Closer to our time, these lines from *The Dunciad* form a haunting original to Sir Edward Grey's prophetic lament on the eve of the Great War: "The lamps are going out all over Europe; we shall not see them lit again in our lifetime." The image, in a new way, fits that war to end all wars. In politics a prophetic poetics reaches out to what in the *Impeachment of Warren Hastings, A Speech in Reply,* Burke calls "the retiring . . . [and] the advancing generations, between which, as a link in the great chain of eternal order, we stand" (Ninth Day, 12: 394). Lincoln will echo this in his appeal to the "mystic chords" of memory, just as "the living and the dead" becomes a common phrase and leitmotif in both Wordsworth and Whitman.

Burke was for decades frequently and commonly compared to Shakespeare. Though no one would press the letter of this comparison, we have lost even its spirit. "Shakespeare himself has come again," said a correspondent on the Continent.[23] Sir Robert Heron wrote on February 17, 1835, that Burke is "an authority for all times . . . in the political what Shakespeare was in the moral world."[24] Coleridge compares Shakespeare and Burke in the first essay on method in *The Friend* (1818), Section 2, Essay 4, and also characterizes Burke's qualities of mind in *Friend* No. 9 (October 12, 1809). Alfred Cobban in *Edmund Burke and the Revolt Against the Eighteenth Century* remarks how Coleridge and Wordsworth thought of Burke and Shakespeare together; as did Hazlitt, evidenced by his *Eloquence of the British Senate* (1808), "On the Prose-Style of Poets" in *The Plain Speaker,* and elsewhere.[25]

Finally, for Burke as poet, we can make use of Coleridge's distinction between poetry and a poem. For Burke unquestionably does not write poems. And while he, like Lincoln, was not considered a captivating speaker, his command of language lends him a modern Cassandra's voice.[26] He gives about a thousand speeches, delivered with notes but in the main impromptu or extemporaneous, from an outline not fleshed out. And most of it is thus lost—as surely as most words of Sophocles and Isaiah are lost. *On American Taxation* (April 19, 1774) is the first speech Burke takes pains to publish, though by then he had delivered above two hundred in Commons. As with his later publications, people flock to buy it.

Despite public eagerness to read his prophecies and arguments, the comparison with Cassandra remains apt. Burke is without honor, that is, without ruling influence in his own country, a scar that, near the end of his career, he can no longer cloak in his *Letter to a Noble Lord* (1795). The words of Milton surely pained him: "Such honor was done in those days to men who professed the study of wisdom and eloquence, not only in their own country, but in other lands, that cities and seignories heard them gladly and with great respect, if they had aught in public to admonish the state." By contrast, some see in Burke's modern prophecies actual derangement. The press treats him roughly. Caricatures are common—Burke the "seer" squinting through his spectacles. He finds himself perpetually in the minority; during thirty years of continual service the only post he holds, paymaster general, a relatively minor cabinet appointment, is his less than a year. After his stand on American trade, he is cast out as MP for Bristol, then England's second largest city and greatest trading port with America. The last of his works published while he lives, *Letter to a Noble Lord,* defends his modest pension against the eighth Earl of Lauderdale and the immensely rich Duke of Bedford. (A merely verbal, hypocritical sympathizer with the French Revolution, Bedford challenged Burke's qualifications and sought to make his pension a point of irritation for the government.) Every major issue Burke takes up he loses on an immediate if not a fundamental level—American conciliation, economic reform, Irish reform, India and the impeachment of Hastings, and steps to prevent French mass murder, tyranny, and eventual European war.

4

For Burke, then, is it too much to see in his imaginative grasp of moral forces and in his remarkable gift of expression, something akin to the genuine spirit of the Hebrew prophets, whose words he knew well? In role, attitude, responsibility, and language, in deep feeling, acutely transferred to practice, in strength of expression, surview of mind, and persuasive ability, we are hearing a voice committed to providential duty and control: in his writings we can find the organon, the living power of word, the all-seeing eye by which a people are governed, the power by which a people determine what actions are good and what are unjust, that is, what will serve and what will decay the moral balance of power for future generations.[27] This is not a form of mysticism, but knowledge of human affairs distilled from history and joined to a grasp of what motivates human belief, custom, and action.

Burke does not claim, nor would anyone claim for him, divine inspiration. That might be held for Milton's heavenly muse, and in a sense Blake claims it

James Gillray's caricature of Burke, "Cincinnatus in Retirement" (1782), satirizing his Irish origins, humble background, need of spectacles to act as a prophet or "seer," and his appeal to religious sentiments. The Roman Cincinnatus was considered a model of virtue, simplicity, and self-sacrificing patriotism. Saint Boniface was an English Benedictine. The comparisons are meant to diminish and belittle Burke. Reproduced by permission of the Houghton Library, Harvard University, Cambridge, Massachusetts.

for himself. But Coleridge introduces his discussion of Burke in Chapter 10 of the *Biographia* (in the section with its apt subheading, "Opinions in Religion and Politics"), by appealing to religious sources: "Causes, which it had been too generally the habit of former statesmen to regard as belonging to another world, are now admitted . . . to have been the main agents of our success." Then, to introduce Burke directly, Coleridge quotes Judges 5:20: We, he says, "fought from heaven; the stars in their courses fought against Sisera."[28]

But even if Burke seems not inspired in the way we now associate with Milton or Blake, though to Coleridge and others he certainly was, we nevertheless find in his language and vision—explicit throughout his writings—a divine or providential sense akin to Vico's, George Washington's, or Lincoln's in the Second Inaugural Address. On the American war Burke reflects that, "Times, *accidents,* the Characters of men, do much, but *accident,* (or an unseen providence for unknown Ends,) does most of all."[29] In 1788, Burke notes, "There is a sacred veil to be drawn over the beginnings of all governments. . . . Time, in the origin of most governments, has thrown this mysterious veil over them; prudence and discretion make it necessary to throw something of the same drapery over more recent foundations" (9: 401). It is as though Burke were participating in Vico's belief that a poetic and providential wisdom—that is, a creative and life-giving awareness—founds and guides civil polity, *if* good people help to will and work it. The Providence to which Burke appeals is neither, then, a streak of fatalism nor a deus ex machina but the cooperative bond of human good will in action, *deus est in pectore nostro*; in Lincoln's words, "with firmness in the right, as God gives us to see the right."

Burke himself even appears possessed by some providential power; to his friends he often seems a genuine visionary. Enemies and contemporary artists picture him mad, foaming at the mouth, a wild Irishman dressed in black appealing to mysterious forces and ancient authors like a sorcerer or alchemist gone manic. Admirers have difficulty explaining him; they often simply resort, as do many modern defenders, to Burke's power of language. But his power of language has sources other than the purely aesthetic.

Gerald Chapman appropriately calls Burke's belief and sense of the divine "a Providential vitalism," a form of "vatic intuition" that "runs through all of Burke's thought." As in few other writers we get a sense of what is sacred operating through powers that govern daily affairs: that there exist wellsprings of history, faith, and cohesion that keep people in a position to pursue happiness, but—once broken—end in hate and prejudice, tragedy, war, revolutionary madness, the destruction of whole nations, and genocide. This sacred, providential vitalism resonates, for example, in the closure of the Declaration of Independence: "And, for the support of this Declaration, with a firm reliance on the Protection of Divine Providence, we mutually pledge to each other our Lives, our Fortunes, and our Sacred Honor." This power is not something we can formulate, but a power of history we become aware of only through experience—and perhaps especially through the bitter discoveries revealed by tragedy, suffering, and failure.

Repeatedly in Burke's writings we witness this invocation of providential power and closure. In early May 1775, when he refers to the Intolerable Acts against the colonies, Burke admonishes Commons, for Commons had "given punishment *& Gov^t* in one—Gov^t given in *Anger*," yet felt "no sort of terrour at the awfulness of the situation" placed in its power "by providence." Of the course and prognosis of this action, "Next to that tremendous day, in which it is revealed, that the saints of God shall judge the World," Burke said that he knew nothing more terrible.[30] Earlier, on February 2, 1775, he warned of "the true crisis of Britain's fate, painted the dreadful abyss into which the nation was going to be plunged." This is the real abyss of blood and death and treachery that is happening every day somewhere, not the abyss of an abstracted philosopher or theoretician unencumbered by any responsibility to exercise power or to advocate specific action.

In *Thoughts on French Affairs* (1791), coming to accept the inevitability of events in France, an acceptance Arnold calls Burke's "return upon himself," Burke places himself as an individual completely subject to this providential power, even though its course seems to him malicious: "The evil is stated, in my opinion, as it exists. The remedy must be where power, wisdom, and information, I hope, are more united with good intentions than they can be with me. I have done with this subject, I believe, for ever. It has given me many anxious moments for the two last years. If a great change is to be made in human affairs, the minds of men will be fitted to it; the general opinions and feelings will draw that way. Every fear, every hope will forward it; *and then they who persist in opposing this mighty current in human affairs, will appear rather to resist the decrees of Providence itself, than the mere designs of men.* They will not be resolute and firm, but perverse and obstinate" (4: 377; emphasis added). This concludes the last paragraph of *Thoughts on French Affairs*. As in so many of Burke's speeches, Providence becomes a form of literary and historical closure. The intellectual argument he has stretched to its limit, recognizing that all societies and governments—and their policies—are constructions prone to accident and corruption. And, so, the appeal to Providence becomes a form of intellectual closure as well, one that sees the limits of human design.

In the course of his *Speech on Fox's East India Bill* (December 1, 1783), Burke lists the enormous complications of administering such a huge, varied stretch of land and heterogeneous peoples. He concludes, "All these circumstances are not, I confess, very favorable to the idea of our attempting to govern India at all. But there we are; *there we are placed by the Sovereign Disposer,* and we must do the best we can in our situation. *The situation of man is the preceptor of his duty*" (2: 465; emphasis added). Burke believes the situation calls for

British withdrawal, at the very least for humane policy as the fulfillment of that duty so strangely and severely provided for, but others see India as a boon for self-enrichment.

And as another mark of Burke's providentialism, in the *Speech Opening the Impeachment of Warren Hastings,* Fourth Day, he reminds the lords who will judge Hastings (again, closing his address with an appeal to the earthly ministers of Providence):

> You have the representatives of that religion [the Bishops in the House of Lords] which says that their God is love, that the very vital spirit of their institution is charity,—a religion which so much hates oppression, that, when the God whom we adore appeared in human form, He did not appear in a form of greatness and majesty, but in sympathy with the lowest of the people, and thereby made it a firm and ruling principle that their welfare was the object of all government, since the Person who was the Master of Nature chose to appear Himself in a subordinate situation. These are the considerations which influence them, which animate them, and will animate them, against all oppression,—knowing that He who is called first among them, and first among us all, both of the flock that is fed and of those who feed it, made Himself "the servant of all." (9: 144)

Such an argument, or rather the essence of Burke's argument here, is later used by eloquent church representatives in South Africa, such as Bishop Desmond Tutu, to end apartheid.

The prosecution of Warren Hastings, governor-general of India, lasts more than fourteen years, his trial more than six. From Burke's closing speech on the *Impeachment of Hastings: Speech in Reply,* Ninth Day, we catch again the iron rod of his piety: "My Lords, it has pleased Providence to place us in such a state that we appear every moment to be upon the verge of some great mutations. There is one thing, and one thing only, which defies all mutation,—that which existed before the world, and will survive the fabric of the world itself: I mean justice,—that justice which, emanating from the Divinity, has a place in the breast of every one of us, given us for our guide with regard to ourselves and with regard to others, and which will stand, after this globe is burned to ashes, our advocate or our accuser before the great Judge, when He comes to call upon us for the tenor of a well-spent life" (12: 395–96).

When the vote is cast on Hastings's impeachment—and by implication on the whole British treatment of India—Burke, like so many prophetic poets before him, finds himself, after fifteen years' effort expended on the issue, once again in the minority.

We noted how Burke frequently fears for the future of America. He warns of "a series of wars and contentions among yourselves," and speculates that the southern states might eventually defect or secede. These dangers are the same ones alarmingly drawn in a contemporaneous American poem, *The Anarchiad,* a work whose spirit derives from another poem familiar to Burke. As we have seen, in speaking prophetically he uses it himself. It is Pope's *Dunciad.* The curious relation between Pope's poetry and the formation of a strong American federal constitution is also a story, like Burke's many efforts, of literary and political fusion.

3

Pope's American Constitution

Politics is the art of the possible at the present moment. But it is also based, as Burke and others conceive it, on principles. And therefore true statecraft is a prophetic art transmitted by an application of the past to the here and now, and to the future. Ironically, the greatest political use and recognition of Alexander Pope derives from writing that English contemporaries identified as his most transient and, according to many, his least satisfactory performance, *The Dunciad*. This poem William Ayre—probably the pseudonym of the bookseller and sometime antagonist of Pope, Edmund Curll—in his *Memoirs of the Life and Writings of Alexander Pope* (1745), declares might, "at this Crisis, when the *publick Dulness* of ten Years past was come under *Inquiry*," rouse "great Expectations" of "*political Satire*, but the ingenious Author has given the World only a satire on *Modern Life*, and the Conduct of it in general."[1] A more unconsciously brilliant and prescient criticism Ayre (or Curll) never made. Its import escaped better commentators.

By satirizing modern cultural life and the conduct of it at large, Pope creates a mythic vessel into which he and others can pour reflections on several political specters of the modern era: decline, democratic anarchy, leveling, blind ideologies, and the bureaucracies that first bloat states with mediocrity then finally sink them in chaos. *The Dunciad* is nothing *less* than a satire on "*Modern Life, and the Conduct of it in general*"; consequently, it creates the potential for application as a political satire in the most profound sense.

Observers separated by temperament, political party, and time—Swift, Johnson, Joseph Warton, and others—all insist on the transient, comparatively unworthy nature of *The Dunciad*. Samuel Richardson thinks it too topical (and too long); he writes George Cheyne in 1743, about "this *everlasting* Work of exposing *transitory* Dunces," and offers that, "Mr. Pope might employ his Time, and his admirable Genius better than in exposing Insects of a Day." A year later, in 1744, Richardson is harsher still. Discussion of *The Dunciad* constitutes—by far—the shortest of any of Warton's sections (13) in his two volumes on Pope. It commands barely thirteen of six hundred pages, wildly incommensurate with twentieth-century judgments. Warton exudes hostility to the poem, especially to the fourth book, calling it foreign, lacking all propriety and decorum, heterogeneous, injudicious, ill-placed, and incongruous.

But one group of American poets brilliantly applies *The Dunciad* at a time of political and cultural crisis. By "application" we should not expect exegesis or a biographical linking of Pope's life or character with his text; nor "imitation" in the usual eighteenth-century literary sense, but in the sense Burke uses it: taking a work or writer, such as a Greek tragedy, or Dante, or *The Dunciad,* and using it as an imaginative rather than formal model in order to address present situations and problems whose tangled roots are political, psychological, religious, and cultural. This application of an older text goes beyond employing it as an epigraph or historical precedent. It goes beyond—though it may encompass—allusion, exact quotation, or evocation. It is in the vein of Edward Young's sense of imitation as catching the spirit and ethos of the old, but transforming its design into something original, newly charged with emotional and intellectual repercussions, an application that, in keeping with the larger aims of literature, calls for action. Burke applies Virgil and Milton this way in his speeches in Commons, and he also applies Pope. In these applications Burke, remarked Gibbon, "possessed the sense and spirit of the Classics."[2]

In his first published work—*The Reformer,* January through April 1748—Burke uses Pope's onslaught against "the empire of Dulness" to criticize the theater and cultural milieu of Dublin. Throughout his life Burke applies *The Dunciad* as an imaginative polestar by which to read the course of the British Empire.[3] Among his many allusions to the poem, we find one from *Parliamentary History* (February 20, 1781 [21: 1292–93]): "Mr. *Burke* said, so many and such great revolutions had happened of late, that he was not much surprised to hear the right hon. gentleman treat the loss of the supremacy of this country over Ireland as a matter of very little consequence. Thus one star, and that the brightest ornament of our orrery, having been suffered to be lost [the American colonies], those who were accustomed to inspect and watch our political heaven, ought not to wonder that it should be followed by the loss of another:

> So star would follow star, and light, light
> Till all was darkness and eternal night.

These lines resemble several passages in *Dunciad* 4 (lines 1–4, 13–16, 639–40).

But while Burke enjoins the spirit of visionary literary works, his is not the major application of *The Dunciad*. The most unexpected, significant one comes by an imitative method worthy of the Scriblerians themselves. This application aims at immediate political purposes, nothing less than to preserve the union of fledgling American states; evidence indicates that this application of Pope helps to ratify the federal Constitution, a ratification hinging on the crucial Connecticut compromise, without which the Constitution could never have succeeded.

The Anarchiad, a poem by Joel Barlow, Colonel David Humphreys (a friend of George Washington's), John Trumbull, and Dr. Lemuel Hopkins—all members of the Connecticut state society of the Cincinnati, whose secretary was Trumbull himself—transports Pope to the New World. At the time, some said the authors drew their plan for *The Anarchiad* from "The Rolliad" (1784), attributed to Fox, Sheridan, and their circle of wits. Humphreys read "The Rolliad" while traveling in England. But any close reading reveals the original inspiration for *The Anarchiad.* The American poem, published complete in *The New Haven Gazette and Connecticut Magazine* (October 26, 1786 through September 13, 1787), also appears partially in numerous newspapers in Connecticut, Massachusetts, New Hampshire, and Rhode Island. The publisher encourages others to pirate and reprint the work locally, which many do. Originally *The Anarchiad: A Poem on the Restoration of Chaos and Substantial Night,* the subtitle already echoing Pope, the American poem comes to its climax during the crucial days of the Constitutional Convention. This is also the time of large, violent, insurrectionary mobs, of Shays's Rebellion. Pro-federalist, *The Anarchiad* aims to check and control the mob leaders; it attacks "Shays' and Shattuck's mob-compelling name."

As the "great Anarch," a name for Chaos, appears at the end of *Dunciad* 4, so *The Anarchiad* echoes those lines:

> Thy constitution, Chaos, is restor'd;
> Law sinks before thy uncreating word.

The play on constitution is obvious. The poem makes a plea to follow the actual requisitions of Congress, not the "mobs" and "anarchy" of roving, armed bands. As does Pope's "Epistle to Bathurst" (see Chapter 7), it decries the abuses of paper money, then issued disastrously by Rhode Island. The poem foresees consequences of American political chaos without some form of central government able to control crises that threaten to spread beyond state borders:

> Behold the reign of anarchy, begun,
> And half the business of confusion done.
> From hell's dark caverns discord sounds alarms,
> Blows her loud trump, and calls my Shays to arms.
> ·
> Now sinks the public mind; a deathlike sleep
> O'er all the torpid limbs begins to creep.

This same image of physical torpor Burke employs many times when he writes on the British response to American affairs. The trope is employed much as we might use "decline" today.

The Anarchiad praises Generals Nathaniel Greene and George Washington as heroes, Colonel Humphreys having served under both. It also parodies Pope's personal invocation to Swift in *The Dunciad,* inverting it to attack rather than to praise the anti-federalists William Willams and James Wadsworth:

> Oh, thou, whatever title please thine ear,
> Judge, General, Delegate, or Registrar
> ·
> Bid insurrection claim thy noblest praise,
> O'er WASHINGTON exalt thy darling Shays.

Commonwealth of Massachusetts.

By His EXCELLENCY

JamesBowdoin,Esq.

GOVERNOUR of the COMMONWEALTH of

MASSACHUSETTS.

A Proclamation.

WHEREAS by an Act passed the sixteenth of February instant, entitled, " An Act describing the disqualifications, to which persons shall be subjected, which have been, or may be guilty of Treason, or giving aid or support to the present Rebellion, and to whom a pardon may be extended," the General Court have established and made known the conditions and disqualifications, upon which pardon and indemnity to certain offenders, described in the said Act, shall be offered and given ; and have authorized and empowered the Governour, in the name of the General Court, to promise to such offenders such conditional pardon and indemnity :

I HAVE thought fit, by virtue of the authority vested in me by the said Act, to issue this Proclamation, hereby promising pardon and indemnity to all offenders within the description aforesaid, who are citizens of this State ; under such restrictions, conditions and disqualifications, as are mentioned in the said Act : provided they comply with the terms and conditions thereof, on or before the twenty-first day of March next.

GIVEN at the Council Chamber in Boston, this Seventeenth Day of February, in the Year of our LORD, One Thousand Seven Hundred and Eighty-Seven, and in the Eleventh Year of the Independence of the United States of AMERICA.

JAMES BOWDOIN.

By His Excellency's Command,

JOHN AVERY, jun. Secretary.

BOSTON : Printed by ADAMS & NOURSE, Printers to the GENERAL COURT.

Governor James Bowdoin. *A Proclamation* [broadside] offering "conditional pardon" to those involved in Shays's Rebellion. The charge was treason. Boston: Adams & Nourse, February 17, 1787. The Gilder Lehrman Collection, on deposit at The Pierpont Morgan Library, New York, New York. GLC 518. Reproduced by permission.

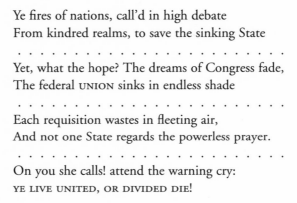

$\cdots \cdots \cdots \cdots \cdots \cdots \cdots \cdots \cdots$
Still may'st thou thus support th'unfederal cause,
The scourge of Congress, and the dread of laws.

If the versification is not always smooth, in Number 10 (May 24, 1787) we receive the central message of the poem. Hesper, opponent of the Anarch, addresses the Constitutional Convention at Philadelphia:

Ye fires of nations, call'd in high debate
From kindred realms, to save the sinking State

$\cdots \cdots \cdots \cdots \cdots \cdots \cdots \cdots \cdots$
Yet, what the hope? The dreams of Congress fade,
The federal UNION sinks in endless shade

$\cdots \cdots \cdots \cdots \cdots \cdots \cdots \cdots \cdots$
Each requisition wastes in fleeting air,
And not one State regards the powerless prayer.

$\cdots \cdots \cdots \cdots \cdots \cdots \cdots \cdots \cdots$
On you she calls! attend the warning cry:
YE LIVE UNITED, OR DIVIDED DIE!

This is published on the eve of the first day of the convention. The connection between Pope and the Connecticut Wits is no state secret and has been mentioned by Leon Howard in his classic study *The Connecticut Wits* (1943), and by William Dowling in *Poetry and Ideology in Revolutionary Connecticut* (1991). But Howard severely downplays any actual effect of the satire and intimates that its authors were, "in general, climbing on the bandwagon of public opinion instead of trying to lead it." While Dowling sees the Wits as engaged in ideological action, an interpretation that fits with literary critical preoccupations of the 1980s and 1990s, he also implies that the political impact of the poem is minimal. Howard feels that Barlow and Humphreys "never escaped from a basic assumption that poetry was not quite real—that polite literature, like polite behavior, was a cultivated affectation." Howard is hard on the poem, and not only because of its harsh versification, falling below what Humphreys, speaking of Pope, calls "the sweetness of his versification."[4]

But more plausible conclusions are reached by William K. Bottorff in his 1967 introduction to a reprinting of the only book-length version of *The Anarchiad,* an 1861 publication we shall touch on at the end of this essay. Bottorff amasses contemporary evidence strongly suggesting the pervasive presence and influence of the poem. He has grounds to speculate that some Connecticut delegates pack installments of the poem in their bags for the trip to Philadelphia. He concludes, "The notion that *The Anarchiad* may have affected public opinion in 1787 seems valid." He also quotes sources within living memory of the event, as well as scholars in the generations before Howard. The satire "was copied into scores of newspapers, became the theme of common conversation, and aided largely in forming the popular feeling that made possible the Federal constitution of 1787"; "The poem was very popular . . . and was of great service . . . in recalling the people to a realization of their responsibilities and duties"; *The Anarchiad* became "the most celebrated political satire of the times"; the poem was "copied in periodicals throughout the United States and had a widespread political influence"; and "The contemporaries of the Connecticut Wits received *The Anarchiad* with great favor. . . . Almost every intelligent citizen of Connecticut was reading *The Anarchiad*."[5]

Beyond this, a review of the massive, more recently published *Documentary History of the Ratification of the Constitution* (vol. 3, 1978) provides more evidence that Howard's assessment is grudging, Bottorff's more accurate. For example, we find from the *Documentary History* that *The Anarchiad is* packed for trips to Philadelphia. Humphreys himself acts as a delegate from Connecticut to a national meeting of the Society of the Cincinnati in May 1787, at Philadelphia, and is among the party "who escorted Washington from Chester to Philadelphia on 13 May." Bottorff's speculation turns out to be true in spades. One of the authors personally accompanies Washington, the hero of the poem, to Philadelphia, two weeks before the stupendous tenth number of *The Anarchiad* appears. Merrill Jensen, editor of the relevant volume of the *Documentary History,* states, "There were of course more serious essays on the subject of government, and on a far different level" than *The Anarchiad.* "Perhaps the best summation of Connecticut arguments for constitutional change, the kind to be hoped for from the Convention then meeting in Philadelphia, was David Daggett's oration in New Haven on 4 July 1787." But when Daggett's speech is read closely, it reveals repetitions of the same arguments already found in the parts of *The Anarchiad* published earlier. Jensen does allow that "Personal attacks in prose and poetry . . . may have had some effect on Connecticut voters. Shays's Rebellion in neighboring Massachusetts had far more by the spring of 1787." But this remark completely misses the point: by the spring of 1787, *The Anarchiad* had done more than any other single document, report, or speech to publicize Shays's rebellion and to galvanize public opinion against it.[6]

Roger Sherman introduces the Great Compromise, known also as the Connecticut or Sherman Compromise, to the Constitutional Convention on June 11, eighteen days after publication of Number 10 of *The Anarchiad*. And while the compromise fails on that day, it emerges a month later as the essential move to salvage and solidify passage of the Constitution. By giving small and large states equal representation in the Senate, it resolves an intractable issue facing the delegates. Sherman, a remarkable politician who signed the Declaration of Independence, is keenly aware of public sentiment and popular publications in his home state. Several months later he himself writes an essay for *The New Haven Gazette* (the same paper publishing *The Anarchiad*) urging Connecticut to ratify the new Constitution.

In short, as the evidence comes together, especially from Bottorff and the facts in the *Documentary History,* the skepticism of Howard and of Jensen's distasteful judgment of satiric verse as not "serious" both evaporate. Readers then took satiric verse seriously—or else they would be ignoring the whole of English-speaking public life since 1660. (Jensen cites only Leon Howard as a scholarly source for the Connecticut Wits.) This poem matters politically, as much or more than any other poem in American history. Yet *The Dunciad,* its model, is not at all Pope's most political poem. There are, in fact, few political interpretations of it.[7] How can we explain its application?

2

Considering how Pope's overtly political verse is treated in the mid and late eighteenth century, and how his reputation as a political poet in England fades, the American application seems all the more an inventive shock. From the start, the use of *The Dunciad* as a model for much of anything seems doomed. Swift informs Pope that only Londoners—and those Londoners alone who follow the fortunes of Grub Street—will be able to track the references and allusions. He writes Pope, "The Notes I could wish to be very large, in what relates to the persons concerned; for I have long observ'd that twenty miles from London no body understands hints, initial letters, or town-facts and passages; and in a few years not even those who live in London."[8] At its birth the poem is already thought stillborn by many. In a few years, Swift—who indicated to Gay how topical the poem is—predicts it will be buried. Three decades later, in *Sir Launcelot Greaves* (serialized 1760–62), Smollett's hero finds it necessary to go out of his way to inform readers that, "Of all those whom Pope lashed in his Dunciad, there was not one who did not richly deserve the imputation of dulness; and every one of them had provoked the satirist by a personal attack" (Chapter 23). Smollett's defense, already singular, is the last to champion Pope in these terms. Smollett writes it because he knows that the personal and political squabbles no longer hold interest. Even among the cognoscenti, few understand the hints after fifteen, let alone thirty, years. Swift's prediction has come true.

Samuel Johnson, reviewing Joseph Warton's first volume of *An Essay on the Genius and Writings of Pope* in *The Literary Magazine*, 1756, says that "the writer is of opinion [*sic*], that he has dispatched the chief part of his task; for he ventures to remark, that the reputation of *Pope*, as a poet, among posterity, will be principally founded on to [*sic*] his *Windsor-Forest, Rape of the lock*, and *Eloisa to Abelard*, while the facts and characters alluded to in his late writings will be forgotten and unknown, and their poignancy and propriety little relished; for wit and satire are transitory and perishable, but nature and passion are eternal."[9]

Despite the complaints of Swift, despite the fact that Smollett's already anachronistic defense comes less than twenty years after Pope publishes the final version of the poem, and despite the growing opinion of Warton, relayed through Johnson, who thinks it important enough to quote at length, we've seen that in a curious twist of reception and application the most obscure of Pope's works—and clearly not the most political, *The Dunciad*—exerts the greatest political repercussions later in the century, in a new country and in a manner no one could have anticipated. In the colonies and the young Republic, styles in architecture and the decorative arts lag several decades behind their "cutting edge" in England and the Continent. The same is often the case in literary taste and style.

The emphasis of much modern scholarship falls on Pope's political attitudes, the minutiae of party politics and party strife reflected in the *Moral Essays* (3 and 4), the *Epilogue to the Satires, Windsor-Forest*, "To Augustus," and other *Horatian Imitations*, with the recognition that, for Pope, politics, morality, and aesthetics are vitally intertwined. We reconstruct topical allusions, personages, and complex political attitudes, and we chart the shifting image of Caesar Augustus and the British monarchy. But this is not how scholars, biographers, or poets of the later eighteenth century treat Pope. As the century passes, the political issues in Pope's poetry fade. We find scant reference to them in criticism, biography, or verse. This erosion is tersely summed up by Joseph Warton's comment in the second volume of his study of Pope (1782). Warton speaks of examining Pope's poetry "now that party prejudices are worn away."[10] They were worn away years before.

It is true that critics, occasionally citing a specific line, refer to Pope's break with Bolingbroke. The life of Pope by Cibber and Shiels (1753) mentions controversy over the "Spirit of Patriotism, and the Idea of a Patriot King," but declines extensive discussion.[11] Most critics mention Pope's "decent freedom" toward monarchy. An anonymous Elegy of 1744, appearing a few days after Pope's death on May 30, ventures:

> Not GEORGE returning to his native sky,
> From these sad Scenes shall with more Glory fly,
> Than Pope who in his loftier Sphere did sit
> Sov'reign of POETRY, and Prince of WIT.

And there are other fairly innocent hits at monarchical tyranny. Percival Stockdale closes the peroration of his *Inquiry* of 1778 this way: "as I know that I am above *low ambition, and the pride of Kings,* I would rather wish to possess *thy* abilities,"—meaning Pope's—"than the power of a monarch."[12] This generic attitude, in phrase and sentiment, falls in line with attitudes frequent in Pope's verse. Owen Ruffhead in his *Life* (1769) agrees with Pope that kings are not fountains of honor but merely bestowers of titles; and Ruffhead praises a single line in *The Dunciad,* "The right divine of kings to govern wrong," though in broad terms. Yet Ruffhead concludes that Pope is "a bigot to no sect or party," a conclusion that neatly avoids discussing what parties or sects Pope favors or attacks.[13] By the time Warton completes his two-volume study in the early 1780s, he and others seem impatient even with Pope's mild disdain of royalty. Warton notes that,

> Our author is so perpetually expressing an affected contempt for kings, that it becomes almost a nauseous cant;
>
> > —*the pride of kings*—
> > —*some monster of a king*—
> > —*pity kings—the gift of kings*—
> > —*Gods of kings—much above a king*—
> > —*Settle wrote of kings*—&c.[14]

Here the "&c." might include the penultimate line of "Bathurst," "The Devil and the King divide the prize" (see Chapter 7; Pope parallels Swift's rather nasty marginal comments on kings, especially Swift's about Henry VIII).[15]

But these references do not qualify as "political" in any finer-grained sense. Most treatment of Pope in biography, criticism, and poetry is explicitly and consciously without politics. To clinch this point, we can turn to a few, at that time, better-known and influential studies. Ayre/Curll, in his *Memoirs of Pope*, protests that Pope was only "a Gentleman, a Scholar, and a Poet. He filled no Office or Place. . . . his Life was wholly a State of Inaction, and spent in Conversation, Study, and Books."[16] This verdict catches the first part of Maynard Mack's subtitle to his modern study *The Garden and the City*, but neglects the second half of the equation: *Retirement and Politics in the Later Poetry of Pope*.

Cibber and Shiels report that young Pope, conversing with Addison, affirmed, "But as politics was not his study, he could not always determine, at least, with any degree of certainty, whose councils were best." Incredibly, these two biographers accept this self-protective, politic judgment at face value. Aside from noting the controversy with Bolingbroke, their life is apolitical, treading gently the verge of partisan issues.[17] Smollett begins his 1756 notice of Warton's first volume in *The Critical Review* with a reference to "*Belles Lettres.*" He notes that Warton's erudition is "perhaps too ostentatiously displayed" but that he nevertheless has written a work of true criticism. Smollett then examines images and representative meter. The poetry of Pope covered in Warton's first volume does not offer many political subjects compared with those poems covered in the second, but it is clear that Smollett does not regard Pope as a political poet, at least not one worth emphasis. It might be objected that Warton delays his second volume because in the 1750s it would have been too charged politically, but no evidence supports this.

Smollett, reviewing Warton's first volume, offers a parallel in Pope's critical treatment shifting from political to literary and belletristic grounds in Smollett's own defense of Milton as a poet against Hume's harsh treatment of Milton resting primarily on the regicide question in Hume's *History*. (Smollett's review of Hume's *History* appears in the same issue of *The Critical Review* in 1756.) Smollett stresses the need to focus on poetic achievement rather than political convictions or crimes. In doing so he counters Hume, who was a friend, and adds to the growing pattern of the reception of Dryden and Pope. The point is not so much that Pope is being consciously depoliticized in a way that other poets are not, but that the general tendency to aestheticize and to put all criticism on more formal, literary grounds has the effect of cutting off and devaluing much of Pope's poetry, particularly the poetry of the 1730s and 1740s.

W. H. Dilworth, for his poor *Life of Alexander Pope, Esq.* (1759), relies heavily on Ayre/Curll. Treating the later political poetry in an odd way, Dilworth uses *To Bathurst,* a highly charged Opposition poem published with overt political purposes on the day Parliament opens in 1732–33, merely as a pretext to discuss how Pope spent his own fortune and kept up relations with Bathurst. Dilworth says nothing about political objectives in the poem. He ignores the devilish machinery of Walpole's financial scheming. His commentary on the fourth *Moral Essay* centers on Pope's egregiously bad taste in attacking Lord Chandos, an affront, Dilworth implies, not to be brooked. Pope's Horatian imitations get two pages of short shrift.

Owen Ruffhead's *Life* treads gently on political issues, too. We have noted Ruffhead's willingness to side with Pope against the despotism of tyrannical kings; but he reports that when Pope came across anything political in Sir William Temple's essays, "he had no manner or relish for it. This disrelish for politics, continued throughout his whole life: and . . . his indifference at last ended in aversion." Ruffhead does not question this simplistic report, left as the sole explanation and commentary on Pope's political nature. He treats "To Bathurst" with tongs, noting only the portraits of Cotta and Buckingham, dead already by the end of the previous century. From the story of Sir Balaam—which we now recognize as charged with contemporaneous party, religious, and financial implications—Ruffhead draws the bland moral that wealth invites a curse, for which lesson, he says, the portrait of Balaam needs no gloss. About "To Augustus," another, even stronger litmus test of cultural and partisan interests, a poem for which Pope was threatened with assassination, Ruffhead concentrates "especially where poetry is the subject"! He avoids all political complications, then turns again to individuals and issues in the distant past. If the living presence of George II were ever a bar to comment on the poem, his death in 1760 removed that obstacle nine years earlier for Ruffhead, who, however, has nothing to say about Augustus, Roman or British.[18]

Percival Stockdale's *Inquiry* defends Pope against Warton, whose taste is "vitiated, and whose head is confused with too much learning."[19] But Stockdale concentrates on versification, imagery, and invention. Though Pope was not of a higher social class than Warton, Stockdale defends Pope as a gentleman (after all, Horace was, too!). Stockdale asserts that nature, not Cambridge—Warton's university—is Pope's alma mater, and that Pope should be judged by that source and test and end of art. Then Stockdale, too, hints that poetry would be sullied by an exercise of any lower inquiries from learning or politics. Against Warton's judgment of twenty-two years earlier, he claims for Pope the transcendently pathetic and sublime, and concentrates on "Eloisa to Abelard," "To Arbuthnot," *The Essay on Man,* and *The Rape of the Lock.*

To add to this list of critics who emphasize Pope's less political work and who, even in treating the political poems, concentrate on the belletristic, we can look at a popular, influential anthology, Knox's *Elegant Extracts.* It contains Pope under two headings, "Elegiac" and "Devotional and Moral." His political side Knox ignores or suppresses, the sharp satire is eliminated, and "Satiric Verse" means one piece from his milder side.

Warton's second volume digresses a little on present politics, as occasioned by Pope's lines from the sixth epistle of the First Book of Horace:

> Or popularity? or stars and strings?
> The mob's applauses, or the gifts of kings.

But Warton then advises contemporary politicians to correct themselves by reading Socrates' advice to Alcibiades, not Pope. Yet he does dwell longer than other critics on "To Augustus," saying, "All those nauseous and outrageous compliments, which Horace, in a strain of abject adulation, degraded himself by paying to Augustus, POPE has converted into bitter and pointed sarcasms, conveyed under the form of the most artful irony. Of this irony the following specimens shall be placed together, in one view, added to the preceding lines, which are of the same cast." Warton quotes four passages, one from the beginning and three from the end of "To Augustus." These contain a scathing, personal attack on the king, one Pope conveys with perhaps the greatest imitative irony in the language. However briefly, Warton locates the deep personal antipathy and political irony of this epistle. Here is some recognition, too, that the political archetype of Augustus calls up contempt—a point we shall pick up in a moment—and that Horace is no trustworthy political model or court poet. Warton, more acute than Stockdale, fingers Pope's ironic use of Horace and the rejection of Horace's sycophancy; in doing so he speaks in the spirit of Pope's 1738 "Epitaph," written for himself, "For one who would not be buried in Westminster-Abbey":

> HEROES and KINGS! your distance keep:
> In peace let one poor Poet sleep,

> Who never flatter'd Folks like you:
> Let Horace blush, and Virgil too.

But before we see in Warton any political sympathy with Pope, or a use of him beyond recognition of the slavish political behavior of *one* of his Roman literary models—Juvenal and Persius are present in the Horatian imitations, too—we should remember how Warton alludes to Pope's two dialogues that form the *Epilogue to the Satires*. They are for Warton a false prophecy: "Yet this very country, so emasculated and debased by every species of folly and wickedness, in about twenty years afterwards," says Warton, "carried its triumphs over all its enemies, through all the quarters of the world, and astonished the most distant nations with a display of uncommon efforts, abilities, and virtues. So vain and groundless are the prognostications of poets, as well as politicians. It is to be lamented, that no genius could be found to write an *One Thousand Seven Hundred and Sixty One,* as a counterpart to these two satires." Not a very Popean conclusion, and one that denies any prophetic power that Pope—or any poet or politician—may hold. Moreover, Warton cites the character of Walpole in the *Epilogue* as one "dictated by candour and gratitude; distinguishing the minister from the man." It is hard to read this as an overtly partisan comment. And, incredibly, it constitutes Warton's only reference to Pope's frequent child of scorn.[20]

3

Measured against this growing aestheticization of Pope and the buried memory of his politics, American taste is, as usual, lagging behind by thirty years or so. Not only is Pope's mode still popular, political embroilments in the colonies keep alive the satiric and politically charged spirit of Pope. This spirit the Connecticut Wits seize. As Pope uses, not copies, Horace, so they use, not copy, him.

The Anarchiad ends with an attack on the Frenchman Michel René Hilliard D'Auberteul, who wrote against the American Revolution. The explanation included with the poem states of D'Auberteul:

> He concludes with the following sublime address to his shade, which has been closely copied by Pope, in one of his smaller poems:

> Swift fly the years, and rise the expected morn!
> Oh spring to light! auspicious sage, be born!
> The new-found world shall all your cares engage;
> The promised lyre of the future age.
>
> . . . .
>
> Virtue no more the generous breast shall fire,
> Nor radiant truth the historic page inspire;
> But lost, dissolved in thy superior shade,
> One tide of falsehood o'er the world be spread;
> In wit's light robe shall gaudy fiction shine,
> And all be lies, as in a work of thine.

Now, this is a direct, conscious inverse of Pope's *Messiah*—with echoes of *The Dunciad* to boot. We witness, in other words, a complete reversal of the image of Augustus in the Augustan Age. The figure of Augustus as Virgilian Messiah is turned on its head. This is diametrically opposite to the way Dryden begins *Astræa Redux,* quoting Virgil's fourth *Eclogue* and proclaiming Charles II a new Augustus. To us is now revealed a newer Augustus, no savior but a tyrant, a French lover of despotism who opposes the American Revolution. The allusions invert themselves. Pope's *Messiah* is inverted in its purpose, too, and the new Messiah becomes a political Antichrist. Instead, George Washington is the true Savior, the leader not of an empire but of a new country that revives Roman republican virtue and will identify with heroes such as Cincinnatus, who, as the Minutemen do, will leave the plow to save the Republic.

At the start of *The Anarchiad,* we are told by the introducer, "I know not whether it is necessary to remark, in this place, what the critical reader will probably have already observed, that the celebrated English poet, Mr. Pope, has proved himself a noted plagiarist, by copying the preceding ideas, and even couplets almost entire, into his famous poem called 'The Dunciad.'" Here the connection with Pope is made explicit. We can recall, too, that Pope's poem was included in President Clap's library at Yale, which Joel Barlow frequented and loved. And for Trumbull, Howard notes that "The most interesting of the surviving bits of his undergraduate verse are in Pope's manner." One admirer calls Trumbull the "immortal Son of immortal Pope." In fact, in January 1774, Trumbull wrote "The Destruction of Babylon," a rendering of biblical passages in Pope's *Messiah.* So, the connections with Pope, *The Dunciad,* and *The Messiah* are deep and long-standing among the Wits. The idea, we discover, is that

The Anarchiad represents an ancient native American manuscript dug up and interpreted by a "society of critics and antiquarians," a ruse worthy of Martinus Scriblerus himself. A year later, in 1788, Timothy Dwight will publish *The Triumph of Infidelity*. His notes, mostly satiric, are by "Scriblerus."[21]

Pope's *Dunciad* is applied politically by the Connecticut Wits because of its power of myth, its visionary nature. It suggests an epic sweep, a condemnation of culture in decline and of the politics associated with such a degeneration. It is a poem whose modern apocalyptic imagination fits the leveling, anarchy, and even the terror and fear of modern political misdirection, excess, paranoia, and plain stupidity. It's also a poem about the city in all its connotations: *civitas* or civilization; the City as financial and cultural center; the city as *polis*, the original site of political action. None of this can be said in the same way about the *Moral Essays* or the *Horatian Imitations*. *The Dunciad* contains, however strung out and vitiated its narrative, an action whose inevitability presages darkly the terrible turn of political events that seem precipitately unavoidable in the way they career out of control at the behest of demagogues, accompanied by the applause of their followers. There is no constant speaker, no *adversarius,* but finally a narration and a narrator that might imaginatively be applied to any similar future *mythos.* This is the vatic and narrative power found in Burke, in Blake, and at moments in Dryden, three of the finest political poets in English.

We can think of Warton's particular distaste for *The Dunciad,* especially Book 4. Yet it is precisely there that Pope unleashes his vision of "*Modern Life,* and the Conduct of it*" that holds greatest promise of political application, and the one most appropriated by Burke and the Connecticut Wits. By its grand and detailed apocalyptic transitoriness, *The Dunciad* attains an eerie, timeless universality; the old names and footnotes are drained and bled away by time, but the political application of its vision finds current dramatis personae. This is what the Connecticut Wits recognize, though with the added joke that they claim their poem precedes Pope's, so it is he, not they, who seems to perform the application. Agnes Sibley, still the chief authority on Pope's reputation in America, notes, "the method would have delighted Pope."[22]

In modern literary scholarship, the political lessons of Pope's poems are embedded in historical fact, minute knowledge, and detailed context. But the political wisdom and application of Pope, while related to that knowledge, is another matter. We already see two examples of applying Pope in a political way, and in ways he could not have anticipated: the principles of Burke and the argument for a particular kind of American constitution in *The Anarchiad.*

Pope's American constitution provides key support for the American Constitution. It is delegates from Connecticut who hammer out the Great Compromise permitting passage of the document. As William Bottroff states, "Perhaps the cumulative effect of these papers [the serialized printings of *The Anarchiad*], including their influence on the delegates' constituency, helps explain the otherwise 'surprising switch of Connecticut'" with respect to approval of the Constitution. In addition, by attacking Rhode Island's issuance of paper money, *The Anarchiad* likely influences Connecticut's Sherman to insist on a constitutional prohibition against any state ever doing do again.[23] Here is a constitution, a poetic and political negotiation of the "old" but generally unknown historicism, one more real, vital, and of greater import than any ornamental connection between a given text and the political powers that prevail during its composition.

The Connecticut Wits and Pope echo in American culture once more. Edited by Luther G. Riggs and published in New Haven by Thomas H. Pease, *The Anarchiad* is issued for the first time as a book in 1861. Now the old Popean poem is intended to address a new, impending conflict that threatens the Union, a crisis arising from issues left unresolved by the American Enlightenment and subsequent interpretations of the Constitution itself—the Civil War. The poem, thus reprinted, does not stay the course of war. Perhaps a newer application or fresh version would have had genuine impact. But that it remains in public consciousness strongly enough to be called upon again at a time of renewed national fragmentation is a tribute to the hope placed in a literary response to civic threats. To believe in a link between writing and conduct is always an act of faith. And if the connection is real, it harbors potential abuse as well as use. Since Pope's time, no one has grasped the double-edged sword cutting between words and action with more skill than his friend Jonathan Swift. Swift knows that governments, writers, intelligence communities, and communities of intellectuals all weave webs of words. To what ends they do so, and how those webs enmesh each other—that makes all the difference.

4

Swift Considers Words, Intelligence, and the Academy

The Engine of Broken Sentences, the Method of Discovering Plots

To serve its own peculiar motives, the academic world has judged the third voyage of Lemuel Gulliver in the manner Dr. John Arbuthnot does: "I tell you freely," he writes Swift on November 5, 1726, "the part of the projectors is the least Brilliant." Irony—or, more likely, genuine self-effacement—may lurk in Arbuthnot's comment if he himself, as some suspected, wrote "the part of the projectors." Twelve days later, John Gay confides, "As to other Critics, they think the flying island is the least entertaining; and so great an opinion the town have of the impossibility of Gulliver's writing at all below himself, that 'tis agreed that Part was not writ by the same Hand, tho' this hath its defenders too." On November 27, Swift thinks it worth repeating to Pope that, "(unless I am much mistaken) Dr. Arbuthnot likes the Projectors least, others you tell me, the Flying Island; some think it wrong to be so hard upon whole Bodies or Corporations."[1]

The third voyage of *Gulliver's Travels* indicts academies. It takes to task their vanities of learning and their naive political complicities. From motives of self-protection, conscious or unconscious, literary scholars and critics have comfortably viewed the third voyage as a satire on modern science or politics or, occasionally, on learning in general. But it pointedly satirizes irresponsible acts that lie at the heart of critical interpretations, including literary ones, and their political applications. On this voyage Gulliver travels to several lands, not one. He converses with creatures who are not giants, Lilliputians, horses, or Yahoos. They are people his own size. Some live on the Flying Island, a kind of controlled, subspace asteroid, whose ruler can use it as a giant impact bomb to quash unruly subjects who ask too many questions, refuse to pay taxes, or build their religious temples too high. Gulliver talks with citizens so fascinated with the formal properties of math and music that they lose track of all else, their theoretical proficiencies so brilliant they cannot handle a plumb line or carpenter's rule: their dwellings are in constant danger of lethal collapse. Later, in another country, Luggnagg, he meets the *struldbruggs,* people who grow old for hundreds of years, but whose decaying age without death creates crises in law, health care, and social behavior. After a brief stay in Japan, Gulliver returns home. But on this voyage he speaks, too, with professors at the Grand Academy of Lagado—not scientists, really, but modern academic specialists. Two of them investigate codes, words, or strings of words. Their motives for doing so range from scholarly honors and prestige to governmental thought control.

Samuel Johnson echoes the opinions he heard as a young man, that the Flying Island is the least successful part. Although Daniel Boone told people that his favorite book was *Gulliver's Travels,* he seems to have left no reaction to the third voyage. Coleridge lets loose an emotional tirade against the third voyage, a desire to "expunge" this "wretched abortion, the product of spleen and ignorance and self conceit."[2] When he speaks in his literary lectures of the *Travels* as Swift's greatest work—he likes *A Tale of A Tub,* too—he comments only on the first, second, and fourth voyages. The third he skips.[3] As if on S.T.C.'s cue, the *Norton Anthology* for years presented chapters from voyages 1, 2, and 4, omitting completely the third. Then, it printed those voyages entire. Only recently has the third crept in. Allan Bloom's "Outline of *Gulliver's Travels,*" half apologizes, "We can make only a short visit to Laputa," and tackles first, as does most commentary on the third voyage, what elsewhere is called "science," "high science," "pseudo-science," "technology," or "Utopianism."

But there is as much about language, words, and their interpretation. The satire explicitly addresses *all* the arts and sciences. The Grand Academy is the closest thing not to our scientific societies and laboratories, but to our universities and institutions of higher learning.[4] The inhabitants of the Flying Island and of Lagado possess something more than a lack of poetry; they possess an excess of bad criticism. Why have we slighted the direct hits of the third voyage against poor interpretation and self-interested criticism, while frequently calling attention to its comments on politics and science? The answer is suggested by what Norman O. Brown says about Swift's writing in another context: "It is a perfect example, in the field of literary criticism, of Freud's notion that the first way in which consciousness becomes conscious of a repressed idea is by emphatically denying it."[5] Not only The Royal Society but all academies are deeply implicated and rebuked in Swift's third voyage, and those who follow certain methods to study words become objects of his satire. The relative unpopularity and the difficulty of teaching the third voyage is not new to critics, but the motive for those reactions and pedagogical practices is not, I think, intellectual perspicuity or innocent imitation of a long prevailing view. The attitude toward the third voyage, particularly to its first six chapters, masks an avoidance of what implicates scholars most. Ricardo Quintana, William Eddy, and others term it the least literary of all the voyages, yet, in Gay's term, I would like to defend it because it attacks pernicious literary practices. Its defenders have, instead, usually dealt with structural unity, Gulliver's character development, a critique of science, Utopian fiction, or the place of the third voyage in the direction of the whole narrative. Douglas Patey has helpfully contextualized the third voyage in the quarrel of Ancients and Moderns and its nomenclature of knowledge—with the slippery question of what, exactly, "science" means—as well as nicely connecting some of its episodes with themes found in the other three books.[6] But I take especially the hints of John Sutherland, who identifies "intellectual pride" as the overarching theme, and of Clive Probyn, Brian Tippett, and Martin Croghan, especially Croghan, who sees Swift throughout his works as a major (and ignored) semiotician interested in the excesses of semiotics. Scholars have generally ignored George Orwell's essay on *Gulliver's Travels*, "Politics *vs.* Literature," probably because it is not very good in its entirety and might seem dated. But Orwell does discern the link between excesses of language—codes and semiotics, politics, and the episodes of the third voyage—noting, "There is something queerly familiar in the atmosphere of those chapters, because . . . there is a perception that one of the aims of totalitarianism is not merely to make sure that people will think the right thoughts, but actually to make them *less conscious.*"[7]

2

The two *longest* episodes of the visit to Laputa (The Flying Island), Balnibarbi, and Lagado (the city of the Grand Academy) are not about science, but about the perils of interpretation. A mechanical frame of haphazardly spinning signifiers, whose random order is used to form sentence fragments then collected in weighty tomes, graces the first of these episodes. A method to improve deciphering the ordinary language of alleged political conspirators rests at the heart of the second. We go from an academic obsession with the undetermined, totally free play of all signifiers, eliciting no action whatsoever—but rather a collection of verbal shards published in multiple volumes—to the overdetermined hunt for suspects whose innocent use of pragmatic signifiers—of ordinary language— can pack them off to prison. The first episode degenerates into an academic "free play" with no discernible purpose, ethical commitment, or meaning. Here, by the contrivance of the frame, "the most ignorant person at a reasonable charge, and with a little bodily labor, may write books in philosophy, poetry, politics, law, mathematics, and theology, without the least assistance from genius or study," producing "volumes in large folio . . . of broken sentences." The second abuse, decoding common discourse into meanings subversive to a powerful government, misinterprets clearly intentioned signifiers by forcing their restricted play into a wildly strict "decoded" construction putatively harboring covert political meanings, and thus holding potentially dire consequences for anyone who uses ordinary language. As Paul Korshin has shown, Swift's knowledge of codes and their connections with government intelligence is extensive and grows out of a rich context.[8]

At one blow Swift strikes at absurdities of the literary academy and at potential excesses of any government's intelligence community. Each corporation or body practices, or is readily capable of practicing, a radical misuse of interpretation. If the professor standing at the frame of freely spinning signifiers seems a political innocent, Swift connects the academy and politics by providing another professor who writes a treatise on deciphering allegedly political coded diets and feces, a treatise in which Gulliver, like any driven academic, soon proudly hopes

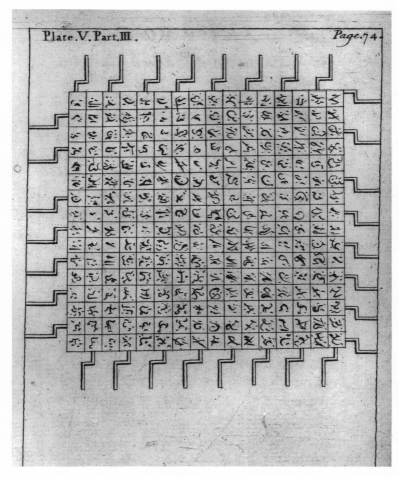

Plate.V.Part.III.

Freely spinning signifiers on the mechanical engine of "broken sentences," an original illustration for *Gulliver's Travels*, the third voyage, Chapter 5. "The professor then desired me to observe . . . The pupils at his command took each of them hold of an iron handle, whereof there were forty fixed round the edges of the frame [only thirty-one are drawn]; and giving them a sudden turn, the whole disposition of the words was entirely changed. He then commanded six and thirty of the lads to read the several lines softly . . . and where they found three or four words together that might make part of a sentence, they dictated to the four remaining boys who were scribes." Reproduced by permission of the Houghton Library, Harvard University, Cambridge, Massachusetts.

to receive "honorable mention" by offering improvements in the method of interpreting language and letters. Swift links the study of language, specifically of words—and, where words fail, syllables and letters used in anagram and acrostic—to the speculative vanity of a completely free play of signifiers. It makes no difference that no one outside the academy pays any attention to this. And, second, he links the study of language to a completely imprisoned and predetermined interpretation that, far from free, threatens the liberty of those who write the most ordinary, politically uninvolved discourse.

These two episodes portray abuses of interpretation in the academy and in party politics—in linguistic criticism and in what was, even in Swift's day, ironically called intelligence. The two are not so different—one where the free play of language means whatever you wish, the other where ordinary language means what you did not want it to, but rather what someone else in power twists it to mean. Academic and political intelligence are held up for examination on the basis of their zealous interpretation of words and the order, or lack of it, in the words themselves. Why link the academy and government intelligence in this way? A history of fertile connections between literary academics and codes exists, in many cases representing a careful, intelligent application of language, though in a few cases spinning out of orbit into wild theories. The great Allied code-breaking center of World War II, Bletchley Park, employed not only many mathematicians and musicians (more practical than those inhabiting the Flying Island), but also a preponderance of literary critics and textual editors. Gwynne Evans, editor and head of the Riverside Shakespeare project, for instance, works at Bletchley and breaks the Free French code for the Allies. Professor, later Ambassador, Edwin Reischauer, who ends his career at Harvard (as does Evans) works on Japanese ciphers for a code-breaking center in the United States. Fredson Bowers, associated with Brown, Harvard, Princeton, and the University of Virginia, directs a naval code group that breaks Japanese encryptions. As a Yale undergraduate, James Jesus Angleton, later head of CIA counterintelligence, invites William Empson to lecture, meets Ezra Pound, and, guided by his teacher Norman Holmes Pearson, falls into the company of T. S. Eliot, Graham Greene, E. M. Forster, Elizabeth Bowen, and H.D. Early in his intelligence career, Angleton recruits Richard Ellmann. Angleton believes that the New Criticism—and consequently Yale—will provide good ground in which to grow and reap agents.[9] But Angleton, once Kim Philby's best friend, sees plots everywhere and eventually believes that Henry Kissinger is a KGB spy. In Henry Hathaway's box-office film hit of the Office of Strategic Services training in World War II,

13 Rue Madelaine, starring James Cagney, chief coach to the apprentice spies is the avuncular Pappy Simpson, professor of English at Dartmouth College. The academic/intelligence connection goes back to the First World War as well, when John Mathews Manley and Edith Rickert work on cryptography.

But in the context of the third voyage, Chapters 5 and 6 suggest a liability common to more naive academic approaches and crassly partisan ones. Rather than grasping the function and criticism of language in an imaginative, inventive manner, these two approaches pervert the imagination and its inventions to serve academic vanity or political control—or the two combined, for academic vanity seeks political control, at least over its own insecure, diminished baili- wick. The two seemingly opposite concepts presented by the engine of broken sentences and the method of discovering plots are cousins under the skin. They find one home in the mind that uses language as the free play of signifiers but uses language as political or cultural intelligence to serve the mystifying purposes of a self-interested and secretive government—or academic movement. One re- cent critic made language a "rigorous" playground while covering up past associ- ations with political authorities eager to spread the fear of "international conspiracies" and "plots" carried out by a supposedly pernicious, inferior race.

If the frame is, as Swift is careful to point out, a *mechanical* device par excellence to produce endless variations of the free play of signifiers—with their resulting volumes of secondary criticism and interpretation—then the philoso- phers' backpacks of objects, which they silently offer one another in place of everyday discourse, represent the givenness of endless signifieds. The argument on this subject, using the same terms we use now, was, in Swift's time (and before and after him), a debate rivaling in bulk, profundity, and professional silliness the "discovery" of these semiotic terms during the last generation of penetrating critics. The mechanical writing of John Wilkins that fascinated Swift has its modern equivalent in the mechanical production of vast numbers of volumes of scholarship and criticism printed in order "to get it out" and to satisfy administrative criteria, often quantitative, for job security.

There exist parallels here, as Kathleen Williams and others have noted, to the treatment of criticism and interpretation in *A Tale of A Tub*—not so much in the "Digression on Critics" as in the "Digression in Praise of Digressions." There Swift describes modern wits and scholars who multiply learning. And in *A Tale,* as Dustin Griffin keenly points out, the control of critical acts of interpre- tation involves political acts of power as much as epistemological acts of inquiry or personal ones of communication.[10] We see methodolatry, index learning, and

"Similitudes, Allusions, and Applications, very Surprizing, Agreeable, and Apposite, from the *Genitals* of either Sex," such as what nowadays are called gynocrit-
ics, the shift, as fearful misogynists or militant feminists characterize it, from
critspeak to clitspeak, or the dangerous presence of the absent phallocentric.
Chesterfield remarks in Swift's century (writing Madame du Boccage) on the
"*Amazons,* and their husbands," who are "the wretched captives, destined to
perpetuate the *gynarchy.*" We have no monopoly on these terms. Such critical
learning may, like the work of the great frame, be achieved with little study or
application. Or it may be deeper. Whichever it is, warns the "narrator" of *Gulliver's Travels,* it is inexhaustible, a fortunate characteristic for those seeking novelty
and untroubled by deciphering the past and the long train of ideas that history
bequeaths us. We become "*Scholars* and *Wits,* without the Fatigue of *Reading* or
of *Thinking.*" So, reports Gulliver in Chapter 2 of the third voyage, "Imagination, fancy, and invention, they are wholly strangers to, nor have any words in
their language by which those ideas can be expressed." Put another way, what
the *Travels* calls "The common actions and behaviour of life" suffer from the
semiotics of learned professors and the codes of the intelligence community.

In the section on discovering plots, we can pass over the Atterbury and
Gyllenborg connections. They have been worked in special studies, and F. P.
Lock observes that they echo back—as Swift probably knew—to Nero, Domitian, and the Borgias.[11] The point is that Swift paints the whole apparatus as a
cover-up designed to protect, serve, and save one person, though that person
cannot be named directly. It is the king or *head* of government. Gulliver's ety-
mology for Laputa, for instance, suggests not *La puta* as the whore, nor the red
herring of the wing and the sea; rather, the old, obsolete language points to
Laputa as "High Commissioner," and this in turn suggests the chief governor
or lord lieutenant of Ireland. As Pope does in one draft of the *Epistle to Bathurst*
(see Chapter 7), Swift lets us decide how to fill in the pregnant blank or cipher
that in his text equates with the code word "codshead." It is, of course, "king,"
and the equivalent of the modern "dickhead" is none other than George I
(George II in the 1735 edition), king of Great Britain and Ireland. No surprise,
then, that Swift wonders to Pope on September 29, 1725, whether there would
be "A Printer . . . brave enough to venture his Ears." A printer guilty of sedition
would lose them. Others feel relieved when Swift's masterpiece clears the censors, as Gay says, "*nemine contradicente*" (3: 183). A few years later, Pope's
political and personal satire on George II, "To Augustus," also clears the censors.
But on closer reading it proves so inflammatory that the king's inner circle
considers assassinating Pope.

3

In the United States, citizens know that their government has spied legally and illegally on them. The massive structure housing FBI headquarters, named after the sharpest practitioner of that art, is located in a larger district named after an entirely different kind of man. But we have even witnessed public inquisitions there, where words are twisted—in the army McCarthy hearings or, more recently, in the Senate confirmation of Supreme Court Justice Clarence Thomas and in the various interpretations of its hearings. In the catalogue of the third voyage, "a senator" is paired with "a lame dog." Whichever witness one credits, Anita Hill or Clarence Thomas, we have, beyond that question, senators who were more than eager to proclaim that statements such as Anita Hill's "I don't know Phyllis Berry and Phyllis Berry doesn't know me," and the like, were "flat-out perjury." This accusation was made, incredibly, before other witnesses were heard. Some senators could not or, in front of TV cameras, would not construe anything other than the barest literal sense of her words; or, as one senator slyly called it, their "natural sense," as if Professor Hill's ordinary, colloquial sense, obvious to millions watching, was somehow an *un*natural lie told by someone disloyal to the government. Senator Arlen Specter, a former prosecutor and soon to be presidential candidate, said—before hearing any corroborating witnesses—that such statements by Professor Hill sounded to him like "a plot." What it all sounds like is the third voyage.[12] Specter remained in the Senate, though was subsequently almost unseated by a woman crusading against his conduct in the hearings. He apologized for it.

Considered as a complex assessment and satire on "science" and learning in general—and broadly the third voyage is that, too—the visits to Laputa and the Grand Academy are safe for those who study language. This perspective proves reassuring. It is all at arm's length. It is about somebody else's profession. It is written to divert, not vex us. We have nearly three hundred years of scientific progress on which to rely; and that hindsight alone gives us a better handle than Swift, even if, in other contexts, some of us are quick to scoff at the ascendancy of science and the ills technology brings, and, as proud humanists, quick to envy the sums and resources expended on the sciences, while we humanists, exactly as Swift portrays his professors, are comparative beggars scavenging for handouts and funding. In the present day, as on November 16, 1726, Pope would still have reason to write Swift what he does when *Gulliver's Travels* first appears: "the mob of Critics, you know, always are desirous to apply Satire to those that they envy for being above them" (3: 181).

Swift's satire, we know, is multivalent. It turns its scrutiny on academics, interpreters, critics, politicians, the politics of culture, the culture of politics, and the politics of academics studying to improve culture, as much—more, I would suggest—as it satirizes what we have come to call science. Alternations and vicissitudes of fashion in the study of language, the vanities of literature, and constantly retooled trends in interpretation, these leave us with a superiority over the Grand Academy far less settled than one might imagine. The human sciences, as Bacon observes, are more on a level and do not develop cumulatively. Or, as Hazlitt aptly notes, the diffusion of culture is not to be equated with its advancement.

So, too, in politics. We have satellites and eavesdropping devices but have hardly changed the ambiguous ethical territory. The intelligence community can still protect and cover up for a sitting administration and its head. Our situation is darker, perhaps, for intelligence gathering now uses not only language and code to secure political and even partisan aims, but every technical application of science it can muster. When the ones "off the shelf" prove inadequate, directors of intelligence can commission new applications. In one sense, Swift witnesses and foresees such activity, as when Gulliver beholds the frame and then recommends technical improvements in the method of discovering plots, improvements, respectively, in hardware and software. If the academy fosters and accepts any self-serving interpretation of the spinning frame of signifiers, is it any wonder that the administration of the government insists on its own spin control? Shortly after George Sherburn, a prominent Swift scholar, died a generation ago, one colleague remarked, "This least inhibited of scholars was especially puzzled at the extent to which the learned world . . . could be intimidated by slogans, catch-words, titles, advertising, professional jargon, and all the varieties of semantic bewitchment that bully opinion."[13]

4

And so we swing, in the fashion of our academies, from arbitrary signifiers to determined agendas of cultural studies. It is hard to know, faced with our academies and our intelligence agencies, and with the connections between the two (where extremes of right and left can kiss and not tell), if Swift would feign being overwhelmed—as Pope feigns in the *Epilogue to the Satires*—and complain that even imaginative satire cannot keep pace with the giant strides of folly and vice. Or would Swift be driven to madness; or continue with the same intensity of humor and savage indignation?

Having seen the slaughter of a dozen innocent children, is it possible to increase one's emotion proportionately at witnessing the slaughter of a hundred or a million? Yet thirty thousand die each day for lack of basic hygiene and minimal nutrition. As Swift knew, it is a case of perspective: of magnifying, multiplying, or diminishing the size in order to see, at bottom, the essential flaw in the specimen. Swift sees that flaw, then reinvents it, in language, in a profoundly imaginative way. In parts of the third voyage the specimen he sees is not merely *homo sapiens;* it is the academic and the politician. In *Gulliver and the Gentle Reader,* in part quoting Swift and noting his desire to vex the world, Claude Rawson says, " 'the world,' gentle reader, includes *thee.*" And I include myself, "a Person of much Curiosity," admitting, along with Gulliver, that "I had my self been a Sort of Projector in my younger Days."

We honor least what indicts us most. That has been the fate of the third voyage in the hands of the academic left and right. If professors play cultural politics with literary interpretations, they will, in all honesty, need to see Swift as a running critique against the academy, against excesses of academic and political culture—a Swiftian thing to do. Do we have the courage?

Read attentively, the power of Swift's satire is that we realize, at some horrible moment, that the reality we live is *worse* than the satire he writes, that he is not exaggerating but understating. Swift gives this final twist to the knife. "A Modest Proposal" offers a more painless, arguably a more humane, way of treating Ireland's starving children than the life and death they experienced. Or, as George Campbell observes in 1776, about the third voyage, Swift's account "is not excessive, as I once thought it. The boasts of the academists on the prodigies performed by his frame, are far less extravagant" than Raimund Lully's magical circles of logic or Athanasius Kircher's coffer of arts, "which in truth they very much resemble." Seth Ward's *Vindiciae Academiarum* (1654) had more than a half century before suggested the use of objects to hand about, much like the backpacks of objects used by Swift's philosophers of language. More recently, Brean Hammond testifies, "Nothing in Swift's satire reaches the heights of idiocy that the [Atterbury] plot itself achieved."[14] Swift repeats the warning, if we are willing to listen: the reality is worse. Byron the ironist knows it in *Don Juan:* "'Tis strange, but true; for truth is always strange,— / Stranger than fiction" (canto 14, st. 101).

There are voices that say there is no need to worry—we are moderns—our scholarship and criticism have greatly advanced, our methods are secure and self-conscious, we historicize our arguments, the excesses Swift attacks in reality are no longer found. Today we are on the cutting edge. We witness such follies only in the fanciful inventions of Malcolm Bradbury, David Lodge, A. S. Byatt, or Robertson Davies. They do not actually occur. In our voyages to Philadelphia or San Francisco, Langley or Beijing, Cambridge or New Haven, Jerusalem or Jerusalem, Oxford or Cambridge, Reykjavik or Washington, D.C., Belfast or Sarajevo, we see nothing like Lagado or Laputa. Abuses catalogued by Swift have vanished. We have progressed; we have refined the state of our academies and governments to the point where language is intelligently employed. The idea of a random free play of signifiers open to any interpretation seems now absurd. And the claim that a government would pervert language to mislead the credulous, accuse the innocent, protect a chief executive, and subvert the will of the people appears patently a fiction of the past. Or, in the hall of mirrors and puzzle palaces constructed by our study of words, our political intelligence, and our politics of the academy, can we see ourselves and, grinning over our shoulder, Swift's ghastly smile?

If the ironies of self-indictment are a bitter emetic to swallow, then a thinker less satirical, though no less critical, might be welcome.

5

Hume's Cultural Critique

Against Polemic, Against Polarization

After decades of the New Criticism, formalism, and linguistic or language-based theories, many literary thinkers have rediscovered cultural relevance with the zeal of new converts. In part fueled by this rediscovery, though not as a necessary result of it, the humanities grow increasingly politicized in many colleges and universities. This is true despite the fact that the internal politics of higher education—and the politics of much of the professoriate in the humanities—resemble the polity of the country only obliquely, and are hard to fathom for many educated people. David Hume's cultural criticism, timely in his own day, invites continued application. However different their particular views, Jefferson, Burke, Voltaire, Wollstonecraft, Hume, and others, chafing at inert knowledge, prize learning that can be—in Johnson's phrase—"put to use," and recommend such applications.

It now seems somewhat ironic that the first practitioners of critical theory in its modern incarnation—those who coin the phrase, Theodor Adorno and Max Horkheimer—envision that theory as a liberating force not for a few but for the many, a movement to protect the autonomy and dignity of the individual against forces of state control, totalitarianism, corrupt language, and propaganda, as well as against the related misuse of public media, communications, and intellectual academies—in other words, against the forces of an imposed correctness. At its outset, critical theory not only aimed for, it was based upon, cultural and political relevance. But—*trahison des clercs*—in American universities particularly, and to a lesser degree in the French, many intellectuals internalize it in the academy, giving it jargon and projects that isolate it from other citizens.[1]

Hume thinks it necessary to discuss cultural subjects in the clearest and plainest language possible. This is not because he or his contemporaries trust language or hold a naive notion of any transparent relations between signifier and signified, word and thing. They distrust language profoundly but realize that only with language can we create culture. In "Of the Standard of Taste," Hume admits that "we must allow that some part of the *seeming* harmony in morals may be accounted for from the very nature of language." Berkeley refers to the "common delusion of words." Locke, George Campbell, Johnson, Coleridge, and others remark on this deception of words. There are no illusions about the "natural" quality of words. Language is, to quote them, an "arbitrary" and "imperfect" medium. Yet precisely because it is so flawed, language must be used as clearly as possible. And if a writer intends to address issues of broad social and cultural import—for Hume and others the issues most worth addressing—then an accessible mode earns a premium. This helps explain the stress on clarity of style from the late seventeenth through the late eighteenth century. When Hume aims in his *Essays Moral, Political, and Literary, History of England,* and *Dialogues Concerning Natural Religion,* for "polite" readers, for a cultural audience rapidly including, at that time, many women readers, he exemplifies an ideal of writing about culture for a wide audience. Hume becomes a public intellectual, an unusually brilliant one.

Though faced with words that he realizes are treacherous, Hume still contends that "the true philosophy approaches nearer to the sentiments of the vulgar, than to those of a mistaken knowledge." He states, "philosophical decisions are nothing but the reflections of common life, methodized and corrected." And "the common sense of mankind" remains for him a strenuous standard.[2] The premium on clarity and accessibility of common discourse stems from a thoroughgoing distrust and awareness of the play of language, an awareness as deep as any later semiotician's or theorist's—of the gelatinlike instability and arbitrary power of words. Hume's clarity and Derrida's obscurity are bipolar responses, not philosophically unrelated, to similar realizations about the nature of language, knowledge, and culture. On technical subjects in philosophy, Hume admits a more technical language, but in every instance he believes that the clearest possible language should be used. Performative ambiguity and obscurity, however cleverly conceived, become gratuitous to him and, worst of all, drive away a large portion of the audience. To discuss problems relevant to society, an author should address the polite audience in that culture, not merely its like-minded scholars or similarly trained specialists. *More important* than serving the academy, one should be intelligible to the intelligent. In "Of the Standard of Taste," his *Treatise,* the *Inquiry Concerning Human Understanding,* "Of Moral Prejudices," "Of National Characters," and *Dialogues Concerning Natural Religion,* Hume remarks on what influences our taste, character, religion, politics, and social practice—constituent elements of culture. Among factors that affect our judgment are, he says, "the different humors of particular [individuals]"— that all-important, often overlooked question of personal character or temperament—and also "the particular manners and opinions of our age and country." Even in one age or country, "Speculative opinions of any kind . . . are in continual flux and revolution." Hume centers on religion but includes any larger "systems" of speculative or philosophic thought. Today we might include ideologies.

For Hume, the case of culture is paramount because it *combines* both the pursuit of knowledge and the judgments of aesthetics and of morality. That is, Hume simultaneously brings to bear on cultural judgments two elements: first, issues of epistemology—involving reason or knowing what is true and false; second, issues of aesthetic taste and moral assessment—involving the judgment or interpretation of what is beautiful or deformed, as well as the assaying of what is vicious or virtuous. These judgments draw on reason *and* on sentiment. As a complex process combining knowledge (metaphysics), taste, and the manner in which we act and conduct life (morals), culture intertwines for him a "mitigated scepticism" in philosophical questions of reason and a "common sense" set of judgments in values and morals, judgments that appeal to feeling as well as to reason. Such skepticism and such judgments are therefore more considered and nuanced than many modern critics, who denigrate "common sense" and are ignorant of its deeper philosophical meanings, are liable to admit or to realize. The tradition from which Hume's view of morality springs and in which it is embedded is not rationalism. Unlike Hobbes (and more in line with Shaftesbury, the followers of Shaftesbury in the Edinburgh Rankenian Club—including James Boswell's father and Francis Hutcheson), Hume does not think that morality can be treated like mathematics or reduced to a rational system. It is more naturalistic. Hume is specific about this and states that "the distinction of vice and virtue is not founded merely on the relations of objects, nor is perceiv'd by reason." In fact, if we were to grasp moral action rightly, then "all the vulgar systems of morality"—those of the rationalists and reasoners of disembodied good and evil, of abstract rights and obligations—would vanish. He is remarkably like Burke in this conviction. Later in the *Treatise* he is more explicit: "Tho' justice be artificial, the sense of its morality is natural. 'Tis the combination of men, in a system of conduct, which renders any act of justice beneficial to society. But when once it has that tendency, we *naturally* approve of it."[3]

This discourse combining reason with aesthetics and morality—joining Hume's "mitigated scepticism" with his "common sense" aesthetics and morality— is what "literature" in its widest signification creates and what constitutes its real definition: it fuses fact, history, and science with matters of taste, imagination, feeling, and ethics. A literate culture joins systematic knowledge with a class of matters judged and interpreted by the combined, complex scrutiny of reason, custom, morality, and taste. These judgments, as we shall see, are always subject to change and alteration. So, Hume claims that, even though he does not write poems, plays, or novels, the whole of his profession is in literature, in letters; for the act of writing or of being an author is to cultivate, create, and participate in culture at large. This is why Mark Box states that Hume's "movement"—his "moderate scepticism" and his empiricism—"is not a dead movement. It has only lost sharpness of definition after pervading Western culture. It is, in fact, the basis for literary scholarship." Box notes that while Hume does not produce fictive or imaginative works in the usual sense, this does "not keep Goldsmith from thinking of him as a competitor in letters." Boswell, before meeting Johnson, flatly calls Hume "the greatest writer in England." In Hume studies, the appeal to return to a broader definition of *literature* goes back as far as Ernest Campbell Mossner.[4] Clearly, Hume was first and foremost considered as a writer, an author, before he was more specially regarded as a philosopher, historian, or moralist. And so he considers himself, judging literary authorship his highest achievement. Arguments have been made that Hume's view of causality no longer carries the force it once did because of advances in modern scientific knowledge,[5] but no similar or sustained attack has been successfully mounted against Hume's cultural criticism. (He himself prefers the term *arts and sciences*—preserved in schools and universities—to *culture,* soon used in the late eighteenth century, for which the *Oxford English Dictionary* gives as its first citation Wordsworth's 1805 *Prelude.*)

One group of Hume scholars has examined his stress on the need for repeated refinement of experience, for *délicatesse* (fineness of being or judgment), and for satisfying both cognition and sentiment as they balance repeated "tastes" in order to form an individual's totality of response to culture. This involves repeated comparison, analogies, and likenesses. Roots of this in Hume's thought are several, including Dominique Bouhours' *délicatesse* and *je ne sais quoi.* Despite varied experiences and our comparison of them, we all develop prejudices. Hume takes this for granted. In another vocabulary, we all have ideologies. But we should identify and analyze them, growing continually in awareness of our limitations, not unlike the process of sincerity outlined by I. A. Richards in *Practical Criticism,* the chapter entitled "Doctrine in Poetry" (Part 3, Chapter 7). This, in fact, is an important part of Hume's philosophical method of proceeding, and is sometimes seen as a technical aspect of it. It is called "general rules" and is also pertinent to cultural values and their critique, not the least because our moral sentiments are corrected by an appeal to these general rules. Hume claims that in our understanding we "rashly" form judgments, "which are the source of what we properly call *Prejudice,*" but then, if we are able to remain open to experience, we continue to perform what is in effect a series of midcourse corrections and adjustments "by a new direction of the very same principle." The process is empirical, not absolute; it can offer a better understanding, not absolute truth. And when one set of general rules collapses under the eventual, accumulated weight of experience, we then develop, in both our understanding and in our moral sentiments, a higher-order set of rules. And so on. As Marie Martin remarks, "Hume is claiming that the basic principles of our understanding are *self-correcting.*" This is counter to *any* dogmatism.[6] As for "objective" truth, and Hume's or any one else's claims for it, Richard Popkin's statement provides a helpful corrective: "most major eighteenth-century thinkers, far from exalting the power of reason, pointed out that it could not *know* about a real world independent of the mind. The subjectivity of all knowledge was usually alleged to have been demonstrated already by Gassendi, Locke, Fontenelle, even Pascal."[7]

Does Hume's emphasis on experience make his cultural criticism particularly "neoclassical"? Elsewhere I have argued that it does not. What he calls his "philosophical skepticism" may proceed along lines congenial with the neoclassical idea of assessing models, further imitating, refining, and building up a stock of values; there are similarities between "Of the Standard of Taste" and, say, Pope's *Essay on Criticism*. (One can see neoclassicism as a method of criticism as much or more as it is a mode for the production of art.) And Hume's vision of society may be termed in some respects conservative. But Hume relies on no authority. Earlier writers do not populate his texts as they do the criticism of recognized neoclassicists such as Corneille or Rymer (or Pope, for that matter). No commentator in the past thirty-five years specializing in Hume is willing to call his literary or cultural criticism "neoclassical," and many state emphatically that it is not. Hume is experimental and classical in Johnson's broader manner.

The argument is for cosmopolitanism of approach, constantly testing and reassessing one's values and tastes, one's character, and the character, values, and crosscurrents of one's culture. Hume belongs, in his famous phrase, to the "party of humanity." His cultural approach is drawn from new experience and practice in conjunction with results of previous experience and practice. Thus, his cultural criticism is at once skeptical *and* pragmatic. It is related to Kant's third *Critique,* just as Hume's *Dialogues Concerning Religion* are related to the last section of Kant's first *Critique.*

A few recent commentators, though not Hume scholars or even much acquainted with Hume studies, suggest that Hume is unaware of the contingencies of his own position.[8] But that is precisely his point. He admits that we—that no one—can ever be fully aware, even as we strive to test our taste and our culture's values against all that we encounter, here and elsewhere, past and present. We will always encounter some paradox. As Peter Jones notes with regard to Hume's aesthetics, "*désintéressé* does not mean *dégagé*"—we all have prejudices; the difference rests in how we struggle with them.[9] Yet, finally, we always possess taste—we cannot, in practice, become complete skeptics or complete relativists. We find ourselves believing some position, not because we have demonstrated it but because we have come to judge it as probable. We act not only because some form of action is unavoidable in life, we act because we have come to believe one thing more than another. Implicit in most if not all our actions are beliefs, which themselves may be seen as "acts of believing." To clarify: a rigorous and demonstrable "rational justification" of action, and an "unavoidability" of action, are not the only two alternatives facing us when we make judgments and act upon them.[10] Furthermore, each belief we hold is not, in Hume's words, "beyond all hope of alteration or improvement." Proceeding by "general rules" (to use his technical term) or by a constantly self-calibrating and self-testing taste or discrimination (to use terms from the fine arts), we can work toward new positions, ones not governed strictly by the beliefs or ideologies we once held. We are not all prisoners in cells of interestedness, cells that share an incarcerated regularity and routine differentiated only by name or number.

Hume gives us freedom but without certainty. As a result, he avows that some tastes are better, more informed, than others, though we cannot prove or demonstrate which; we can only argue and try to persuade. A relative contingency is possible *only* in a theory that leads to no practice, no action, no belief. Time and again Hume rejects the skepticism of the Pyrrhonists as he understands it: "Should it be asked me . . . whether I be really one of those skeptics, who hold that all is uncertain, and that our judgment is not in *any* thing possessed of *any* measures of truth and falsehood, I should reply that this question is entirely superfluous, and that neither I nor any other person was ever sincerely and constantly of that opinion." The underscoring of *sincerely* anticipates Richards's discussion, for it employs the word in the same philosophically personal sense. "We retain a degree of belief," contends Hume, "which is sufficient for our purpose, *either* in philosophy or common life." And,

> though a man . . . may entirely renounce all belief and opinion, it is impossible for him to persevere in this total scepticism or make it appear in his conduct for a few hours. External objects press in upon him; passions solicit him; his philosophical melancholy dissipates; and even the utmost violence upon his own temper will not be able . . . to preserve the poor appearance of scepticism. . . . So that, upon the whole, nothing could be more ridiculous than the principles of the ancient Pyrrhonians if, in reality, they endeavoured, as is pretended, to extend throughout the same scepticism which they had learned from the declamation of their schools, and which they ought to have confined to them.[11]

That is, these last thinkers should confine such pseudo-philosophy to their own academies and their own internal politics. It can have no true cultural existence. While both a speculative and practical philosopher, Hume has little respect for a purely theoretical point of view in either philosophy or the common life we share culturally, just as Burke has little respect for abstract, purely theoretical systems of government. They know, like Milton, not that we must descend into the dust and heat of the arena, but that we are always already there. We construct certain beliefs in the world. We live our culture. There is no other way. It is how we do it, in a sense how honest we are about it, that counts.

For example, in the Declaration of Independence—and few documents carry greater political consequences and cultural weight—the signers do not subscribe that the truths guiding their actions *are* self-evident. They would never make such an absolute claim. Jefferson, influenced by Hume and the philosophical debates in Scotland, instead writes deliberately, "we *hold* these truths to be self-evident"; that is, we *believe* them to be. This belief guides their actions but they do not claim absolute objectivity for it. Rather, it is in this holding, this believing, that they go so far as to risk their lives, their fortunes, their sacred honor.

More important than Hume's affinity with some aspects of neoclassicism is his affinity with Kant. Kant's famous remark that Hume woke him from his "dogmatic slumbers" has a point in cultural criticism, too. Hume contends that any dogmas of complete relativism, total skepticism, or thoroughgoing contingency, are, in their slumbers, equally oblivious with the dogmas of any rigid ideology, whether orthodox or subversive. Hume's skepticism is empirical but not dogmatic. It is, to use the phrase of one commentator, "skeptical realism." Hume calls it "mitigated scepticism." It may be seen as pragmatic, but its pragmatism is not a default mode because the rest are pis aller. Hume offers a pragmatism that is, in this sense, more than "an extended pragmatic mitigation" of relativism and skepticism; once faced with the untenable nature of pure skepticism, his pragmatism is an alternative based on our desire—our free will—to construct a workable set of beliefs and judgments, and on our ability to improve upon them. This suggests that Hume's solutions are themselves not self-confident; they do not seek an absolute resting place, nor pretend to finality.[12] In the first *Enquiry,* the section on "Sceptical Doubts concerning the Operation of the Understanding" is answered by one titled "*Sceptical* Solution of these Doubts." We must be skeptical of all solutions, yet we can and must solve, and resolve. In this vein, it is interesting to recall that in its origin, skeptic meant an inquirer— not a doubter, but one who never stops inquiring. Adam Potkay asks some larger questions and, studying one of Hume's essays, comes to a helpful stand: "Was the Enlightenment itself ideologically consolidated? Was it as monolithic as we have sometimes conceived it?" Potkay concludes that a "contextual reading of Hume's 'Of Eloquence' would suggest not," even though Hume displays certain cultural and political sympathies. Then Potkay states, "Hume's attitude toward eloquence certainly expresses contradictions that a single ideology cannot quite manage."[13]

The emphasis on belief without taking refuge in a single ideology that cannot manage contradictions—an emphasis to which we will return near the end of this essay—cannot be underestimated. As Hume notes in part 2 of "Sceptical Solution of These Doubts," the basis for these solutions, "its true and proper name . . . is belief, which is a term that every one sufficiently understands in common life. And in philosophy, we can go no farther than assert, that belief is something felt by the mind, which distinguishes the ideas of the judgement from the fictions of the imagination."

2

In our surge back to relevant criticism that analyzes and strips away cultural assumptions in order to assert new beliefs and opinions, a simplistic model of two parties has emerged. (We should recall that Hume's *Dialogues Concerning Natural Religion* present three speakers, not two.) On the one hand, we are often told, stand the older traditionalists, Arnoldian and Eurocentric (Derrida's "ethico-religious" lot), the self-assured, presumably insular, privileged caste who preserve political power and defend *the* canon of literary works, cultural artifacts, and moral values. These created straw figures have a naive faith in the "eternal verities"; they are "absolutists" or "essentialists." On the other hand ranges a liberated, forward-looking, theoretically sophisticated, younger group who have subverted, called into question, and fatally shaken the assumptions of the former, or at least frequently outvoted them. "Diverse" and "pluralistic," they are often suspicious of the "transcendent." I do not belong to either of these (all too fatally and simplistically constructed) camps, at least not as they usually describe each other or themselves. But such entrenched parties, close to caricature as they may seem, are exactly what we become, says Hume, when we associate our identities with groups and factions. In "Of National Characters" he notes, "The propensity to company and society is strong in all rational creatures; and the same disposition, which gives us this propensity, makes us enter deeply into each other's sentiments, and causes like passions and inclinations to run, as it were, by contagion, through the whole club or knot of companions." In our

David Hume by Allan Ramsay. Ramsay's other subjects included Gibbon and Chesterfield. Reproduced by permission of the Portrait Gallery of the National Galleries of Scotland, Edinburgh.

cliques we succumb to the common delusion of words. We submit ourselves to a common polemic rather than to our own experience. (This, Bacon warns in *The Advancement of Learning,* is one of the vanities of learning most rampant among scholars.) And while it is true that conclusions drawn from experience have no ultimate and demonstrable proof, no self-evident justification or warrant, yet they are the only conclusions we can draw. Hume detests polarizations. He sometimes refers to them in terms that conjure religion and politics ("enthusiasm" and "superstition"), but everywhere his enemy is "the spirit of zealotry," intellectual or otherwise.[14] Ironically, Hume himself was victimized by such polarizations. He had cause to lash back at those accusing him of atheism or irreligion. In 1745, Edinburgh University placed him on the final short list for its chair of ethics and pneumatical philosophy, but then rejected him because of reports and rumors regarding his reputation for attacking religion. And for generations, until quite recently, Hume has been regarded—at times tarred and feathered—as an *un*mitigated skeptic rather than one who argues that we all do believe in the "fictions of reality" we construct because we judge them best to meet the case of our own experience. Part of the "reason" for this is that in Hume's own day, the word *skeptic* not only no longer means an inquirer, or even a doubter; it means a doubter of the Judeo-Christian revelation. Yet Hume apparently believes atheism itself to be a nonskeptical form of dogmatism that no person of reason can accept.[15]

But, to return to the issue of polarization and, in the process, pigeonholing one's opponents. We can consider one cultural and educational debate between Lynne Cheney, then director of the National Endowment for the Humanities, and heads of various humanities centers. The NEH report *Humanities in America* set itself forward in terms some citizens might agree with, at least in part, but caused dismay to some professors of literature, fine arts, and cultural history. The directors of humanities centers at Cornell, Harvard, Rutgers, the State University of New York at Stony Brook, and Yale responded with a booklet, *Speaking for the Humanities,* published under the auspices of the American Council of Learned Societies. It should be noted that the NEH report could not pretend to represent national sentiment in any experimentally accurate way; nor could the directors of the humanities centers and institutes, who were not elected but some of whom were appointed after having actively sought their positions, be said always to represent much beyond their own personal stance, as they freely admit.

In this case, as often in cultural and academic debates, dogmatic orthodoxy encountered dogmatic skepticism. New Presbyter is old priest writ large. By way of analogy, as Hume says in *The Natural History of Religion* (Section 15), "in a future age, it will probably become difficult to persuade some nations, that any human, two-legged creature could ever embrace such [religious] principles." But "it is a thousand to one . . . [that] these nations themselves shall have something full as absurd in their own creed, to which they will give a most implicit and most religious assent." So, in our age, contending over cultural inheritance and humanistic education, we have dogmatic believers of an older stripe, and dogmatic skeptics, many of whom turn out to be dogmatic believers of a newer sect under the pose of skepticism or even pragmatism. Yet dogma is the common denominator. In fact, Tzvetan Todorov calls the booklet *Speaking for the Humanities* "dogmatic skepticism" and counters that there are those instead, a third group, "who maintain that truth is neither a dogma nor a chimera, that it is, rather, the horizon of dialogue, the regulating principle of exchange (these thinkers range from Kant to Habermas and beyond)."[16] For Kant he could have substituted Hume. Kant said Hume woke him from his own dogmatic slumber.

While the NEH report sounds some alarms worth sounding (Cheney's arguments against overspecialization are especially sharp), that report states untested assumptions about cultural values and literary canons—and gives evidence of partisan political motivation. The NEH is, after all, a government agency headed by a political appointee. Yet, when the ACLS reply finds a book about crisis in the humanities "disturbingly popular," with the implication that the generally educated populace reading and responding to it must be misguided, misinformed, or prejudiced, its authors might recall Hume's desire to set philosophical and cultural discourse on a more popular, not a more elitist or mandarin footing. Beyond this, *Speaking for the Humanities* attempts to establish, mostly by assertion, the putative truth that there is no such thing as truth or objectivity: ideology will "delude us into promoting as universal values that in fact belong to one nation, one social class, one sect." "Claims of disinterest, objectivity, and universality are not to be trusted and themselves tend to reflect local historical conditions." If one hopes for something of Richard Rorty's liberalism, irony, and solidarity here, qualities not unlike Hume's, they do not surface. Instead, many statements announce secondhand opinions and appeal to anonymous authorities: "The consensus of most of the dominant theories is"; "From the perspective of many of the best practitioners of modern thought"; "the best contemporary work in the humanities"; "the best contemporary thinking" is promoted by the very centers headed by the booklet's authors; "the most distinguished philosophers of science of our time [understand]"; or, "the most powerful modern philosophies and theories have been demonstrating." This is itself the rhetoric of a totalizing, dogmatic skepticism based on received opinion. At bottom insecure, it will not stoop to the particular, the practical, or to the fact that we all do hold cultural beliefs upon which we act, and that we kid each other if we state that we each think that all these beliefs and actions are equally acceptable and desirable. At one point the authors touch on the central issue: "Many who are distrustful of the modern critique of objectivity assume that it gives license to anything since there would appear to be on this account no objective grounds of argument, only various versions of personal or political interest." Immediately, they resolve the issue by avoiding it: "This is not the place to enter into an extensive discussion of the philosophical positions that have been taken up around this problem." Yet what more ingenious and politically savvy way to gain power than by denying that there is any other than a relative and local basis for all judgment and power to begin with, and that anyone who claims otherwise must be "distrusted" and, presumably, ousted from any position of responsibility? While the authors state that past texts should be studied, they contend, ironically, that in the humanities "past curricula, past conceptions of value and meaning" cannot provide any models. Instead, these are the very cause of "failure." The report opposes what it calls "a gentlemanly ideal: a vision of the humanities as repository of known truths and received values." At one blow this statement caricatures all opposition and implies that the idea of a repository of *any* known truth or value is worthless, part of an outmoded "positivist ideal." Later, with no apparent sense of self-contradiction, the authors state, "Innovation and tradition together are needed if the past is to be made a living force within the present." *Speaking for the Humanities* does not speak for many humanists.[17]

The debate outlined above, which has continued for years, has drawn us away from more important problems. John Searle notes that "it tends to be shrill and vindictive, and the level of argumentation is not that appropriate to the presentation of a philosophy of education. . . . [T]he issues being argued about, for the most part, are not the major problems in American higher education," which include lack of money, poor basic preparation of entering college students, and lack of jobs for graduate students, even for excellent ones who have completed their degrees. Yet Searle then characterizes the "great debate," and says, since "I do not know of a neutral vocabulary, I will describe the participants in the debate as the defenders of the tradition and the challengers."

While he attempts a candid assessment of both "traditionalists" and "challengers," he sees the two sides in more or less the same light as the participants do, though not in a tone as "shrill and vindictive." There are only two sides, they oppose each other, they fight over the canon, multiculturalism, and political issues. Searle's analysis, lengthy and thoughtful, contends that higher education—and literary criticism in particular—is undergoing changes that may permanently be for the worse, ones that show a loss of confidence and consequently substitute a focus on immediate "hot button" political issues for one on larger subject matters such as literature. And Searle's conclusions, while more or less in the "traditionalists" mode, do not argue for a status quo or return to some past set of circumstances. He argues that to be a public intellectual presupposes a public language, and that therefore it "is self-refuting" for such a public intellectual to argue that there is no such thing as "metaphysical realism," that is, no such thing as some truth that is objective, even though we cannot be certain what that truth is. This argument is devastating and squares with Hume's stance. Searle selects *Speaking for the Humanities* as one example of this kind of self-refutation.[18] Yet what has happened here, once again, even in an attempt to draw attention to more important problems, is a return to the same polarizations. If we cannot get beyond "traditionalists" and "challengers," and beyond the model of a two-party political system for the study of the humanities and culture at large, then we are doomed to the fruits of our division, and a house divided cannot stand. Opposing one side does not mean that we automatically champion the other. Accepting that would be to accept the tyranny of a view prepackaged and Manichaean.

3

None of us keeps our cultural beliefs in a pristine, theoretical dogmatic skepticism of complete contingency. The new dogmatic skeptics are actually practicing the most rigid kind of neoclassicism—the kind Hume rejects—that is, the acceptance of authority (or current fashion) for statements about cultural criticism. Howard Weinbrot asks, "When was neoclassicism?" and concludes, with much justice, "It is now." The dogmatic skeptics are their own version of the old guard turned inside out. As Longinus says, later echoed by Sainte-Beuve, "nothing so much resembles a hollow as a swelling." The problem with so many arguments about culture carried out with ideology or politics as the main engine is that the contestants will cleave to their own set of political beliefs as absolute. Their compass needle is nailed down (or else blows opportunistically with the prevailing wind). They compromise only as a last resort (to do so earlier would defeat or diminish their institutional power) and would rather appear on a dog-and-pony show of debate, always the "right" against the "left," where both sides collect honoraria.[19] A declaration of complete contingency is no mitigated skepticism, it is a convenient escape hatch. So is a general swearing of faith to "Western culture." An *absolute* belief in complete contingency is a logical contradiction; a belief in absolute truth fully known claims nothing less that godlike perfection.

Hume does not urge (and I am not urging) some one transcendent Truth, received wisdom, or idealistic speculative system. Moreover, some of Hume's own specific cultural, historical, and racial opinions are ones with which many, including myself, profoundly disagree. In "Of National Characters" he says, "I am apt to suspect the negroes and in general all the other species of men . . . to be naturally inferior to the whites. There never was a civilized nation of any other complexion than white."[20] Here I disagree violently and trust that if Hume had lived longer, he would have shed this prejudice, and that experience, self-correction, and, stemming from these, a higher order of "general rules" of judgment would have altered his opinion.

What I am urging, as Hume urges, is that culture, that life, does not thrive under dogmatic skepticism anymore than it thrives under dogmatic positivism. We believe. We hold opinions. We feel as well as think. "Reasonable men may be allowed to differ where no one can reasonably be positive" (*Dialogues,* "Pamphilus to Hermippus"). Hume would subscribe neither to the dogma of cultural authority and canon nor to the dogma of skepticism or pure contingency, which denies any claim to the worth of cultural values outside some local habitation. Both dogmas are equally suspect and between themselves share common delusions. In politics they both lead to totalitarianism of the right or the left. There may exist an ultimate truth but we cannot claim to know it or, if we venture to make such a claim, we can never demonstrate it. Yet our beliefs, our values, our actions, these exist *in* us and in our culture.[21] They are an inextricable part of individual and social existence, and their contingency does not make them less valid. The point is to secure for them a contingency that escapes the merely local and transient, one that is better informed, more open to experience, one that is—to use a key word of Johnson's thought—more general. This is what

Johnson claims for Shakespeare as a poet—more than other English writers—he achieves truth to general nature, not to some abstract or universal ideal, but to a range of real experience removed from the predominant influences of accident, locality, narrow custom, and prejudice.

Hume suggests that an answer to the two opposing dogmas, dogmatic tradition and dogmatic skepticism, is a "philosophical" or "mitigated skepticism"— experimental, experiential, practical. We must, in the end, come to some preferable *belief*, however provisional and subject to change. Otherwise our actions are random, solipsistic, or paralyzed. If all seems *equally* contingent to us, a culture of cannibalism or hate becomes equal to one of cosmopolitanism and toleration. Mark Box eloquently sums up Hume's stance:

> His contribution was his tenet that complete suspension of belief is impossible. We must have beliefs, which must be fallible; but we can and should temper our credulity: plausibility, or what Hume called *"moral Evidence"* . . . still provides a criterion for belief and action. . . . As new experience contradicts our beliefs, we must be willing to revise our estimates of plausibility. This does not mean that truth changes, only that our best approximations of it are perpetually subject to revision.[22]

As a writer Hume tries to perfect a style, a mode of expression, a rhetorical effect, that will instill these habits of thought in readers. As an author, he knows he faces this challenge, and his progress as stylist and rhetorician results in an accomplishment of which he is justly proud, perhaps more than of anything else. Though their work has not been published in specialized philosophical journals and thus has fallen on some deaf ears, John Richetti and others emphasize the importance that Hume assigns to the manner as well as to the matter of writing; Hume cannot, indeed, be read in the same way Kant is read. More recently, Paula Brown has ventured, "Hume's rhetorical techniques produce a suspension of judgment in his ideal skeptical reader, an openness to arguments independent of their source and their religious or political implications." It may be argued that Hume's emphasis on social give and take, on dialogue, conversation, sympathy, and openness, is for culture *more important* than "getting it right" or nailing down, with "monkish virtue," a technical point in some larger academic scorecard. With too few exceptions, modern studies of Hume (and of many other figures, as I suggest throughout this book) have diverged into two roads leading to two different camps, two different disciplines: philosophy or literature, literature or politics, religion or literature, literature or history. All these divisions would puzzle, even disturb Hume. So would the claim that intellectual progress has created such divisions—and the divisions of language they foster—as an unquestioned good. Again, there are affinities here with certain positions offered by Richard Rorty. But it is Raymond Williams, a generation ago, who asks with greater, almost caustic urgency, parodying the language of a blue-book examiner: "Is David Hume . . . moralist, logician, historian, essayist? Under which of these categories are you proposing to read him? Remember, before answering, the serious penalties involved, if you get on the wrong side of any of these lines."[23]

In 1977, Isaiah Berlin, in "Hume and the Sources of German Anti-Rationalism," charts the ironic fact that Hume's confirmation of the necessity of secular belief, no matter how provisional, coupled with his undogmatic skepticism, leads, through Hamann and Jacobi, to the German Counter Enlightenment: "Belief is more properly an act of the sensitive, than of the cogitative part of our natures." This statement from the *Treatise* fits with what Hume says in "Of the Standard of Taste," that is, taste is a sort of conviction or belief, however tentative, and we develop it (to borrow Keats's phrase) not only from "consequitive reasoning" but from feeling. As Hamann tells Kant in 1759, recognizing the pragmatic aspect of Hume's belief, "If you want a proof for everything, you cannot act at all—Hume realises this."[24] Hamann and Jacobi turn the necessity of belief to religion and culture.

Hume realizes that belief is always and inevitably being turned to cultural ends that are not specifically religious. His sense of belief exerts an effect on German and English culture. An open, undogmatic belief in taste or cultural values, an experimental, experiential, skepticism that nevertheless comes to grips with the necessity of belief, is the kind of self-testing and experimentalism that leads to personal *Bildung* and, ultimately, to social or national *Bildung* or culture. This kind of non–a priori, undogmatic *Bildung* (whether it opposes dogmatic skepticism, dogmatic traditionalism, or dogmatic antitraditionalism) ultimately informs the bildungsroman, such as *Wilhelm Meister*; it informs Keats's cast of mind and vale of soul making, seemingly so different from Hume's, but equally undogmatic, self-questioning, open, and resistant to the embrace of any one speculative system or established religion.

The resistance to system and to the a priori, the questioning of orthodox religion, yet the sense that neither dogmatic skepticism and its relativism nor rigid ideology and its pure correctness are viable alternatives, come as hallmarks common to Hume and to certain strands of later eighteenth-century English and German thought. Hume does not "cause" any of the developments we have come to call Romantic—especially about Hume one would not want to say that—but his stance is related to the "obstinate questionings," "internalized quests," "mysteries, doubts, uncertainties," and *Bildung* of the generation that follows him.

In cultural politics, ethics, and criticism, Hume remains a potential guide. He would keep the language in which these issues are discussed open and accessible to the generally educated understanding, not closed inside a professionalized or cultured elite. He rejects dogmatic tradition and received authority. He also rejects dogmatic attacks on cultural traditions. He rejects dogmatic skepticism, complete relativism, and total contingency: while these may be valid constructs in theory, they can never exist in cultural practice, which must involve beliefs and the necessity of acting, however provisionally, in the van of circumstance.

6

Vico Tells the Story of Stories

Culture, Identity, Education

Hume's vision becomes comprehensive. He sees how the arts and sciences create more than a set of special interests; together they constitute culture and affect individual choice. Yet cultural vision and personal conduct must submit to constant revisions. This synthetic task is for Hume best achieved in language by a quality he calls eloquence. Slightly older and unknown to Hume, Giambattista Vico holds this quality in esteem, too. He devotes his career as educator and intellectual to discovering how the connection between language and culture can be taught and learned. When we first hear the articulate sounds of our children, we bask in delight. Soon, we tell them stories.

Vico in the *New Science* (*Scienza nuova,* 1725, revised last in 1744) emphasizes that imagination acts most strongly in our childhood and youth. And the imagination present in childhood—as well as in nascent societies—should never be discarded or "grown out of." All cultures depend on its continued activity.

Care must be taken not to lose it, Vico warns, in the welter of technical procedures that characterize modern learning and the professions. Civilizations hob-
ble themselves when they overrefine, looking only for rarefied, theoretical
abstraction on the one hand, or immediate material utility on the other. Seemingly poles apart, these both depend on fine branchings of critical analysis and
technical, efficient methodologies. Vico emphasizes that before descending into
theories and techniques of specialties, we need to educate our imaginations
firmly and fundamentally. At the start we should turn to capacious subjects. For
instance, to confirm observations on the Greek and French languages, Vico
states that with "regard to young people at an age when memory is tenacious,
imagination vivid, and invention quick," then "they may profitably occupy
themselves with languages and plane geometry, without thereby subduing that
acerbity of mind still bound to the body which may be called the barbarism of
the intellect. But if they pass on while yet in this immature stage to the highly
subtle studies of metaphysical criticism or algebra, they become overfine for life
in their way of thinking and are rendered incapable of any great work" (159).
Vico is defending against what Bacon in sections of *The Advancement of Learning* identifies as a vanity of learning.[1] Vico knew the book virtually by heart.

The issue Vico raises, educating the imagination, is if anything today more
urgent. It demands a sharper vigil because of the exponential increase in technical procedures and method that many educators have adopted to replace liberal
education. Because there are so many procedures and methodologies to master,
each requiring more effort than imagination, and because a student brushes up
against many subjects, such an agglomerative approach never asks the student
to think through the purpose of education as a general *end*—over and above a
series of means or methods. Nor does it pose the question of what connected
purposes and relative values might be attached to differing bodies of knowledge.
Most regrettably, such a technical approach never opens up that world of human
experience, finally irreducible to method and procedure.

The child's imagination gathers a storehouse of images from sense experience directly. But soon imagination incarnates itself in new, recombined images,
in words—in childish poetry. The storehouse has become a factory, a place to
make, with its own source of power. The images are not just collected, they are
re-collected, reordered, and recombined. "In children memory is most vigorous," says Vico, "and imagination is therefore excessively vivid" (211). Perhaps
the best record of this imaginative growth in the child's mind as a subject of
poetry is Wordsworth's *Prelude*. In *De nostri temporis studiorum ratione*, Vico

remarks that *ingenium,* the faculty of invention or creative imagination, "is the faculty of youth."[2] But the youthful transformation of experience into images, and then into evocative language, must be retained as *the* central part of knowing the world and its relations as an engaged adult.

Our imagination forms our individual character before it alters or contributes to any particular body of knowledge.[3] Once the imagination opens a capacious vision, it can proceed not only to form new knowledge but to see such knowledge in relation to human character: to history and social institutions, to public policy and the beneficial or disruptive uses of technology. We can hardly recapture the imaginative force of the first men in their "primitive" societies (378). But that does not mean we should not try to emulate the virtues of those "first natures" and "first customs" (916–21). At an early age it is vital that we address the imagination in a way fanciful and marvelous, yet also immediate and real. That is why in all cultures children's teaching texts have for millennia been fables, animal stories, fairy tales, nursery rhymes, and ballads. In these narratives and myths, we locate elements of ethical decision, family life, law, and social reality. "The first fables," says Vico, "must have contained civil truths, and must therefore have been the histories of the first peoples" (198; see 352, 408). Thus, to understand what and who we are, "the first science to be learned should be mythology or the interpretation of fables" (51).

The psyche creates its "self," its individuality, and its values, only as it simultaneously discovers the culture that, through language, fosters this self-creation. The psyche forms its identity as it learns and leads itself out through the verbal structures of culture—narratives, stories, myths, and the patterns of words—as it becomes educated, from *ex ducere,* leading out. All attempts to understand either individual psychology or collective culture hinge on seeing the two symbiotically, exploring those images and narratives, those personal and collective histories that create and connect self and culture in lively interdependence. The argument foreshadows Shelley's *Defence of Poetry* and the work of the modern psychologist Jerome Bruner. Vico emphasizes that the mature arts are the first poetic activity of human imagination, analogous to the first imaginative activity of the child (217).

Vico's project is then the humanization of knowledge. This does not mean salvaging an arid roster of "traditional values." It is an attempt to render knowledge relevant to human life and social institutions, to save knowledge from becoming inert, to help serve human welfare, justice, and health. The key faculty for this synthetic endeavor is a mature imagination, and its key instrument is language, which places knowledge before society in public debate, places of worship, legislatures, businesses, universities, and courtrooms. Technical, mathematical, and crafted media are not ruled out but subsumed; primarily through language society communicates, defines values and problems, and reaches solutions. As Vico formulates the connection, we are led to conjecture "that ideas and language accelerated at the same rate" (234). Knowledge of facts alone may be represented by different symbolic systems, but the relevance of facts to human values is expressed and anchored by language. Language constitutes the social and human relevance of all knowledge.[4]

We see the importance of rhetoric if we accept Vico's capacious formulation of it: "wisdom speaking eloquently." He feels revulsion at deceptive language, the ingenuity of argument simply to persuade, and rhetoric severed from an ethical foundation. Similar to Bacon's view, rhetoric for Vico is not based on formal or analytical procedures of categorizing figures of speech. That is not its essential function or entelechy. Rhetoric performs that as a means. The goal is to elevate language in the service of human virtue, to learn language in order to act and exert power for good. Imagination—we might say the products of imagination—are most completely centered in rhetoric, in "poetic wisdom," the language that speaks eloquently to our habitual thoughts and feelings. (For modern ears Vico's use of "poetic" is often better rendered as "imaginative.") Poetry—imagination—is necessary to create, shape, understand, and transform the world. "The theological poets were the sense and the philosophers the intellect of human wisdom" (779, 821).

Individual education should recapitulate the processes that create collective culture. As education begins with imagination, so for educated adults imaginative wisdom remains necessary to grasp the world. Its elusive nature is therefore to be sought most assiduously at the outset, while the mind is pliable and vivid with images. This wisdom in its developed form is conceived as nothing less than the synoptic ability to express—and in expressing to imitate, embody, and create—a series of images of human life and history at different times and in different cultures, finally bringing these pictures and myths together to form a mural or surview, a picture of the human condition conscious of its status in the world at large, its history, and its possible future (*storia ideale eterna*). This surview gives a context for individual ethical and social decisions, decisions we can never analyze in isolation, for they arise out of the dense and knotty relief of human conditions. Vico apprehends poetry and poetic wisdom not primarily in technical terms (his remarks on prosody and style seem insignificant), but in the way poetry, myths, and metaphor—which is myth in miniature—reflect institutions, collective experience, and the development of ideas or ideologies. In his search to construct truth relevant to human experience, Vico favors a *topical* art, the art of *topoi,* rather than a *critical* or Cartesian method that judges what is assumed to be already existing as either true or false.[5] Vico is what one of Alfred North Whitehead's colleagues distastefully admitted Whitehead had become in his later years: "Oh, you mean he's a *sage.* Yes, but then he's no philosopher"![6]

"Qui dit langage," says Lévi-Strauss, "dit société," an axiom in harmony with Vico.[7] Mind, language, and society become mutually self-enabling, self-realizing. And insofar as the capacity for language, whether as articulate speech or symbolic inscription, is embedded in the structure of the mind, society is known, in large part, by studying how the mind imaginatively portrays the knowledge of the world in words—imaginatively, because this portrayal cannot occur except by an act that calls on sense, abstraction, perception, and memory remolding them into larger forms, customs, traits, and weltanschauungen. The language need not be written, it can be oral, to have the effect of producing a nation or society (67). But for decades those in literary studies distanced themselves from rhetoric, or else redefined it in terms of public speaking, "getting your point across." Anthropology seems to have done the most here. But even in "primitive" societies, language and social institutions prove complex. To ferret out even simpler decodings of common verbal symbols, let alone myths, taboos, laws, and the importance of what is unspoken or tacitly understood, becomes difficult and controversial among inhabitants of any society.

Language can have the effect of creating a reality, of making a human world, or at least acting as midwife to one. This is part of the principle of *verum/ factum* in Vico: human truth resides in human construction. One passage that exemplifies *factum* as poetic making and *verum* as social truth comes when Vico mentions "Orpheus, considered as a theological poet, who through the fables, in their first meaning, first founded and then confirmed the humanity of Greece" (81). Poets are not scientists, they lack "objectivity"; but their imaginative use of language is necessary for—in fact, creates—the reality and virtue of civil society, a reality that changes over time, but one that language and myth always capture. In his excellent study *The Rehabilitation of Myth: Vico's 'New Science,'* Joseph Mali understands that Vico sees myth embodying a distillation of all our knowledges; myth never becomes obsolete. It is, in other words, hard-wired into us. It is the way we come to know the world and to deal with it, tinctured by the unique paths of our own particular culture.[8] It is our humanity, what separates us from scientific automation. Yet myth is not irrational. It does not oppose science. Combining drives in us both reasonable and resistant to pure rationalism, myth is arational and "eternal."

Often ignored in contemporary literary discussions of "rhetoric" is the crucial operation of language in the affairs of society—an operation understood not solely through linguistics but through rhetoric conceived broadly, not as classification of terms but as the formation of moral judgment and argument, the elucidation of a worldview. Rhetoric (or "discourse") and ideas, rhetoric and ideologies, become inseparable, so that when we speak of the rhetoric of Marx, Rousseau, Nazi propaganda, or Scripture, we imply, with those different "rhetorics," the ideas or ideologies from which they cannot be extricated. The imaginative use of language connects, as nothing else can, our disparate, specialized knowledges. Rhetoric and imagination are synthetic principles, counterforces to the atomization and trivialization of knowledge.

This is why Vico calls for an alliance between philosophers and philologists—an interpenetration of the "knowledge of the true" created by reason, and of the "consciousness of the certain" created by words and human choice. Here philology does not mean only the history of language; it involves the history of peoples, their institutions, values, social systems, even their gods (138–40). Vico expresses this synthetic principle of language, ideas, and history by claiming, "The etymologies of the native languages also agree, which tells us the histories of the institutions signified by the words, beginning with their original and proper meanings and pursuing the natural progress of their metaphors according to the order of ideas, on which the history of languages must proceed" (354).[9] Language is the primary vehicle for imagination; nurturing one strengthens the other. As a corollary, a purely utilitarian language produces a purely utilitarian people, devoid, as Emerson said, "of analogies," and poverty-stricken in their sense of transcendence.

2

Jerome Bruner begins his *Acts of Meaning* (1990) by observing, "I have written it at a time when psychology, the science of mind as William James once called it, has become fragmented as never before."[10] This characterization of his own field fits many humanistic studies: "The wider intellectual community comes increasingly to ignore our journals" (xi). Researchers rest on postage-stamp-sized topics that cite others of small scope; it is estimated that eighty percent of all articles published in the humanities are never cited. Talk of interdisciplinary studies brings to mind Wilfred Cantwell Smith's remark that "interdisciplinary" is a ladderlike word designed to help humanists climb out of a hole that they never should have fallen into in the first place. Bruner sees hope that basic questions on "the nature of the mind and its processes, questions about how we construct our meanings and our realities, questions about the shaping of mind by history and culture" (xi) are still being raised. Yet, in the drive to make it new, what is basic in Bruner's sense gets lost in the shuffle and looks unglamorous or vague, not vogue. Returning to basic questions takes courage because we do not possess ready-made, basic answers.

In opposition, one brand of current skepticism holds that any answer is no better than any other; that there exists no question more essential than any other; that cultural conditioning, or a cultural marketing strategy, means all. For all its purported shock value, this updated skepticism is simplistic. It amounts to a rigid form of cultural behaviorism, devoid of a search for meaning. Similarly, a pure literary textualism—exclusively formal arguments over the technical nature of writing and interpretation—is akin to the splintering technical nature of cognitive studies in psychology. For Bruner, failing to see human meaning and value as central betrays the flaw in psychology's cognitive revolution. Why should it be less of a betrayal in literature?

Truths and beliefs are culturally conditioned and contingent, and truth—as Bruner suggests in a discussion of Richard Rorty—is not an eternal, immutable essence, or a list of exact correspondences with "reality." Vico would agree with this, too. But to suggest that the decisions we make for ourselves about meaning or truth—what grounds we take for life's myriad, interconnected acts charged with affect, emotion, cognition and value, how we teach, vote, raise children, love our partners, spend money, die, choose careers—are somehow not truthful or meaningful decisions because they are relative or contingent: this does nothing less than rob us of free will, what Coleridge calls our true and absolute self.

Bruner contends that any study of psychology divorced from the influence of culture is impoverished, and he is right. Culture provides us with many semiotic systems (Locke points this out in his *Essay Concerning Human Understanding*, 1690), systems ready-made and charged with customs, habits, interpretations, and values built up over time—in history—and shared or debated by a community. Language is at the base of cultural psychology because, as Locke notes, it is the most pervasive of semiotic systems, clearly recognized by Vico, by classical rhetoricians, and by recent thinkers such as Lévi-Strauss.

For Bruner, what "A culturally oriented psychology . . . takes as central . . . is that the relationship between action and saying (or experiencing) is, *in the ordinary conduct of life,* interpretable [a Vichian phrase, echoed by Emerson, originally from the classics and schoolmen]. . . . This is what makes interpretation and meaning central to a cultural psychology—or to any psychology or mental science, for that matter" (19). Issues of meaning and interpretation forge links with literary and hermeneutic studies, with I. A. Richards, Empson, Dilthey, Ricoeur, and Gadamer; Bruner mentions Ricoeur and Dilthey. Bruner urges psychology to stop its various attempts to be meaning free—and, we could add, value-free. Why? Because the mind and the culture to which the mind contributes—and which it can also change—never are.

Bruner's stance will be familiar to readers of Vico, Northrop Frye, narrative studies, or any thorough discussion of storytelling, narrative, genre, and myth as they relate to culture, not just literary taxonomy. Bruner argues, under the term "folk psychology" (he does not mean the primitive, but "folk" as customarily part of a culture), that the elaborate yet commonly received structures of language forming the basis of culture must be applied to psychology, too. These structures of language help constitute the individual psyche as well as supply the vehicle for its expression. If structures of language and narratives, Frye's "verbal universe," cannot be quantified or predicted, if they become matters for interpretation and cultural history, this does not place them outside of psychology. It places them at its center. If we return to William James's *Principles of Psychology,* we find that storytelling, anecdote, and quotation—many different stylistic voices and cultural signals—populate it.

The recognition of folk psychology expressed through language is, says Bruner, "where psychology starts and wherein it is inseparable from anthropology and the other cultural sciences" (32). This makes psychology inseparable from literature conceived as the study of language in relation to experience and values. This was once the compass of rhetoric, though often degenerating into a classification of tropes and figures. Rhetoric is intended by its great practitioners—Vico is a prime example—to embrace what Bruner advocates. As Shelley points out in the *Defence of Poetry,* it is Bacon—one of Vico's heroes—who believes that "similitudes or relations," expressed in metaphorical language, give power to "the faculty which perceives them as the storehouse of axioms common to all knowledge." "Folk psychology" or "common sense" is philologi-cally and practically related to the Greek *topikos,* "commonplace," which Vico takes up in his philosophy of topics, contrasting it to critical or analytical philos-ophy. Not coincidentally, Bruner says that if "folk psychology" or "folk social science" are unattractive terms, we may call them "common sense." Related to the older *sensus communis,* this common sense is what Adam Smith, Kant, and rhetoricians and philosophers of the later eighteenth century call it, too, being careful to distinguish this connotation from its crude characterizations. Yet com-mon sense, a complicated philosophical idea with a long history, has been at-tacked by commentators such as Christopher Norris and Catherine Belsey. They use the term to represent a reductionist straw concept, charging it with naive faith in a supposedly self-evident, but false, "objectivity."

Vico's concept of the imagination reflects his profession and values. Survey-ing the idea of imagination as it developed from Hobbes and Leibniz through Kant, Coleridge, and Hegel, it could be said, summarizing swiftly, that three main sources of the idea work in interplay: the empirical, the Platonizing or idealistic, and the transcendental, all of which develop aesthetic applications.[11] Aware of the empirical and attuned to the Platonic sources, Vico pursues them less avidly than do many contemporaries. His idea of the imagination reflects the embracing vision of the humanist rhetorical tradition as it confronts the modern world of self-consciousness and social history. In his attempt to see the human relevance of knowledge gained and discovered by human effort and expressed in eloquent or poetic language, in his premium on the polymath over the side blinded specialist, he is, as Alain Pons remarks, "the last philosopher of the Renaissance."[12] Vico contends that science—and the quantitative and experimental social sciences—do not alone provide the best understanding of what *is* human, nor how human needs and problems might be articulated and solved in society. An imaginative vision must finally address these issues.[13] The nature of societies—what Vico is driving at—is determined by how we direct what is at our disposal, how our passions and desires wield the knowledge hang-ing at our fingertips. About this we tell stories; culture is something we narrate.

Vico's stress on the imagination points to the synthetic and comprehensive rather than to the analytic and divided. His forte is not psychological nuance, nor is it formulating categories to fit modes of cognition and related mental "faculties" of understanding, judgment, and sense; he does not pursue the finer-grained aesthetic implications of imagination; he does not assess the fine arts in thorough practical criticism, nor does he achieve a theory of the fine arts, insofar as one considers theory linked to close consideration of technique and form. Nor is Vico rooted primarily in analytic philosophy. Perfectly aware of—and often sympathetic toward—these many sources and angles from which the idea of imagination is growing by confluence, Vico, however, develops—and simultaneously exemplifies and exercises[14]—a concept of imagination with broad historical, social, and speculative resonance.

He sees that the imagination is not a monolithic faculty but entails several levels or degrees of operation.[15] When he remarks that, "In children memory is most vigorous, and imagination is therefore excessively vivid, for imagination is nothing but extended or compounded memory" (211), it is not the identification with memory that should arrest our attention, but the complicated nature of extension and compounding. And when Vico says, "Imagination is more robust in proportion as reasoning power is weak" (185), we need not jump to a simple polar model of the mind. He is repeating a commonplace repeated countless times before him. In this instance, Vico appears to be discussing people who are credulous, susceptible to superstition, and not generally educated. In Lessing, Joshua Reynolds, and Coleridge, and in a famous passage near the end of *The Prelude,* reason is seen either as inadequate in some areas, or else becomes enlarged to include intuition and imagination such that "reason" evolves as the total, subsumptive nature of the whole mind. For Wordsworth, imagination is "Reason in her most exalted mood" as well as "intellectual love." We might think of Matthew Arnold's later phrase "imaginative reason," or Bacon's own "insinuative reason," as short definitions of imagination.

Vico's sense of imagination is thus not a distinctly analyzed "faculty" of mind, but a complex mode or *topos* of human activity. It is assimilative, combinatory, and sympathetic, always crossing the borders of specialized knowledges. It's for this reason that Bacon, one of Vico's "four authors," calls in *The Advancement of Learning* for "a science of the imagination." In the same spirit Bacon contends that our studies should not be like rooms with walls that separate one another in a large house, but like veins and sinews that connect one living body. Since our factual knowledge will never be complete, nor all connections within our body of knowledge obvious, metaphor constantly remains as a key mode of imaginative thought. At the edge of knowledge the mind will naturally begin to think metaphorically. Physics Nobel laureate Edward Purcell believed that science and art in their creative acts share a sense of metaphor as a connective act binding and relating phenomena seemingly separate. Metaphor challenges the boundaries of known, literal definition in order to bring more knowledge—to create more knowledge—within the ken of language or even mathematical relationships.

3

We have dwelt on structures of language but, as Bruner notes, "At their core, all folk psychologies contain a surprisingly complex notion of an agentive Self" (41). Narratives of folk psychologies organize, present, pass on, and collectively "remember" the relation between the self and that culture of "common sense" with which the self coexists but which it can also affect. We often start our own language narratives by naming our own creators, "mama" or "dada." Our later, larger narratives are, as Frye notes, quests. Their language depicts *acts* of meaning. Every questing self is potentially a hero, an idea at the core of Frye and Vico, especially Vico's *De mente heroica.*[16] The variety of cultures leads to Joseph Campbell's "hero with a thousand faces." One reason the hero in the modern world has become problematic is that we are all potential heroes—and hence all potentially failed heroes observing our own quests. The idea of the Logos even takes on this active sense of quest or narrative, too, not of some absolute and unchanging essence. The living Bible, one of the great narratives, begins simultaneously with Logos and an act of the ultimate agentive Self. Frye starts his study of the Bible, *The Great Code,* by avowing indebtedness to Vico. For Frye, reading the Bible is never done: we reach the end to return to the beginning, a never-ending story. As Wallace Stevens says in another context, we merge with the book.

Bruner takes up the rhetorical term *fabula* to identify the story that helps the self establish its relation to culture. We can recall the admonition of romance narratives: *de te fabula,* this story is about you, your self. Here we are not far from the first injunction of Western philosophy, know thyself, knowledge that becomes evident only through acting, telling, interpreting, and retelling. To do this, we participate in and learn cultural narratives, diverse and pluralistic, then create our own. Every story reinforces but also deviates from what culture provides. Our personal quest is a search for something new or lost, something not present and therefore imagined. Bruner puts it this way: "The function of the story is to find an intentional state that mitigates or at least makes comprehensible a deviation from a canonical cultural pattern" (49–50). That deviation joins and alters the canonical patterns so that tradition and culture grow but change. Myths take on new forms when they are retold, embellished, even denied. "This method of negotiating and re-negotiating meanings by the mediation of narrative interpretation is, it seems to me, one of the crowning achievements of human development in the ontogenetic, cultural, and phylogenetic sense of that expression" (67).

Vico claims this in less technical language. He feels that such imaginative processes of personal development begin when we are young, educated for the first time through contact with culture and language, before we enter into specializations. Donald Verene says Vico "holds that studies should be introduced to cultivate first the powers of memory and imagination in the young and that too early an emphasis on the mastery of philosophical criticism and logic will make the mind sterile. The sense of wisdom and eloquence found in the Ancients should not be easily thrown over for the rapid assimilation of the techniques of modern invention and science. The arguments and ingenuities of the Moderns should be mastered, but only by mature minds that have been educated in the art of topics."[17] This anticipates Shelley's reflection on Bacon, as well as Bruner's sense of folk psychology conceived as the topics of common sense found in cultural narratives. Bruner addresses how "the young human being achieves (or realizes) the power of narrative" (68). Another word for this power, the word Vico uses, is imagination.

This learning of and through language—its relations, situational appropriateness, and cultural shadings, as well as memorization of words and grasp of syntax and grammar—begins to constitute the imaginative construction of meaning and value for the individual. We each end by uttering a personal voice, a self, not quite like any other. This crucial process is put in a deceptively simple phrase by poets and writers when they speak of "finding a voice."

Every author who re-creates the world in a new perspective uses language in arresting, defamiliarizing ways and constructs an identifiable style. Talented writers are parodied more than others. We can pick up one paragraph of a novel and say, this sounds like Austen, or James. A line or two may be enough to recognize Dickinson's voice. Shakespeare creates many selves and writes many styles, his particular dramatic genius. Every such construction in language is an interpretation of self and culture. We rely on interpretive procedures or strategies to make sense of the world, our culture, and our self. Being "an author" is bound up with one's own self—as personality or autobiography—but also with the languages of culture and how such languages interpret the act of being an author in the first place. Hence, we ask with Foucault, *what*—and not only who—is an author? Our interpretive strategies and cultural experiences, that is, our answers, may differ.

The self develops out of the imaginative, language-sensitive acts of meaning that we construct. We do this first as children, getting a handle on words and stories; eventually, we realize with Kierkegaard that life is lived forward but understood—interpreted—backward. In these inventions, tellings, and interpretations, which take place in time—in the history of a culture, and also in the span of one individual's life—we descry that our knowledges and identities cannot partition themselves into separate fields and categories. The essence of narrative interpretation is to make connections. Such acts of meaning build relations. Our education, our leading out into the world, our transformation of that world, recognize that knowledge is akin to a vast set of narratives, myths, and interpretive procedures. Or, as Nietzsche says in *The Birth of Tragedy,* a vast set of systems of knowledge nest one inside the other, pushing out into the black unknown. But they apply to human life only when they are subsumed in the larger system of art and its mythologies—that is, in the larger system of imaginative language, Vico's "poetry" or "eloquence." In the *Poetics,* that most influential of critiques on art, language, and education, Aristotle signals the ancient Greek confidence in art as *psychagogia,* the leading out of the individual soul or self into the world and its cultures.

In his address of 1737, "The Academies and the Relation between Philosophy and Eloquence," Vico reiterates the importance of feeling and language, heart and tongue, in conceiving of knowledge as a series of relations and processes. At the end of the address, he defines wisdom briefly as "mind and language . . . the perfecter of man in his properly being man." This could stand as a gloss for Bruner's *Acts of Meaning.* Bruner titles his first chapter "The Proper Study of Man"; the phrase is from Pope ("The proper study of mankind is man"), a contemporary of Vico who shares with him conceptions of poetry and rhetoric as key to education, civil polity, and ethical character. The complete couplet harkens back to that basic tenet of philosophy: "Know then Thy-self, presume not God to scan; / The proper Study of Mankind is *Man.*" In the next chapter we will see how Pope fulfills this role of the poet and addresses specific public issues.

4

Even the most devoted Vichian may find it difficult to explain adequately Vico's trust in "Providential sense."[18] Our intellectual age is secular. It is hard to remind ourselves that figures such as Washington, Burke, and Lincoln invoke a providential sense of human history at key moments in their writings and speeches, not as a sop to the credulous but because of their own deep, almost inarticulate belief. Today, we might say that a providential sense or hope is based on a communal outlook toward the human species as a whole; that we might cooperate with the forces of nature to work out our own salvation without destroying nature; and that in order to do this we require faith in our Providence, our destiny, as one race made of many races and nations, and that such faith is a self-potentiating act, not an abstract catechism.

If we accept this view, we begin to understand Vico's emphasis on piety—*pietas,* the sense of connection and sympathy between self and others, leading to a sense, however dim, of what Vico said the first poetic souls conceived of as "Sympathetic Nature." Piety embraces family, duty, country, spiritual life. It sees life as a series of connected wholes. One of the more remarkable (and least understood) dedications in the history of literature is the one Samuel Johnson gives to his fifty-two prefatory *Lives of the English Poets.* He dedicates that work to the advancement of piety. Taken as a whole, the *Lives* is a profound commentary on poems, poetry, poets, and the values—aesthetic, moral, political, religious—held by the authors and their audiences, by individual selves and their culture. Where we hardly expect it, Johnson's sense of poetry and its wisdom overlaps with the close of the *New Science*: "To sum up, from all that we have set forth in this work, it is to be finally concluded that this Science carries inseparably with it the study of piety, and that he who is not pious cannot be truly wise" (1112). Johnson's dedication and Vico's conclusion realize that human knowledge, especially when directed by human desires, remains imperfect. Poetry, or the poetic language of figuration and metaphor, is the most persuasive way to express this very imperfection. In short, for Vico and for Johnson piety is the virtue profoundly associated with imaginative wisdom, with eloquence. There seems an internal logic beyond coincidence in the fact that Virgil, Dante, Vico (who cites Plato in this regard), Burke, Johnson, Washington, Lincoln, Churchill, and King, to name just a few, not only understand rhetoric in its fullest sense, but also believe in piety, instilled by the wisdom of words, as the active retention and expression of Providence in human affairs.

As Vico conceives of it, piety, which embraces suffering, duty, and sacrifice, is next only to love as the virtue readying us to act, to bind us together as human beings in sympathy and interconnection. Only by exercising this virtue can we create a common humanity. It does not exist otherwise. Nature does not give it to us automatically. Thus, Vico says poetry "founded gentile humanity, from which alone sprang all the arts" (214); the piety of poetic wisdom creates common humanity. And so it must sustain it: "poetic morality began with piety, which was ordained by providence to found the nations, for among them all piety is proverbially the mother of all the moral, economic, and civil virtues" (503).

We do not need to adopt Vico's complete, often elusive system for his insights to retain value. To ask the intellectual world to convert to Vico is quixotic. Yet perhaps that is Vico's point; no such single conversion will take place. As the human spirit plays itself out in different societies throughout history, the important thing is to see what drives us to create these different views, and what motives bind them together. Vico's own view is itself a special form of knowledge constructed by the imagination and expressed rhetorically in language, at its highest in narratives and poetic wisdom. The organization of all knowledges and the organization of human knowledge—what we know about the world and what we know about ourselves—become inseparable tasks.

With imagination as the faculty of youth, and imaginative wisdom and piety as the mark of adult social virtue, reading Vico gives new resonance to Wordsworth's lines, "The Child is father of the Man; / And I could wish my days to be / Bound each to each by natural piety." In *De mente heroica* Vico exhorts his students, "Cultivate knowledge as a whole," not merely what is considered knowledge by an academically bound curricula, or by an aesthetic divorced from affairs, but cultivate all types of knowledge, all topoi and their images—and then grasp the interconnections of knowledge in human terms. The examples Vico offers—Alexander, Galileo, Descartes, Grotius—indicate a respect for different feelings, different intellects. Vico proposes to us, first in the vivid experiences of youth, then in mature ethical conscience speaking eloquently, an education of imagination. It means not only how we educate the imagination, how we store it with memories, select from it recollections, and recombine them in new, extrapolated, patterns sympathetic with other memories and experiences; it also signifies how we are educated by imagination, a growth that calls on sacrifice, sympathy, and dedication. With his call to cultivate all arts and sciences, and his vision that the best form of knowing is that which is made relevant, through eloquent language, to human needs—is it too much to claim that when we ask, what should a modern liberal education be, Vico provides an excellent starting point?

The sense of education as a leading out of the self into the entirety of the

Frontispiece to Vico's *New Science* (3d ed., 1744). The all-seeing eye of heaven, reflected by Hermes or Mercury, enters Homer, or the poet, who founds civil society. The symbols of culture, the arts, the sciences, the professions, and government surround him. Reproduced by permission of the Houghton Library, Harvard University, Cambridge, Massachusetts.

world—a *psychagogia*—matches Vico's scorn of "solitude." He does not mean to attack the solitude of contemplation or the disaffected alienation of a virtuous individual slandered and persecuted. Vico is revolted by the solitude of self-interest and solipsism, by the cult of selfishness in a refined, technical society: once deadened to sympathy, human feeling, and justice, mental ingenuity eventually becomes mental cannibalism. This is the solitude of solipsism and self-absorption, the opposite of Vico's piety. As Vico's "Age of Men" now prevails, its own barbarism is the ever inward focus of the self, the closing spiral of the self turning away from history, away from other societies, and then eventually away from the history and otherness within its own society, away from the challenging idea of holistic knowledge and—most sadly—away from the pain of fellow human beings.

Each generation, each individual, needs again to be led out into the world, to discover in the world what has already been imagined into reality—and then to imagine more. As T. S. Eliot's poem of the fragmented imagination of the first half of the twentieth century nears the end of its concluding section, "What the Thunder Said," we hear the injunction of thunder itself, *"Datta, dayadhvam, damyata"*: Give, sympathize, control. Vico's poetic, imaginative wisdom starts, as James Joyce knew, with what the thunder says, then it calls us to explore a diverse world where we might say—not in solitude, but with freedom, duty, and community—*Dovette, deve, dovrà.* Vico wants urgently to remind us that the quality and fate of our vision, our Providence, requires technical method but ultimately rests with the education of our imaginations.

The poet or artist accomplishes this by providing stories, narratives, and images that represent the otherwise unseen and unapprehended ways in which our different, interwoven acts of meaning create personal identity and collective culture. Poets are the founders of civil society. They are its critics, too, ideally seeing how economics, language, law, government, religion, business, and history conspire together for good or ill. This synthetic view Pope achieves in an extraordinary poem, his *Epistle to Bathurst.* In it, the Man of Ross and Sir Balaam are individuals who act in different ways in a larger shared culture, one Pope fears is becoming warped by selfishness and greed.

7

The Politics of Greed—Wealth and Words, or Balancing the Budget on the Backs of the Poor?

Pope's Epistle "To Bathurst"

"You know the use of riches"
—Mosca to Volpone in *Volpone*

"By speech you mean money?"
—*"Yes."*
"Just so we're clear on that."
—*"Why, I don't think there's any question about that. The Supreme Court voted nine, ten times on that matter."*
—Senator Mitch McConnell (Ky.),
chair of the Senate Ethics Committee,
appearing on *This Week,* Dec. 22, 1996

The list of similarities between our own age and Pope's, more than superficial, is worth noting at the outset: the largest financial scandal ever to face a major world power in the modern age, a large national debt, deficit spending, and protection for white collar criminals offered by the innermost—and highest—levels of government: "stonewalling" or, as the eighteenth century called it, "screening."[1] There is more, including securities fraud, junk bonds, complex paper trails hiding duplicity and fraud, insider trading, and the use of new technology to evade detection, mystify law enforcement, and stifle public outcry. To this add relaxed government regulation, and "soft-money" (hard-cash) contributions to elected and appointed officials, whether senators, ministers, olympic delegations, or members of Parliament, who help moneyed interests to avoid troublesome requirements or who look the other way at financial chicanery, even felony. Then there is the patriotic self-righteousness of speculators, often dressed with religious fervor, the flag and altar-cloth piety of directors at Lincoln Savings and Loan, or of Sir Balaam in Pope's epistle. They craft the image and the pretense of helping a decent, hard-working middle class while actually fleecing them to boost the income of a top few, and along the way think nothing of exploiting the poor and marginal. The rich who loot the public trust develop an ostentatious appetite for luxury—Timon's Villa and the Phoenician Hotel (once owned by a savings and loan mogul) are not far apart—while unethical lawyers and "independent" accounting firms reap huge fees from everybody. Over these sad events hangs the threat of foreign conflicts and partisan political accusations, even though blame enough exists for all.

This scenario characterizes the United States at the present time. It also accurately depicts, with uncanny parallels, the situation of Great Britain in the 1720s and 1730s. To make such a comparison is no product of an imagination straining for relevance. It is about as clear an analogy as history can provide. Like any such analogy, it cannot be taken literally, but suggests that the past, and what was written about it at that time, can serve as a guide or commentary for present conduct and values. We write columns, essays, exposés, or books about our predicament. We talk a lot on television. In the early 1730s, Pope writes a brilliant verse epistle, itself modeled on a poem by Horace, who lived in another imperial age and satirized its scandals and financial injustices. Pope's poem, in dialogue form, addresses political and financial greed of the 1720s and 1730s. It casts one link back to Rome's Augustan Age, one ahead to ours. The poem operates through an extraordinary yoking of the power (and value) of wealth and language. Pope's *Epistle To Bathurst,* subtitled "on the Use of Riches," the third of Pope's four moral essays or epistles, is compact and topical, political to the core, laced with outrage, pointed with a moral, and adorned by a cautionary tale.

Pope's poem has such genius of compression that we might think of it as four hundred lines, but four hundred times that scope. In 1960 Earl Wasserman noted that the poem moves on several levels in a "climate of attitudes."[2] This essay examines one level: the commingling in phrase, imagery, and theme of two key systems of signification and value, money and language. As structuralist and post-structuralist critics (among them Barthes, de Man, Culler, Kristeva, Derrida, and Riffaterre) have pointed out, language is a system of symbolic differences whose meanings come from an essentially tacit social agreement, established through education and memory, in which individuals treat each word as signifying roughly the same idea. Possessing no intrinsic or natural connection with things in themselves, words in this sense are "arbitrary" or artificial. Only by communal consent do they represent specific value. Some structuralist and deconstructive critics have called this view of language revolutionary, a contribution primarily of Ferdinand de Saussure and his followers. Many of his insights were fresh and have been extended. Yet this general view of language may be traced back at least to the Middle Ages—as Umberto Eco and others assert—and gained one concise, modern articulation in Locke's 1690 *Essay*. In Book 4 he introduces *semiotic* into modern English discourse. Semiotics constitutes his third branch of knowledge:

> [T]he third branch may be called Σημειωτικὴ or *the doctrine of signs*; the most usual whereof being words . . . the business whereof is to consider the nature of signs the mind makes use of for the understanding of things. . . . therefore to communicate our thoughts to one another, as well as record them for our own use, signs of our ideas are also necessary. (4.xxi)

Linguists have noted, too, that language is a form of currency. Numerous analogies and metaphors reveal that words and the counters of wealth are connected habitually. To coin a phrase, money talks. Horace plays directly on this sense of linguistic currency in *Ars poetica* (lines 58–62), which Roscommon translates

> Men ever had, and ever will have, leave
> To coin new words well suited to the age.
> Words are like leaves, some wither ev'ry year,
> And ev'ry year a younger race succeeds.

Pope, who praises Roscommon at the end of the *Essay on Criticism,* knew these lines and their original. The half-line simile, "Words are like leaves," Pope applies to a different context earlier in the *Essay*:

> *Words* are like *Leaves*; and where they most abound,
> Much *Fruit* of *Sense* beneath is rarely found. (lines 309–10)

Words as coin, words as leaves: the two images, connected through good usage guided by "sense," are embedded in Pope's associations and language.

But as artificial or arbitrary signifiers, neither money as units of capital nor words as units of language stand absolutely or naturally for particular things or virtues. Instead, words and wealth, whether land, gold, credit, or paper notes, acquire meaning and value through social convention and action. Coleridge speaks of the language of daily life as "words used as the *arbitrary marks* of thought, our smooth market-coin of intercourse with the image and superscription worn out by currency," where "currency" gains double meaning.[3] Emerson, in the section entitled "Language" in *Nature* (1836), warns, "old words are perverted to stand for things which are not; a paper currency is employed, when there is no bullion in the vaults." Various uses and usages within each semiotic system of money or language may be judged proper or improper. Furthermore, the two systems have always been, on one level, perfectly interchangeable at no discount. As Fernand Braudel, eminent historian of capitalism and material economy, points out, "As soon as men had known how to write and had had coins to handle they had replaced cash with written documents, notes, promises and orders. Notes and cheques between market traders and bankers were known in Babylon twenty centuries before the Christian era."[4]

2

Pope begins his poem with an argument about the origin of gold. Like two schoolmen, he and Bathurst exchange explanations. Their introductory dialogue is verbal disputation, doctors disagreeing over a theosophical point: "You hold the word, from Jove to Momus giv'n," while Pope contradicts this and will "Opine, that Nature, as in duty bound, / Deep hid the shining mischief under ground."[5] But when the dispute ends, their words signifying different views are found to have concealed identical beliefs. Both agree that gold creates the prodigal and the avaricious miser.[6] The opening argument, with its "soundest" casuistry of opposites, a casuistry Pope elsewhere scoffs at and discredits (e.g. *Lock* 5: 122, and *Dunciad* 4: 642), seems balanced, at least temporarily. One account of the situation clears the other. There is a Christian-pagan tension here, whether gold comes from Jove or God, but the opening is more a rendering of *Buchgeld* or "bookmoney," the contemporary German term, reflecting its written act of settling one account—or argument—against another. Gold itself, and generally all wealth, though extreme in its gifts and debatable in origin, owes its moral worth completely to tenets directing its use. Plenty or penury makes no difference in virtue or salvation. Riches are not a sign or, to use Pope's word—with its monetary echo even louder then than now—a "token of th' Elect."

Gold, the traditional currency, is less cumbersome than wealth in kind, the production of goods, such as hogsheads of wine or bellowing oxen. Even so, the bribe of golden guineas taken by the "old Patriot," described in Pope's note, is discovered when the hypocrite leaves the king's closet and descends the back stairs, the old-fashioned equivalent of heading for deposit in a shady off-shore account. (We might recall, too, that a bribe itself involves an oral or written promise, in this case to make an insincere speech aimed at gaining William III more money. Politicians often have "speaking fees" paid by special interest groups.) The Patriot's purse splits, out drops a guinea, and the coin betrays him to his Party by speaking:

> And gingling down the back-stairs, told the crew,
> "Old Cato is as great a Rogue as you." (lines 67–68)[7]

Although gold is less bulky than physical objects on which we base wealth, it, too, grows heavy and speaks. It can weigh one down and turn tattletale. But Pope carries the parallel of money and words further. The ultimate in silence, and virtually weightless, is the gentle whisper of a paper leaf. Even more silent is the electronic transfer. Here the fusion of wealth and words, becoming complex, centers on writing as well as speech. Paper money is watermarked and inscribed, usually as a promissory note that bears a signature or signatures denoting a guarantee, someone's or some government's word of honor that the note can be exchanged for gold or silver at will. Until recently, U.S. notes promised in writing to pay the bearer on demand the stated sum in silver. Paper money represents a bill or real debt, which the holder may claim anytime. Its denomination refers to the amount written in words and accompanied by a signature, for as with personal checks, numbers can be altered with ease. Words—paper and ink—become the least bulky of all currencies, the well-languaged form of riches and deceit:

> Blest paper-credit! last and best supply!
> That lends Corruption lighter wings to fly!
> Gold imp'd by thee, can compass hardest things,
> Can pocket States, can fetch or carry Kings (lines 69–72)

Today, we refine on the elusive nature of paper by introducing digital funds and computer trading. But in 1694, when Pope is six years old, the Bank of England introduces government paper notes for the first time. All Europe admires the innovation.[8] Pope seems to have the bank notes uppermost—though not exclusively—in mind, especially since the episode of the speaking guinea occurs in 1698, and immediately precedes the apostrophe to money's "last and best supply!" Paper credit had a long history for personal and bank debts. As Tapwell sneers at the prodigal Wellborn in Massinger's *New Way to Pay Old Debts,* performed more than a century before Pope's day, "You grew the common borrower; no man 'scap'd / Your paper-pellets" (1.1). For centuries, writing stands as a sign of not having actual coinage, gold, silver, or copper, in hand. Government bank notes emerge by a process of evolution sped up in late seventeenth-century England.[9] But paper notes, in denominations too large for the populace to find practicable or even to possess, retain a mysterious aura decades after their first appearance. Echoing Paul (2 Thess. 2:7), Bolingbroke speaks of the establishment of public credit as a "whole mystery of iniquity." "Even in 1752," notes Braudel, "a man of the intellectual calibre of David Hume . . . spoke of 'that new invention of paper money' when the Bank of England had been issuing notes since it was founded in 1694."[10] Suspicion and discomfort cling to this novel way of writing value.

But beyond his ironic paean to paper credit, more specifically to England's new paper notes, Pope transforms paper wealth into *Sibylline leaves.* The *Sibylline Books,* or at least three of the original nine, were consulted by Roman officials in times of state emergency. The Sibyl at Cumae wrote poetic prophecies on her palm leaves and cast them to the winds. In a single simile (lines 75–76),

> A leaf, like Sibyl's, [shall] scatter to and fro
> Our fate and fortunes, as the winds shall blow,

Pope connects writing, the prophecy of empires, leaves, words, paper money, wind, flying, corruption, and, through a note of his own, refers the whole to Virgil. As Maynard Mack stresses, here is "'fortune-hunting' of another kind," where "the evocation . . . of the palm leaves on which the Cumaean sibyl was reputed to scratch her prophecies . . . strikes a note that vibrates through the poem."[11] The passage and its context merit examination. In Virgil the lines are

foliis tantum ne carmina manda
ne turbata volent rapidis ludibria ventis:
ipsa canas oro . . . (6.74–76)

Aeneas asks Apollo and his Sibyl specifically *not* to write, not to use a leaf as paper or note, but to relate Aeneas's duty orally, *ipsa canas oro*. Dryden, as Wasserman observes, renders this passage

> But, oh! commit not thy prophetic mind
> To flitting leaves, the sport of every wind,
> Lest they disperse in air our empty fate:
> Write not, but, what the powers ordain, relate. (lines 116–19)

Whenever and wherever paper money was introduced, many found its nature and influence satanic. "If most contemporaries found money a 'difficult cabbala to understand,'" says Braudel, "this type of money, money that was not money at all, and this interplay of money and mere writing to a point where the two became confused, seemed not only complicated but *diabolical*."[12] The invention of paper money in Goethe's *Faust* (2), which greatly helps the Emperor, is one of Faust's major modern achievements, aided by the Devil. Goethe associates it, as does Pope, with gaming and luxury.

Now, combine this sense of a prophetic, devilish currency with the common opposition portrayal of Robert Walpole as the great Satan or tempter, and through the images and allusions, a finger is clearly pointed at government financial measures—and the men behind them. *Craftsman* no. 297, for instance, portrays Walpole as a tempter casting apples down from the "tree of corruption" variously labeled forfeited estates, charitable corporation, bank contract, and South-Sea. Pope has such a nexus in mind when he writes about money as corrupt, prophetic leaves written upon with "lighter wings to fly." These are winged words of a special kind. Pope later in the poem calls the devil the Prince of Air. He flies, causes shipwrecks, and rouses whirlwinds. Probably Pope is unaware that the Cantonese had for centuries called paper currency "flying money." Yet very possibly he heard the Dutch term for the type of share speculation fueling the South Sea Bubble and compounding the national debt: *Windhandel,* or trading in air. Whitwell Elwin and W. J. Courthope, in their edition of Pope's *Works,* quote a similar metaphor later used by Adam Smith, but in his case used with approval: "The gold and silver money which circulates . . . may very properly be compared to a highway, which, while it circulates and carries to market all the grass and corn of the country, itself produces not a single pile of either. The judicious operations of banking, by providing . . . *a sort of waggon-way through the air,* enable the country to convert . . . a great part of its highways into pastures and cornfields, and thereby to increase very considerably the annual produce of its land and labour."[13]

Prior to Smith, even after, moralists routinely damned speculation, credit, paper money, and banking. Yet Pope skirts this group of naysayers. He and Bathurst seem resigned to the relatively new phenomenon of paper money; its tide is irreversible.[14] But, more important, Pope recognizes how money in the form of the written word can be misused with particular ease and stealth. Intent to keep an eye peeled for the "use of riches," whether in goods, gold, or paper, he is painfully aware how paper—that is, how writing—offers opportunities for an empire without bound of deception and avarice, whether in notes, share speculation, or conveyances and wills drawn up by attorneys. As Braudel warns, "Money was indeed a miraculous agent of exchange, but it was also a confidence trick serving the privileged."[15] If advantage lay in paper money and credit, so did treachery and betrayal of public trust.

Like words that connote values such as goodness or honesty, money—especially paper money—merely signifies. Its medium grows so transparent or invisible that it can be "Pregnant with thousands" but still "flits . . . unseen," playing off the earlier line: "Oh! that such bulky Bribes as all might see." The powerful paper scraps should not be strictly identified nor equated with wealth or capital. But a society can easily develop a monetary economy based on paper rather than on actual wealth. For example, it has been estimated that the amount of metal on deposit at the Bank of England by the end of the seventeenth century was a mere seven percent of the outstanding value of paper notes—not fifty percent, as some contemporaries assumed.[16] In a manner similar to accepting that the face value of paper money or bonds represents the true worth of society's production of goods, social usage easily lets words and rumor, not deeds, pass for its members' virtue and reputation. Easy virtue, easy money, easy words: they have more in common than their modifier.

The connection between writing and money had for centuries been imbedded in European financial practices, not through government issue but as bills, shares, and private banking notes. Pope calls Sir John Blunt the "great Scriv'ner!"—here literally a money writer. Blunt was a key director of the South Sea Company, which tried to buy the national debt, the difference between the

Bank of England's reserves in metal and its paper notes outstanding. In 1720, Pope invested five hundred pounds in the South Sea Company but later castigates himself for the mistake. The debt had in effect been created by writing; it was now to be resolved by scriveners and paper credit. "The scrivener," Peter Dixon remarks, "combined the functions of estate-agent, broker, moneylender, and solicitor, and operated with a freedom unknown to his modern counterparts."[17] The wonder of the public debt was not that it was long term but that it was perpetual, yet any holder could gain personal liquidity by selling shares to someone willing to assume the role of creditor.

When writing becomes money, deeper possibilities of subterfuge include fraud, forgery, and counterfeiting: crimes of false writing and signature. John Ward was guilty of forgery, and perhaps Blunt falsely conveyed, to Ward, part of his estate (Pope later drops mention of this charge). Peter Waters—or Walter—too, is a money scrivener or writer who loans out at interest. The power of such scriveners was, as Braudel observes with anecdotal evidence, "a constant source of amazement. The Italian merchant who settled in Lyons in about 1555 with a table and an inkstand and made a fortune represented an absolute scandal, even in the eyes of people who understood the handling of money and the process of exchange fairly well."[18] Moreover, as Pope's own note reports, Blunt grew "eloquent" and "declaimed against the corruption and luxury of the age" in prophetic style. His money writing, like his prophecies, are false and inflated, his junk bonds heavily discounted. The same happens with his florid rhetoric, often phrased as national prophecy. And how is it that Blunt makes such promises and predictions, resulting in his paper scheme? "A wizard told him in these words our fate." The sense of false prophecy again is emphasized, here with a hint of Walpole as Lord Treasurer.[19] The Charitable Corporation, along with one of its chief directors Denis Bond, makes a pledge, a verbal or written act, to help the deserving poor. But Bond ends by damning them "and hates them from his heart." The easy, always available deception of writing and speaking now entails direct deception in the use of riches, the two systems having become virtually synonymous.

3

"Worth" often punctuates Pope's notes to his poem. He indicates the wealth of individuals by saying how much they are "worth" in terms of pounds, often

italicizing *worth* in mocking emphasis. One obvious play on *worth* comes in the note to Waters: "But this gentleman's history must be deferred till his death, when his *worth* may be known more certainly."[20] Here Pope uses worth in its obverse *and* reverse senses. He seems to be waiting for Waters's funeral, as he had waited successfully for John Hopkins's in 1732, to add "-lessness." But Waters would die in 1746. The desired transvaluation Pope achieves in a note by describing Hopkins, barely cold, as one who "lived worthless, but died *worth three hundred thousand pounds.*"

The final tale of Balaam links material well-being and virtue, assigning worth in both its senses through the intervention of death, which settles all accounts, as Prince Hal, the Chief Justice, and Falstaff discover. Immediately preceding the tale of Balaam we hear:

> Cutler and Brutus, dying both exclaim,
> "Virtue! and Wealth! what are ye but a name!" (lines 333–34)

Each a mere word? Is there some higher system of value that will save or damn the soul exercising or abusing its virtue and wealth? Pope's final examination of word, wealth, and worth—of language, money, and virtue (or lack of it) comes in Balaam's portrait. The stage is set by the next lines, with the key phrase "such worth" referring back to wealth and virtue both:

> Say, for such worth are other worlds prepar'd?
> Or are they both, in this their own reward?
> A knotty point! to which we now proceed.
> But you are tir'd—I'll tell a tale. 'Agreed.' (lines 335–38)

When Balaam is introduced, "His word would pass for more than he was worth" (344). Before his meteoric rise and downfall, his word is better than his written bond, his language trusted to the utmost degree in all dealings. But if worth is the name for virtue, the line inverts its meaning and Balaam becomes a hypocrite or false prophet. What happens to Balaam's word is curious. As his money grows, his word declines until it descends, like Bond damning the poor, into a curse.[21] The play on worth and words emerges as an aural pun, too. Elizabethan pronunciation makes a final *th* into *t*—as in Shakespeare's quibble on *death* and *debt* between Falstaff and the Lord Chief Justice. So, *worth* becomes *wort,* close to *word,* and identical to the German "word." This may seem far-fetched, but we should recall the language of the House of Hanover. Any *th,* at least in the mouth of George I, becomes *t,* his *wort,* another name for *word.* The verbal pairing is evoked again by Johnson in *London,* his imitation of Juvenal's third satire, where Thales decries that worth is not even praised in worthless words:

> Since Worth, he cries, in these degen'rate Days
> Wants ev'n the cheap Reward of empty Praise. (lines 35–36)

But, to return to Balaam, his *exemplum* contains a further connection between the use of riches and of language. Throughout the poem, wealth or worth is bound up, as in Cutler's and Brutus's exclamation, with names and naming— with what others call us and what we call them—and (not always the same) with what things, and even human beings, actually *are.* Names seem to change with the person's worth or supposed value. The philanthropic Man of Ross helps to build a church and raise its steeple. But in the church he "Will never mark the marble with his Name."[22] In fact, as Pope explains in his note, his "true name was almost lost," and Pope had to write Jacob Tonson to ascertain "his Xtian and surname."[23] By his virtuous works, by the simple lines in his Parish Register, the Man of Ross is instead "Prov'd, by the ends of being, to have been." (In *Silas Marner,* one character argues that marriage does not occur with the couple's love or vows, nor with the minister's pronouncement, but only when man and woman sign the register.)

Names have conjuring power. In darkly predictable fashion, the most notorious of the failed savings and loan institutions in the United States, Lincoln, carried the name of the president known for sincerity and rectitude, Honest Abe, who as a youth walked miles to return a few pennies to a tradesman. The parent company of Lincoln Savings and Loan was American Continental, hinting at a patriotic manifest destiny.

Balaam, too, ironically begins Lincoln-like, "A plain good man"—a title also sounding like the Man of Ross—"and Balaam was his name." But then, poking fun at Puritan hagiography, Pope reports "the Dev'l was piqu'd such saintship to behold." With newfound riches clearly of the written kind, the plain citizen becomes someone different—yet frighteningly like everyone else who is corrupted ("Sir Balaam now, he lives like other folks"). And he names everything else in different fashion as well:

> Behold Sir Balaam, now a man of spirit,
> Ascribes his gettings to his parts and merit,
> What late he call'd a Blessing, now was Wit,
> And God's good Providence, a lucky Hit.
> Things change their titles, as our manners turn (lines 375–79)

Or, we might conclude, as Balaam's own title turns to sir.

This change in judgment—and the alteration of the names we use for things as a result of financial success—runs parallel to Pope's *Essay on Criticism,* in which judgment of an author's language is determined by rank or "Quality" and its associated wealth:

> Some judge of Authors' *Names,* not *Works,* and then
> Nor praise nor blame the *Writings,* but the *Men.*
> Of all this *Servile Herd* the worst is He
> That in *proud Dulness* joins with *Quality,*
> A constant Critick at the Great-man's Board,
> To *fetch and carry* Nonsense for my Lord.
> What *woful stuff* this Madrigal wou'd be,
> In some starv'd Hackny Sonneteer, or me? (lines 412–19)

The "*fetch and carry*" of the false critic plying his Lord with written trash reappears in *Bathurst* to characterize the devious servant of paper wealth, who turns out to be the real master able to "fetch or carry Kings." In the Epistle *To Dr. Arbuthnot* (line 226), "To fetch and carry sing-song up and down," voices Pope's scorn for the "race that write." The passage contains an ironic slight of George II as well.

Finally, the Devil, a fine, false rhetorician on the evidence of both Miltonic epics, whispers, tempts, and persuades Sir Balaam. Language, as well as wealth, is the diabolical medium, and the Devil masters both by making them one. What captures Sir Balaam's soul is his attainment of the ironic title "Director." And the Devil "dubs" him this, the verb reinforcing an irony that equates the royal act of bestowing knighthood with dubious gain in Exchange Alley.

But how does the Devil actually secure the soul of Balaam? The traditional arrangement is an instrument of conveyance or actual security itself—something signed—a pact attested by actual signature. The classic example is Faust's bargain witnessed by the Devil's agent or risk arbitrageur Mephistopheles. In Marlowe's *Doctor Faustus,* the learned man writes such a "bill" in his own blood:

> What might the staying of my blood portend?
> Is it unwilling I should write this bill?

After writing, Faustus says, "this bill is ended" (1.5). It is a "scroll" or "deed," too. Though Pope does not explicitly mention that Directors sign stock and notes, everyone knew the practice. We can extrapolate to see how Balaam's situation entails a compact with the Devil, represented as the writing of a bill. As Director, Sir Balaam must sign the securities of the Corporation or Bank.[24] In a sense, signing is his most important act, just as the chief financial officer of a government must sign printed currency to make it good. Balaam's pact with the Devil is thus repeated and reinforced each time he writes his name on a note or bond showering "Cent. per Cent." The Devil's contract is each signed security and, because there are plenty of copies on hand, he can afford to spend as many as he pleases.

4

On the optimistic side of the relation between wealth and words, we discover that for Pope the best use of both riches and words is directed by the same quality of intellect and personal character. What guides their finest exercise is "Sense":

> The Sense to value Riches, with the Art
> T'enjoy them, and the Virtue to impart,
> Not meanly, nor ambitiously pursu'd,
> Not sunk by sloth, nor rais'd by servitude. (lines 219–22)

This formulation resonates with the same "good Sense" that governs writing and criticism. Excess in verbal style Pope compares to gold and jewels that ostentatiously "cover ev'ry Part" in a mass (*Essay,* lines 295–96); in *Bathurst* wealth "In heaps, like Ambergrise, a stink it lies." In moral economy, too, as Clarissa reminds Belinda in *The Rape of the Lock,* "good Sense" is a guiding light of conduct. It, and not the outward sign of a pretty face, maintains virtue in the theater's front box. In *Bathurst* the gambling and corruption caused by paper money make peeress and butler each lose their sense and share the same— dice, theater, sexual—box. The loose mores in Balaam's tale have their analogy in contemporary references to paper credit as promiscuous copulation. Fitting with this fornication, the shower of "Cent. per Cent."—as Maynard Mack observes—alludes to Jove descending on Danae as a shower of gold,[25] a kind of seed money.

In the connection between criticism and spending, the *Essay on Criticism* metaphorically fuses the "Sense" of language with the cent.'s of wealth:

> Be Niggards of Advice on no Pretence;
> For the *worst Avarice* is that of *Sense.* (lines 578–79)

Pope applies the idea of a golden mean with equal appropriateness to the use of riches and the use of language. Bathurst exemplifies it, or at least Pope asks him to do so (lines 219–28). And Pope's address to him is cut from the same cloth as the description in the *Essay on Criticism* (lines 631–42) that calls for critics to practice a golden mean in literature. In *Bathurst* there is even a hint that if the Man of Ross were a poet, his works would be "clear and artless" as the river he bade flow.

> Who hung with woods yon mountain's sultry brow?
> From the dry rock who bade the waters flow? (lines 253–54)

The Man of Ross exercises true wit in the use of riches. What he does is precisely to produce *"Nature* to Advantage drest." In clear, economical style he gives us the "true expression" of riches, and "without method" shows us their sense. *Bathurst* intermingles two of the most important and pervasive semiotic systems of society, words and wealth, writing and money, at a time when— during Pope's own life—they were becoming indistinguishably conjoined. "For money is a language (we too must be forgiven for using a metaphor)," says Braudel; "it calls for and makes possible dialogues and conversations; it exists as a function of these conversations."[26] Each system, money and language, is a powerful signifier of value. But behind them stands the complex nature of Sense, of virtue as human action, the benefit or damage caused by motives directing the use of words and wealth.

Virtue, argues Pope, is thus more than the mere signifiers or arbitrary marks of its worth, whether words or paper notes, a syllable or a leaf. Virtue becomes what we do with—and inescapably within—the semiotic systems at hand, how we bestow value through motives and acts. The constructedness of culture does not make virtue come or go; it does not *make* virtue itself, though it may attach a conventional name or word to it. This stands behind what Howard Weinbrot sees as the guiding principle of the poem, how "virtue is not just a word but a concept of active benevolence that has its pattern in heaven and heavenly workings."[27]

5

We can return to Sir Balaam, having left him a knight and Director signing endless contracts with the Prince of Air, into whose arms the paper notes and government currency fly, swirling like so many misdirected Sibylline leaves. The Man of Ross distributes his modest means to the poor, raises public works, or builds an aspiring steeple for a church without his own name. His works eliminate written money, making scriveners and "vile Attornies" into "an useless race." Sir Balaam, on the other hand, resorts to small coins to do his good works and salve his conscience: "I'll now give six-pence where I gave a groat." Written money is too dear for his charity: having started paper notes with the smallest sum at twenty pounds, the Bank for a time issued five-pound notes but settles on ten pounds as the lowest denomination. Yet the Charitable Corporation specifies forwarding only "small sums" to the industrious poor. At that level, coins must be employed; paper money is too high in denomination. So, Bond and a majority of the Directors of that Corporation take their assets and invest them in the City, London's Wall Street: "Damn the Poor," says Bond, "let us go into the City, where we may get [paper] Money."[28] As a Director, Balaam's fortune comes from paper's "Cent. per Cent.," where the end of riches is self-propagation.

In Pope there is always another nuance. He caps Balaam's rise to MP with this line: "And one more Pensioner St. Stephen gains" (line 394). The connection with the House of Commons and Walpole is soon evident. Sir Balaam has become an inside trader, a team player in a situation where government economic policy is a form of state religion. His pension is a bribe. Johnson's *Dictionary* (1755) equates the two, and his lines in *London* (51–52) echo Juvenal's image: "Here let those reign, whom Pensions can incite / To vote a Patriot black, a Courtier white." (Pope said he would be glad to take credit for the anonymous *London,* and many gave it to him.)

The House of Commons continued to meet in St. Stephen's for a century after Pope wrote *Bathurst.* But St. Stephen's was a Catholic chapel originally, built by the Edwards to emulate or surpass Sainte Chapelle in Paris. Only after the Reformation does it assume a parliamentary venue. Sir Christopher Wren puts it into "plain" style, much like Balaam's original self, about 1707. In contrast, the Man of Ross helps to build a "heav'n-directed" steeple and refuses to desecrate it with his name. (Wasserman draws attention to Pope's later alteration of "Town" to "Church," stressing even more the presence of the church, first without a stone to mark Kyrle's grave, and then "with·' any Stone or Inscription.")[29] But "Vulture Hopkins" commissions, so Pope mistakenly thinks, a vile statue of himself to bear up God's altar. To cap these contrasts, the reader first encounters Balaam under London's paganlike great Column, not "heav'n-directed" but simply "pointing at the skies," its false inscription imputing the Great Fire of 1666 to papists, its shaft overlooking Exchange Alley where paper schemes are hatched. Next, Balaam receives a bribe from what was once a consecrated Catholic chapel, its original identity now defaced, its new brand of morning worshipper pouring in the door. St. Stephen's becomes the Sibyl's cave, her leaves its paper bribes. Its wizard prophet, its satanic Antichrist, is Walpole. To move ahead in time: the Column's inscription is erased in 1831. Oliver Wendell Holmes will later recall that as a schoolboy he read *Bathurst,* and wondered in particular about two lines and "what was the meaning of the second one: 'Where London's column, pointing to the skies / Like a tall bully, lifts its head and lies'" (lines 339–40). When Holmes first visits London, the inscription is already gone. Fifty-two-years later, in 1886, receiving honorary degrees from Oxford, Cambridge, and Edinburgh, he recalls Pope's lines again, apparently still puzzled by the lie the Column tells, or told. The year of his first visit, 1834, fire burns St. Stephen's. The site of Pope's villa now belongs to St. Catherine's Convent, a Catholic school. Pope's Grotto, his own Sibyl's cave, remains on the convent grounds.[30]

To his line about St. Stephen's (394), home of the new written word, Pope appends in 1735, a cryptic note: "—atque unum civem donare *Sibyllae.* Juv[enal]." (P. *1735c–51*).[31] This quotes from the third line of Juvenal's third satire. Wasserman interprets Pope's citation, "Just as Sir Balaam has made his progress from the City to St. James and thence to St. Stephen's Chapel in Westminster, where Walpole performs his mysteries, so Juvenal's friend, Umbritius, is escaping Rome to live in Cumae, where the Sibyl has her shrine and prophesies men's futures. . . . [B]ut the irony, of course, lies in the fact that whereas Umbritius was escaping to the simple, agrarian culture of Cumae, Sir Balaam has fled from sordid London to the very source of its corruption."[32]

Wasserman's reading is apropos. But an additional level of allusion is at work, especially in view of references to the Sibyl and her association with paper money, credit, and bribes. Pope likely knows that the Sibylline Books are transferred to a new locale during the reign of Caesar Augustus, the temple of Apollo Palatine, not at all in the country but near the imperial residence. Their transfer to that marble temple, built in 28 B.C.E., one year before Octavian becomes Augustus, meant that he could hold special worship in the presence of their leaves. Quoting five words, Pope associates his poem with Juvenal's; he also implicates Augustus himself, for Augustus, who customarily worshipped Apollo in the Palatine temple, oversaw the transfer of the Sibylline Books. Pope strengthens the Roman echoes by mentioning, in the previous line, "Britain's Senate," which, like Rome's, has been bought by the emperor and his ministers. Pope arranges to have *Bathurst* first published on the day before the king opens Parliament in 1732–33.

The terse Juvenalian reference opens multiple perspectives. St. Stephen's, once a chapel of Catholic royalty, becomes Apollo's temple on the Palatine, the ruling party's new church and place of false prophecy. To it are taken the latter-day Sibylline Books and with them—or as wizard Walpole's leaves out of them—the bribes doled out to "pensioners" in paper notes, shares, and false conveyance of estates. And as the Sibylline Books played a vital role in Roman religion, Pope casts paper money and the paper instruments on which Balaam and the government gamble their fortunes, and the country's, as misued instruments of Britain's new religion and new Augustus—not so obliquely identified as a business associate of the Devil, King of Whirlwinds. Even stressing the parallel with Cumae rather than with the Sibylline Books, we can reflect on what Gibbon relates in the *Decline and Fall*: during his life Augustus received worship as a god in several temples dedicated to him, one at Cumae.[33]

The gold from God, the paper shower from Jove, funnel through Balaam back to Augustus. Devil and King "go snacks"; in the slang of the day, they share equally: the souls go to Satan, the paper money, stocks, and liquid assets, to the Crown. In the middle of one line in one manuscript version, "The Devil and ____ divide the prize," Pope writes then scratches out "the King."[34] In other versions, including the first edition of 1732, this line does not appear.

But Pope finally includes it, with the scratched words printed out.[35] George II, Augustus, collects his due, and unto Caesar is rendered what is his.

When paper credit was introduced to France by the Scottish economist John Law, whose scheme Blunt professed to emulate, the Princess Palatine—her title here a pure coincidence—exclaimed, "'I have often wished that hell-fire would burn all these notes,' and swore that she understood nothing of the detestable system." In the case of Pope's Balaam, depicted with such representative and compressed brilliance, the princess is far from getting her wish. Instead, the souls burn. The notes are forfeit—that is, they revert—to Augustus. Presumably, they are blown into his Sibyl's hands again to pay more bribes. At any rate, "this uneasiness," exhibited so forcefully by the princess and others, says Braudel, "was the beginning of the awareness of a new language."[36] Pope, master of Locke's "usual" semiotic system of words, understands with the same acuity the implications and machinations of the unusual new system of money writing, particularly as an instrument of social behavior and national policy. At bottom, at least for Pope, their common rate of exchange is moral sense, or its corruption. And corruption is never local but infectious, it spreads. The greed-driven grab in the United States 250 years later will implicate business schools, lawyers, accounting firms, and government bureaucrats in one mesh of complicity. It represents, according to one commentator, a "decline of moral fiber and ethical standards" in all those professions.[37] The Justice Department will admit that there are far too many cases to prosecute within the statute of limitations.

With receipt of a bribe from France disclosed—now bereft of family, place, and means—impeached in the House of Lords and about to hang—poor Balaam at last employs the old language in its linguistically sinful sense.[38] He curses. The corrupted systems of words and wealth, unscrupulously fused as one, have corrupted him. Here there is no room for casuistry or polite debate, no *Buchgeld*. The account must be paid in the soul's currency. His very wind, his body's trading in air, cut off by the rope, Balaam's last word is nevertheless the most impious of performative speech acts. As he hangs he damns God. In doing so, he is also heard cursing what was God and was with God in the beginning—before paper money, even before gold—the Word.

In Western culture, that Word is first expressed in the sacred Hebrew Scriptures; its language conveys power and transcendent presence. At the time of Pope's death, Robert Lowth decides to study that writing on a new basis. He soon realigns modern conceptions of literature, culture, and poetry, as well as their relation to spiritual life.

The final lines of Pope's "Epistle to Bathurst" on "the use of riches." In this autograph draft, the words "the King" have been scratched out. They were printed when the poem was later published. This item (HM 6007) is reproduced by permission of The Huntington Library, San Marino, California.

8

Robert Lowth, Unacknowledged Legislator

Most thinkers extend, preserve, or refine. Robert Lowth, without setting out to do so, radically redirects modern literary culture and religious scholarship by studying ancient, sacred texts. But how can one convince a reader of the value and importance of a writer whose name is so relatively obscure that few are certain how to pronounce it, and whose work is not readily available? Yet Lowth changes profoundly all definitions of poetry and alters its practice permanently. He sees literature as inextricably bound up with the totality of experiences of a people—a nation—over time, and as fundamentally connected with their daily practices, high and low. Thus, he establishes a new, mixed mode of criticism at once historical, cultural—we might call it anthropological, too—and aesthetic. Though he discloses no sense of an impending Romantic movement, he empha-sizes prophecy, power, sublimity, and a poetic form that, above all, conveys these qualities as potentially present in the common things and revelatory moments of daily life, a poetic form expressed in "simple and unadorned" language achieving an "almost ineffable sublimity" rather than adhering to strict formal patterns or classical models.[1] These values provide an intellectual cornerstone for Romantic poetry and poetics. When Stephen Prickett calls Lowth's *Lectures on the Sacred Poetry of the Hebrews* "epoch-making," the epithet is literal in its full force, not flamboyant.[2] It's the combination of Lowth's subject matter and the way he approaches it that gives his work extraordinary, if unacknowledged, power. The tendencies he establishes become so woven into the fabric of Western literature and culture that his role in creating them has nearly vanished. If he had promoted himself as a seminal thinker, perhaps things would be different. But, a modest man, he does not, and only a few have attempted to estimate his achievement. This essay aims to make the case more compelling. George Gregory, in the opening sentence of his preface to the first edition of Lowth's work in English, is not indulging in hyperbolic puff when he says, "It may not be improper to apprize the public, that although the following Lectures be entitled Lectures on the Hebrew Poetry, their utility is by no means confined to that single object. They embrace all THE GREAT PRINCIPLES OF GENERAL CRITICISM."[2]

As a young man, Lowth (1710–87) writes poetry and, thirty years old, is appointed Professor of Poetry at Oxford, succeeding Joseph Spence. First in 1741, but also through 1750, Lowth presents his *Lectures on the Sacred Poetry of the Hebrews,* published by the Clarendon Press in 1753, as *De sacra poesi Hebraeorum: praelectiones academicae Oxonii habitae.* George Gregory's English translation appears March 1, 1787—shortly before Lowth dies—though the *Lectures* are partially serialized in 1753 by the popular *Monthly Review* and more completely by *The Christian's Magazine* in 1766–67. A German translation is sold in 1793, and French ones in 1812 and 1813. Despite their academic setting and the fact he delivers them in Latin, a requirement of the professorship until Matthew Arnold is elected in 1857, the lectures grow popular, attracting large audiences. They constitute, during the past three centuries, one of the most profound, influential set of critical statements about the intersections of poetry, language, religion, aesthetics, and culture. Howard Weinbrot asserts that, aside from Johnson's *Lives of the Poets,* Lowth's *Lectures* offer the "most important extended discussion of poetry" in England in the eighteenth century.[3] Not even Arnold's later work regarding religion and poetry exceeds the importance and impact of Lowth's; and Arnold's would not have been possible without the groundwork laid by his predecessor in the Oxford professorship. Lowth later rises in the Church of England to become, in the span of two years (1776–77),

Bishop of St. Davids, then Oxford, and finally London. Regarded in his early seventies as the next Archbishop of Canterbury, ill health hampers any serious thought of elevating him further.

In his analysis of the sublime, Lowth anticipates Burke and Kant. He sets out a definition of "mystical allegory" that foreshadows, in detail, Coleridge's discussions of the symbol, whose famous remarks on that topic come in the same context—though almost always overlooked—as an integral part of his comments on the Bible, and on the Hebrew prophets in particular as the authors of the history of their own people. Lowth sees deep connections between politics, poetry, history, and prophecy, by no means a new idea to his audience.[4] But Lowth is emphatic: "It is sufficiently evident, that the prophetic office had a most strict connexion with the poetic art" (2:18). When a prophetic mode that is not chiefly satiric gains strength in the later eighteenth and early nineteenth centuries,[5] Lowth is its avatar, an ally for writers, such as Blake, who disdain close imitation of Roman and Greek models. Despite later competing claims and refinements, some contrived and unnecessary, Lowth's view of Hebrew poetry and its parallel structures is regarded still as standard; at the least, it has determined present attitudes and, even if contested, remains a touchstone. Lowth's approach, itself at times too formal for the texts it treats, stimulates others to develop even more rigid and tightly balanced—but less successful— systems of parallelism. However unsatisfactory these are, and however imperfect Lowth's own categories, it should not tempt us to a "revisionism," as Robert Alter puts it, that throws out the "baby-with-bathwater."[6] Lowth did more than explore "the Bible as literature."[7] His *Lectures* represent a cultural and comparative approach to ancient texts. They can be used, as they have been especially in Germany, for purposes of historical criticism.

Yet his work also establishes new ways for the modern world to think about poetry in aesthetic terms, and opens a path for new poetic practices in the Old and New Worlds. As Prickett notes, "The debate over the Bible opened up by Lowth is as much aesthetic as historical."[8] Though he does not inaugurate the idea of studying biblical texts as literature, he carries that idea further, with greater fertility, than critics before or after. The questions he poses and the answers he provides not only alter all previously known theoretical definitions of poetry: his work transforms the practice and composition of verse. His attention to the ode, ballad, idyll, and elegy gives new, contemporary life to those genres. Through Johann Gottfried Herder and Johann David Michaelis, he exerts a lasting effect on German literature, biblical scholarship, and hermeneutics down through Hans-Georg Gadamer in the twentieth century. Every exponent of the Higher Criticism on the Continent studies Lowth's work. Johann Gott-fried Eichhorn, who first uses the term *"die höhere Kritik,"* remarks of Lowth, "Let no one forget that we have become what we are . . . by his aid." Herder names Lowth's book in the first sentence of his own *Vom Geist der ebräischen Poesie.*[9] An 1815 German edition (Lipsiae: Sumtibus Io[hann]. Aug[ustus]. Got-tl[ieb]. Weigel) lists booksellers in Amsterdam, Leyden, Rome, Florence, Ham-burg, Vienna, Paris, and London selling Lowth's *Lectures.* Nor do continental interest and supplements take long to flow back to England. As early as 1763, the Clarendon Press republishes Lowth's Latin *De sacra poesi* with notes and commentary by Michaelis himself, first printed in Göttingen five years earlier.

Lowth fuses biblical hermeneutics and interpretation with criticism and cul-tural study. He believes that Hebrew poetry should be understood not only in the context of religion at that time but also as it is informed—and created—by daily culture, vocations, trades, and habits of thought, including what today we would call the cultural practices and mentalities of that people, for whom sacred poetry represents the Word of God and the record of their own history.[10] Lowth argues, in effect, that the training of a potter, the shape of a utensil, or the particular knowledge of shepherds all bear on the poetry of a people who embrace these facts of life while believing in a set of moral laws derived from one God. And, further, that these simple facts and profound practices become complex in the aggregate, requiring historical imagination to re-create the spirit and interpret the fabric of the verse that expresses them. But it is not enough, he argues, "to be acquainted with the language of this people, their manners, disciplines, rites and ceremonies; we must even investigate their inmost sentiments, the manner and connexion of their thoughts; in one word, we must see all things through their eyes, estimate all things by their opinions: we must endeavour as much as possible to read Hebrew as the Hebrews would have read it" (1: 113). Here is an immersion in what we have come to call *mentalité.*

Dryden could claim that English drama should be different than French or Greek because English people enjoy different literary traditions and do not live like the French or Greeks, but this falls short of the thorough, close examination Lowth performs. And, true, critics since Horace, including Pope, who puts it well, stress the need to

> Know well each ancient's proper character;
> His fable, subject, scope in ev'ry page;

Religion, country, genius of his age:
Without all these at once before your eyes,
Cavil you may, but never criticise. *Essay on Criticism* (119–23)

But there remained a lot of caviling. Moreover, the Holy Scriptures simply had not received this manner of treatment in the extended way Lowth provides. When texts so central to the life and literature of Western culture are markedly reevaluated, life and literature soon reorient themselves around the axis of that new assessment, and this is what happens as a result of Lowth's work.

Often willing to jettison painstaking identification of classical tropes and figures in his study, Lowth nevertheless feels convinced that metrical patterns subsist in Hebrew poetry, though they may be beyond recovery.[11] He anchors his conviction by analogy with Greek and Latin, whose meters and genres he commands superbly. A century and a half before, Sidney in his *Apology* summarized the long-standing view about Hebrew poetry: "it is fully written in meter, as all learned Hebricians agree, although the rules be not fully found." (Sidney's remarks on David the Psalmist as poet and prophet, however brief, are suggestive and prefigure Lowth's.) But, because Lowth never successfully deciphers metrical patterns in Hebrew texts, substituting for them rather his own system of parallelisms—he identifies three main and as many as eight specific types—his work actually ends up providing a new, different kind of poetic original to be imaginatively imitated and exploited. This poetic original comes from an ancient language less known than Greek or Latin, and considered by many the most mystical, a language whose poetry could not be reduced, despite his own efforts, to set meters. Yet he declares it still as poetry. And, by its age, it is arguably closer to the beginnings of all poetry and religion, a fact important to Western culture in and of itself, and reinforced by an intellectual thirst for the primitive and by the cult of origins. This Hebrew poetry, then, older than Homer, is now seen as another model—an origin, an original—for modern writing in an age obsessed with originality, the sublime, and the natural. Weinbrot judges, for example, that in Lowth's view, "David triumphs over Pindar."[12] Hebrew poetry, widely read, at least in translation, becomes freshly analyzed in terms that serve literary criticism and encourage new literary productions in the vernacular. The forms of poetry and prose poetry written by Blake, Smart, Cowper, Macpherson, and Whitman—their unrhymed verse without strict metrical scansion, yet composed in rhythmic and syntactical patterns, often in parallel phrasing (and all, except Macpherson's, considered by their authors of immediate or ultimate religious import)—are not possible without Lowth's work. Macpherson attends his lectures in person. It is well established how Lowth influences Smart. Blake knows Lowth's work no later than 1788, the year after Joseph Johnson prints Lowth's *Lectures* in English at his publisher's and bookseller's house in St. Paul's Churchyard, a house Blake visits frequently. And with equal force Lowth shapes the attitudes and practices of Coleridge and Shelley, Lamartine and Chateaubriand, Wordsworth and Hopkins.[13]

Starting in 1933, the Whitman scholar Gay Wilson Allen establishes a direct connection between Whitman's verse techniques and Lowth's discussion of parallelism in the Bible (Whitman also says, in grand verbal gesture, that he hopes to produce a new Bible). The *Princeton Encyclopedia of Poetics* cites Lowth, Whitman, and Allen among its references to parallelism. Allen reinforces his case in subsequent work, including statements and reprintings more than forty years later. But his view is accepted more with silence than support. A few alternate discussions of the fundamental techniques of Whitman's verse exist, an unpublished one using musicality mentioned by Allen himself and, more recently, one grounded on syntactical—yet still parallel—structures argued by James Perrin Warren. Yet Allen continues to have confidence that "the basic Hebraic 'thought rhythm' will, I believe, remain."[14] Few follow Allen's lead or elaborate on it, perhaps because his work is thorough and makes the case convincingly. But it may also be that Lowth remains unfamiliar to most readers of American literature or, in addition, because it has not been established, until now, that Whitman read Lowth, though Lowth's work is widely circulated in America, and is first published in 1815, based on a German edition of the same year. A new American edition appears in 1829, with notes by Calvin E. Stowe, husband of the author of *Uncle Tom's Cabin.* Stowe can advocate a less formal approach than the one Lowth often takes. If Whitman sees this edition, he takes Stowe's advice to heart. But even if Whitman never reads Lowth directly, he does read another English book, one republished and hugely popular in the United States, Hugh Blair's *Lectures on Rhetoric and Belles Lettres* (1783). Its discussions of eloquence and poetry, poetry and prose, are often cited with regard to Whitman's ideas and poetic practice. Four years before Lowth's *Lectures* appear entire in English, Blair's forty-first lecture, "The Poetry of the Hebrews," carefully condenses and presents a major portion of them. Multiple Lowth-Wordsworth and Wordsworth-Whitman connections exist. Even if Whitman may not have Lowth directly, he read his work through Blair. Ranking, too, among Lowth's admirers is Emerson, who in his junior year at Harvard, encouraged by Edward Everett, reads both Blair and Lowth's *Lectures*. Shortly afterward, Emerson writes a poem condemning rhyme and meters that have "Clogged the free step and mighty march of Mind."[15] It is hard to imagine Emerson's statement that poetry is "not meter but a meter making argument" without his having encountered Lowth.

Yet, despite the impressive catalogue of critics and writers Lowth touches, irony persists in the way he is regarded. If scholars now take up the question of religion and literature in Lowth's own day, or religious aspects of Romantic studies, he is, it is true, mentioned and discussed, notably and recently by Robert Alter, *The Art of Biblical Poetry* (1986), James Kugel, *The Idea of Biblical Poetry: Parallelism and Its History* (1981), and Steven Goldsmith, *Unbuilding Jerusalem: Apocalypse and Romantic Representation* (1993), which relies on Prickett's admirable book. But, if biblical commentary or the idea of "religion and literature" is not the primary focus, Lowth drops from sight. Other scholars seem content to keep him within that somewhat specialized category, "the Bible as literature," a phrase T. S. Eliot detested, perhaps because of its paradoxical tendency to cordon off the Bible from literature and literature from the Bible by putting them together in a single category that can then be safely ignored by people who think either spiritual life or aesthetic experience too serious or too pure a subject to be mixed one with the other. Perhaps Eliot was himself too serious in that regard, or was reacting against Arnold's sweeping remark, echoed by Hardy, that religion and poetry would become one.

At any rate, this relative restriction on Lowth's range is a loss. He is a gifted commentator, a keen cultural thinker, and a critic who helps direct all modern, that is, all postclassical reassessments of poetry and the poetic function of language, formal *and* cultural. Exploring the importance of Lowth on this broader stage are Stephen Prickett's *Words and* The Word: *Language, Poetics, and Biblical Interpretation* (1986), and Murray Roston's *Poet and Prophet: The Bible and the Growth of Romanticism* (1965). As Prickett states, the *Lectures* "were to redefine the conception of Hebrew poetry; less obviously, but perhaps no less significantly in the long run, they were to redefine the notion of 'poetry' itself. . . . The eighteenth-century rediscovery of the structure of biblical verse was not, as Lowth and his successors had imagined, just the discovery of a special case, but served to highlight a hitherto neglected quality latent in all verse, and so effectively to modify poetic theory as a whole. . . . Lowth's work inaugurated a critical revolution."[16] This achievement, this legacy, is apart from any connection with religion as the main topic (the last thing his *Lectures* do is proselytize). Lowth can and should be seen in that light, too, standing at the intersection of poetry and prophecy, as Murray Roston elucidated. But since most scholars and readers in English studies have categorized Lowth by association with the texts he discusses—Alter, Kugel, Roston, Shaffer, Berlin, Lipkowitz, even Prickett and others are, after all, either comparatists, intellectual historians, biblical scholars, or interested chiefly in the intersection of the Bible and literature—Lowth's critical insights, if not ignored, still seem specialized and isolated when, in fact, they are so pervasive that we have lost sight of them. In the *Oxford Companion to English Literature,* between "Malcom Lowry" and "*Loyal Subject, The,*" the drama by John Fletcher, there is no entry for Lowth. Between 1963 and 1980, not one article listed in the Modern Language Association Bibliography discusses Lowth in any significant way. While Addison, Dennis, Johnson, or other writers are invoked, anthologized, or read, Lowth, it is often presumed, should be connected only with biblical issues rather than with literature and culture at large.

2

Others might be better Hebraists, but Lowth excels in his combination of literary tact, power of critical analysis, and range of learning. He exhibits supreme control of Greek, Latin, and several modern languages, and he knows several religious doctrines. His familiarity with Hebrew, though he lacks other Eastern languages, is more than adequate. Edward Gibbon, commenting on the edition of Homer issued in 1757 by the Foulis Press in Glasgow, reports that "Bishop Louth [*sic*] has said that he could discover only one error in that accurate edition, the omission of an *iota* subscribed to a dative." (How, wonders Gibbon, "could a man of taste read Homer with such literal attention?")[17] But such close reading—or "literal attention" as Gibbon phrases it tellingly himself, is precisely what, coupled with a broader critical search, permits Lowth to make sharp, close, and suggestive readings of a kind found only in the best criticism. His full-length *Life of William of Wykeham . . . Collected from records, registers, manuscripts, and other authentic evidences* (1758) is one of the first English books to employ evidence ordered and assessed by modern principles and scholarly, historical documentation. Emerson reads this *Life* in the late 1840s.

Perhaps because of an affiliation with specific religious doctrines in the course of his life as a cleric (a requirement of the Oxford professorship until

Robert Lowth. Reproduced by permission of the Houghton Library, Harvard University, Cambridge, Massachusetts.

Arnold is elected), or because he delivers and first publishes his *Lectures* in Latin, or because his textual interest rests in a book now less at the heart of academic literary culture, Lowth receives scant attention in studies of criticism and culture, even by specialists—or in the many debates centering around theories of the sublime and of the symbol. Yet for these he holds vital interest.

Many readers assume, understandably, that Lowth should be mentioned because he is the first critic to examine the Bible as literature: to discuss explicitly the genius of its stylistic power; to analyze its sublimity and variety, its qualities of lyric, didactic, and dramatic expression; and to investigate its various figures of speech, literary devices, or tropes. But Lowth has several predecessors. On the Continent these include Grotius, Johannes Buxtorf II (1599–1664), Marc Meibomius (fl. 1700), and Christian Schoettgen's *Horae Hebraicae Talmudicae* (1733); in England, Henry Lukin's *Introduction to the Holy Scripture* (1669), John Edwards's *Discourse concerning the Authority, Stile, and Perfection of the Books of the Old and New Testaments* (3 vols., 1693–95), and, more proximately, Anthony Blackwall's *Sacred Classics Defended and Illustrated* (2 vols., 1727). It was common to compare Old and New Testament texts with Greek and Latin classics for stylistic features, beauties of expression, rhetorical resourcefulness, and power. Yet in making some of the same kinds of comparisons and assimilating the work that had gone before, Lowth rejects the tropes and figures of classical rhetoric.[18] Because his father, William Lowth, wrote a highly regarded, short hermeneutic handbook, *Directions for the Profitable Reading of the Holy Scripture* (1708), popular for two hundred years, Robert might have felt freer to engage in literary criticism rather than stick close to interpretation in the service of religious doctrine. While he thinks the Bible contains some qualities whose power would be diminished in "a profane and common subject," he still explores qualities of language, metaphor, and figuration in Hebrew poetry apart from any question of divine spirit, adding, as he puts it, "art and knowledge" to belief. His purpose, then, is not to spread or uphold belief, and few objected to the propriety of his secular approach.

Several interrelated points about Lowth's *Lectures* might serve to reinforce his critical restoration. Exerting strong influence in Germany through Hamann, Michaelis, Herder, Eichhorn, Meyer, and Rosenmueller, the work of Lowth is also studied keenly, as we have seen, in the United States. Lowth is one of a loosely knit group of critics I have elsewhere called the New Rhetoricians— among them Hugh Blair, James Beattie, Adam Smith, Joseph Priestley, and George Campbell. Several of them ministers or divines, several dissenters, and the majority of them Scots, they start from the premise that traditional rhetorics and handbooks of literary criticism are increasingly useless. Adam Smith sets a tone when he refers to older rhetorical figures, divisions and subdivisions of them, as constituting "a very silly set of books and not at all instructive." He echoes views expressed even earlier, including Samuel Butler's lines in the first canto of *Hudibras*: "For all a rhetorician's rules / Teach nothing but to name his tools." When Lowth begins critical analysis in his fourth lecture, the first in the second part entitled "Of the Parabolic or Poetical Style of the Hebrews," he anticipates the complaint Smith makes in the late 1740s. Lowth says, "The phraseology, however, peculiar to the poets, the bold ellipses, the sudden transitions of the tenses, genders, and persons, and other similar circumstances, I shall leave to the Grammarian: or rather I shall leave (since I do not find, that the Grammarians acknowledge any distinction between poetical and common language) to be collected from practice and attentive reading. It would be a no less indolent and trifling occupation to post through all those forms of tropes and figures, which the teachers of rhetoric have pompously (not to say uselessly) heaped together." Such figures can be found in "every composition, however trite and barren." This fits with the conviction of the New Rhetoricians that theories of criticism, including those of metaphoric language, must be constructed a posteriori from practice and not be imposed as rules and nomenclature that, as time passes, lean on increasingly distant authority or abstract ideology. What Lowth seeks are rather "the peculiar marks and characters of the Hebrew poetry," what makes it unique (1: 75, 76).

Instead of such a "useless heap" of "tropes and figures," the New Rhetoricians seek poetry in what James Beattie and others call a "natural language of passion." They privilege primacy of emotion and feeling as the psychological spark of poetic language, not a doctrine of poetic diction. They reject the idea that figures of speech serve as learned ornamentation and regard effective figuration as a natural rather than artificial expression, one that depends in each language on the genius and individual evolution of that particular language and culture and the manner, at any given moment in its historical trajectory, in which each language expresses states of excited consciousness. The essential force of poetry is not any paraphrasable didactic intention or doctrinal message—though that may be included and subsumed—but what is emotional, passionate, full of affections, and suited to the linguistic resources of the language at hand. For the New Rhetoricians, poetic language is regarded not as instances of individual vocabulary or as specific words mentally listed as appropriate to low, middle, or high styles. Rather, poetic language implies a combined effect dependent especially on the selection and combination of words, the Gestalt of phrasing, meter, image, and word choice—what Jakobson and others call the "poetic function" of language, which can occur other than in strictly metrical composition. More specifically, as Claudio Guillén notes, "A well-known thesis of Roman Jakobson affirms that parallelism is the 'fundamental problem of poetry,' its essential characteristic."[19]

Lowth's close reading helps produce the New Rhetoric of the second half of the eighteenth century, one that lasts, through its highly popular texts, well into the last part of the nineteenth century. His *Lectures* represent its first extended practical application and he is, chronologically, the first of the New Rhetoricians. Though it seems futile to establish the origin of any critical school with precision, Anglo-American New Criticism owes much of its lineage to Lowth, Blair, and other New Rhetoricians. I. A. Richards became intimately familiar with them, as did Cleanth Brooks. Sailendra Kumar Sen has argued that Lowth is, in the modern sense, "the first imagery critic."[20] As an aid to doctrinal interpretation by unraveling the processes of language habitually employed in the Hebrew Scriptures, Lowth's work was welcomed, but this is not his chief intention. He is setting apart the poetic function of language from the functions of prose and ratiocination, yet does so without falling back on mundane catalogues of meter, rhyme, and tropes.

From this preeminent position, chronological and intellectual, in the group of New Rhetoricians, Lowth examines qualities of style characteristic of the Hebrew poets. The figures of speech he examines—not the same as classically defined rhetorical tropes—and his analysis of the poetry directly contribute to a slow, relative decline of satiric and didactic verse, displaced to some degree by a revival of lyric and prophetic forms, and by a new interest in poetry as a natural, direct expression of human feeling roused to a state of increased awareness and emotional pitch. Not that Lowth is a romantic precursor: that would be misleading. But his critical approach investigates qualities and modes of language that become important in Romantic theory, rhetoric, and practice, particularly in lyric poetry, on which Lowth spends much of his close reading and analysis.

What are some of the characteristics of Hebrew poetry that Lowth finds important? First, a new and broader sense of meter—so broad that it seems to leave behind all meters familiar from Latin or Greek—connected with parallelism. Also, personification, the sublime, and a particular kind or level of metaphor he calls "mystical allegory." Lowth discusses other elements of Hebrew poetry, including its oral as opposed to its written qualities. This last is tremendously important, a pregnant recognition, one picked up by Blair—interested in its Scottish and Ossianic implications—and through Blair passed on to James Fenimore Cooper, among others. *The Leatherstocking Tales* pay constant attention to the origin, power, and possible demise of oral literature and culture.[21] The forests of North America and the Highlands of Scotland are considered, with justification, places where oral qualities of folk poetry and culture might be recovered before they are lost forever.

Although working within an established tradition of critics examining the Bible as literature, Lowth is alone in emphasizing that the Hebrew prophets write poetry and that such poetry is unique in its parallel structures. (Earlier, a few others, including Hermann van der Hardt, hinted at something like this, but it was counted one of his obscure and odd intellectual fancies.) Lowth becomes convinced that the meter is unrecoverable as such, but that it clearly has nothing to do with syllable, stress, or quantity in their usual senses, but rather with recurring patterns of syntactic and grammatical units, with couplings of phrase that repeat, amplify, or specify meaning in strongly rhythmical patterns. In Lecture 19 he breaks these recurring units or parallelisms into three main types: synonymous, antithetical, and syntactic (synthetic or constructive). John Livingston Lowes bases part of his later famous essay on the King James Bible, "The Noblest Monument in English Prose," on Lowth's approach, proving how well the parallel structures of this poetry survive translation. The purpose here is not to unravel each type of parallelism Lowth examines (he provides concrete examples and ample quotation in Hebrew with Latin translations). The key point might be summed up by noting his contention that, in Hebrew at least, what we call "meter" consists of, or makes its effect felt by, essentially repeated structures that affiliate and align a number of otherwise disparate elements—among them word choice, grammatical unit, logical opposition and apposition, significations of contraries and of similarities—into one complex, harmonized register. "Metrical composition," that old, supposedly most classical definition of poetry, ceases to mean composition in repeated, recognized meters and becomes inadequate, even misleading. As Wordsworth claims, only "a very small part of the pleasure given by Poetry depends upon the metre." Instead, parallelism comes to stand for recurrent but not precisely repeated divisions in phrase, in elision or alteration of individual words, to assist larger divisions and parallels, and in modulations of sentence—and of verses within one sentence—such that many passages, in Lowth's formulation, "treat one subject in many different ways, and dwell upon the same sentiment; when they express the same thing in different words, or different things in a similar form of words; when equals refer to equals, and opposites to opposites." This is no strict rule but a principle or characteristic of such poetry (1: 68–69).

Soon, definitions of poetry show, concomitantly, a tendency to minimize numbers, meter, or rhyme as determining factors. Many stress instead harmony, music, and depth of feeling: language elevated and informed with emotional power and internal cohesion. Lowth's idea of meter in Hebrew poetry—the true rule of which (if it ever had been put down as a rule) he feels can never be

think of oral poetries: forms à la Parry-Lord

recovered—corresponds closely to changes in the way poetry is discussed by the New Rhetoricians and Wordsworth. Lowth prompts these changes.

Personification may be regarded as the quintessential Romantic trope. Geoffrey Hartman, Barbara Johnson, Cynthia Chase, and others assert this. Looking at the New Rhetoricians and particularly at Lowth, we find a stress on personification as the boldest of images, stemming from profound, transformative feelings and thoughts of the poet experiencing nature and circumstance. This personification is not the "capitalized" kind such as Justice, Hope, and Envy, common then and the use of which has almost never been absent in English since the early Renaissance. Instead, personification here creates what Coleridge calls "nature humanized"; it is a "humanizing imagery," which he feels Shakespeare commands supremely:

> . . . here the gentle lark, weary of rest,
> From his moist cabinet mounts up on high,
> And wakes the morning, from whose silver breast
> The sun ariseth in his majesty,
> Who doth the world so gloriously behold
> The cedar-tops and hills seem burnish'd gold.
> (*Venus and Adonis,* lines 853–58)

Or, we have personification in *Paradise Lost,* cited by Hugh Blair, where inanimate as well as living things in Paradise are imagined by Eve as listening to her:

> Must I leave thee, Paradise? thus leave
> Thee, native soil, those happy walks, and shades,
> Fit haunt of Gods? where I had hope to spend
> Quiet, though sad, the respite of that day,
> Which must be mortal to us both. O flowers!
> That never will in other climate grow (9.269–74)

Such personification intimates a bond, even an identity, between human and external nature, soul and cosmos. It is an objective correlative come to life. If we think Ruskin's pathetic fallacy related to personification, we might recall that for Ruskin such personification can and does work the highest effects; it can evoke great feeling or pathos. Only when it is trumped up, or false to what Ruskin perceives the truth of the situation or perception, is it a "fallacy" in the sense of a fault. The proper use of this trope elicits truthful vision and feeling, or pathos—with deep roots in rhetoric as a human as well as a linguistic study—and is no intellectual error to be pitied. Personification occurs when, in Lowth's description, "action and character are attributed to fictitious, irrational, or even inanimate objects" (1: 281). We might think of a west wind, an urn, or of living mountains that stride after us over the waters and instill fear, making us feel like a guilty thing surprised. It is the bond and reciprocity of nature and human feeling. At its highest, this personification even personifies persons, as Lowth points out "that remarkable personification of Job, denoting the most miserable death, 'The first-born of the progeny of death'" (1: 288). He singles out a form that Blake will employ repeatedly, that "expression, by which the subject, attribute, or effect of any thing is denominated the Son" or daughter of it (1: 287), as in Blake's Daughters of Albion. Lowth gives personification a new basis for practice, one that calls for a different apprehension of nature rather than a mechanical application of abstractions. The New Rhetoricians, and then Words-worth and Coleridge (who cull from the New Rhetoricians examples, such as Thomas Gibbons's discussion of repetition in the Song of Deborah, a point Wordsworth places, without acknowledgment, in his note to "The Thorn," and that Coleridge repeats in *Biographia Literaria*), use similar analyses and even examples of personification and figuration identical to those noted by Lowth. Instances include the Book of Job, David's Psalms, the Song of Deborah, and passages in Ezekiel and Isaiah.

There is no doubt, too, that Lowth's comments play a role in the increasing importance of lyric, for he notes that "Lyric poetry, in which the imagination seems to have the fullest indulgence, and which abounds with strong figures, is most favorable to Personification" (1: 281 n.).

3

Renewed interest in the sublime during the past ten to twenty years rarely mentions Lowth while Longinus, Burke, and Kant always are cited.[22] Yet the analytic of the sublime in Lowth, central to his discussion of Hebrew poetry, should be compared to discussions in Burke and Kant, as well as in Hegel. Lowth was familiar to them all. In his first lecture he notes, "As some of these writings exceed in antiquity the fabulous ages of Greece, in sublimity they are superior

to the most finished productions of that polished people." While admitting that
Lowth gives currency to the idea of the sublime (as late as 1926, Oxford University Press reissues a translation of Longinus with selections from Lowth), some
critics, such as Kugel, suggest that Lowth adds little to the analysis of the sublime
because he relies heavily on Longinus. But that repeats what Lowth *says* he is
doing when, in fact, he goes far beyond his own self-effacing characterization.

He secures the sublime not in empirical qualities open to the senses, as
Burke frequently seems to do, but more, like Kant, in the suprasensible apprehension by the faculty of reason that it has encountered the infinite, unfathom-
able instilling of power or fear beyond comprehension or understanding,
accompanied by feelings whose intensity is increased by obscurity or by the
activity of repeated imaginative efforts that fail to grasp their object fully: "Here
the human mind is absorbed, overwhelmed as it were in a boundless vortex, and
studies in vain for an expedient to extricate itself . . . while the imagination
labours to comprehend what is beyond its powers, this very labour itself, and
those ineffectual endeavors . . . demonstrate the immensity and sublimity of the
object [see Ps. 36:6,7]. . . . [T]he mind seems to exert its utmost faculties in
vain to grasp an object, whose unparalleled magnitude mocks its feeble endeav-
ours; and to this end it employs the grandest imagery that universal nature can
suggest, and yet this imagery, however great, proves totally inadequate to the
purpose." This experience, says Lowth, is amplified "by a kind of continued
negation; when a number of great and sublime ideas are collected, which, on a
comparison with the object, are found infinitely inferior and inadequate. Thus
the boundaries are gradually extended on every side, and at length totally removed; the mind is insensibly led on towards infinity, and is struck with inex-
pressible admiration, with a pleasing awe" (1: 353–54).

Lowth uncannily frames the sublime in psychological and aesthetic terms
more akin to Burke or even Kant than Longinus. Though he says of *sublimitas*
that "in this use of the word I copy Longinus," and while his statement that the
sublime "overpowers the mind" might be related to Longinus's "transport of
the soul," Lowth has stronger affinities with a psychological than a rhetorical
analysis. He is interested in the reaction of different faculties of the mind as well
as in "the language of the passions." His concept of the sublime in Hebrew
poetry dwells in the infinite and incomparable, it supersedes representational
language, art, and imaginative power, all of which, however, return to it as if
drawn by a magnet. It overpowers the imagination, it is associated with infinity,
it works "by a kind of . . . negation." These points Kant soon echoes. Lowth's

citation of biblical passages with image piled on image, all straining to grasp the attractive infinite, strikes a parallel with the crux of section 27 of Kant's analytic of the sublime in the *Kritik der Urteilskraft,* where imagination and reason are at once attracted to and repelled by the sublime, drawn to its infinite and insensible or—in Kant's term—"suprasensible" magnitude, yet still unable to encompass that magnitude; and, so, imagination and reason remain in constant process and agitation, returning "insensibly," as Lowth says, with image after image, but each and all of them inadequate. This is unlike the restful contemplation of imagination and understanding engaged in judging the beautiful. Lowth's emphasis on the sublimity achieved in Hebrew poetry opens a new vista in the exploration and expression of that quality in English verse and criticism. No other critic, including Addison on *Paradise Lost,* produces as much practical as well as theoretical analysis of poetic texts exhibiting the sublime, an aesthetic quality growing in importance since the decade before Lowth's birth. As Kugel states, in a cautious form of litotes that underscores how important Lowth's contribution is: "Certainly Lowth's identification of *sublimitas* as a characteristic of biblical poetry was not an insignificant event in English literary history."[23]

We can now move to what Lowth calls the highest and most resonant form of imagery, the "mystical allegory." And what it is, as Lowth describes it, is amazing, for it is equivalent to Coleridge's famous definition of symbol in *The Statesman's Manual,* itself drawn by Coleridge directly from a discussion of the Bible and its portrayal of an intersection of temporal and divine history in the stories and prophecies of the Hebrew people. After Lowth sets out two other types of allegory—first, where one thing stands in for another, the literal for the figurative, and second, the figurative for the literal—he then says, "There is likewise this further distinction, that in those other forms of allegory, the exterior or ostensible imagery is fiction only; the truth lies altogether in the interior or remote sense, which is veiled as it were under this thin and pellucid covering. But in the allegory, of which we are now treating [the mystical], each idea is equally agreeable to truth." That is, both the thing and what it stands for may be taken as the correct interpretation. The mystical allegory is *both* what is literally signified and representative or signifier of something else as well, something larger to which it belongs and with which it can be metaphorically identified: "The exterior or ostensible image," Lowth continues, "is not [only] a shadowy colouring of the interior sense, but is in itself a reality; and although it sustain another character, it does not wholly lay aside its own. For instance, in the metaphor or parable, the Lion, the Eagle, the Cedar, considered with respect to their identical existence, are altogether destitute of reality; but what we read of David, Solomon, or Jerusalem, in this sublimer kind of allegory, may be either accepted in a literal sense, or may be mystically interpreted according to the religion of the Hebrews, and in each view, whether conjunctly or apart, will be found equally agreeable to truth" (1: 239–40).

"[T]he mode of form of this figure, which possesses the most beauty and elegance . . . is, when the two images equally conspicuous run, as it were, parallel through the whole poem, mutually illustrating and correspondent to each other" (1: 242). While Lowth keeps some terms from Greek rhetoric, such as simile and allegory, metaphor and personification, his analyses of them in the Hebrew texts reflects something other than common classical definitions. "Mystical allegory" does not correspond exactly with any classical definition of allegory or symbol. It is a new, more philosophical definition. It corresponds to Gadamer's crisp statement two hundred years later: "The symbol [equivalent to Lowth's *mystical* allegory] is the *coincidence* of the sensible and the non-sensible," while allegory, equivalent to Lowth's two lower forms of allegory, is "the meaningful *relation* of the sensible to the non-sensible."[24]

Now, Coleridge's famous distinction and definition in *The Statesman's Manual* (1816) has a very particular context:

> in nothing is Scriptural history more strongly contrasted with the histories of highest note in the present age than its freedom from the hollowness of abstractions. . . . In the Scriptures they [the histories] are the living *educts* of the imagination; of that reconciling and mediatory power, which incorporating the Reason in Images of the Sense, and organizing (as it were) the flux of the Senses by the permanence and self-circling energies of the Reason, gives birth to a system of symbols, harmonious in themselves, and consubstantial with the truths, of which they are the *conductors*. These are the Wheels which Ezekiel beheld. . . . *Whitherso the Spirit was to go, the wheels went, and thither was their spirit to go, for the spirit of the living creature was in the wheels also.* . . . the Sacred History becomes prophetic, the Sacred Prophecies historical. . . . In the Scriptures therefore both Facts and Persons must of necessity have a two-fold significance, a past and a future, a temporary and a perpetual, a particular and a universal application. . . . It is among the miseries of the present age that it recognizes no medium between *Literal* and *Metaphorical*. . . . Now an Allegory is but a translation of abstract

notions into a picture-language which is itself nothing but an abstraction from objects of the senses. . . . On the other hand a Symbol (which is always tautegorical) is characterized by a translucence of the Special in the Individual or of the General in the Especial or of the Universal in the General. Above all by the Eternal through and in the Temporal. It always partakes of the Reality which it renders intelligible.[25]

It is not just that Coleridge's definition appears in the context of Hebrew poetry and Hebrew history.[26] Elsewhere, he links biblical study with the idea of the symbol, too, remarking on Genesis 2:3 in *Aids to Reflection*: "must not of necessity the first man be a symbol of Mankind, in the fullest force of the word symbol, rightly defined?"—a statement that echoes Lowth's characterization of Job as himself a personification. It is, more specifically, that in essential respects Coleridge's definition of symbol and Lowth's definition of mystical allegory as the highest form of metaphor are identical. As Lowth sees mystical allegory to be necessary to a prophetic mode that involves history—temporality—so does Coleridge. Coleridge borrowed from the Bristol Library Blair's *Lectures*—with its summary of Lowth—in January and February 1798, when Wordsworth read them, too, if not earlier. The preface to *Lyrical Ballads* echoes Blair and Lowth in numerous places. Lowth's seemingly casual remark, "I do not find that the grammarians acknowledge any distinction between poetical and common language," may be compared with Wordsworth's assertion, "that there neither is, nor can be, any *essential* difference between the language of prose and metrical composition." Coleridge the next year in Göttingen studies with Eichhorn, an acknowledged admirer of Lowth.

Paul de Man claims that what Coleridge is defining is really a special kind of allegory (indeed, as Coleridge says himself, "tautegorical" and as Lowth calls it, "mystical allegory"). For de Man, this allegory is involved in "the rhetoric of temporality," the interpretation of its figure through time, an interpretation that becomes clearer, as Lowth and Coleridge and Blake point out, in history as prophecy and prophecy as history, not in crystal-ball gazing. This is not fortune telling or prediction (or typology), but a figuration and knowledge essentially apocalyptic, an uncovering of what Coleridge calls history. The debate over "symbol" versus "allegory" becomes something of a semantic one, involving how the terms are defined in the first place. Coleridge chooses to use the word symbol and to disparage what are, in effect, Lowth's lower levels of allegory. But Coleridge, who had read Lowth at least in Blair's version, defines the tautegorical symbol in a duplication of the properties Lowth attributes to mystical allegory, and which de Man, following Hegel and Walter Benjamin (as he does in other instances as well), attributes to allegory in his essay "The Rhetoric of Temporality." Yet there de Man reads only one slice of Coleridge's discussion and ignores—perhaps suppresses—the fact that Coleridge draws his definition of the symbol, as participating in temporal processes, from the text Coleridge quotes— the biblical *history* of the Hebrew people. This fuller context of Coleridge's definition is rarely mentioned let alone given full weight, and many readers remain unaware of it.[27] Nicholas Halmi argues that while it is tempting to see Lowth's mystical allegory as sharing "an affinity with the Romantic symbol," Lowth's mystical allegory is drawn from a prophetic tradition of "typology— which is a method not of composition but of interpretation." Elsewhere Halmi denies that Coleridge's idea of the symbol is consistent with orthodox Christianity. But this takes into account only one side of Lowth's project, an older one that Lowth is trying to supplement if not actually to overcome. His examples (1: 242–45) deal with prophecy but not expressly with typology. Everywhere he insists that, "He who would perceive the peculiar and interior elegancies of the Hebrew poetry, must imagine himself exactly situated as the persons for whom it was written, or even as the writers themselves; he is to feel them as a Hebrew" (1: 114). As Prickett and others point out, before Lowth's criticism, biblical allegories are routinely interpreted on typological grounds, but Lowth changes that.[28] One central definition of what we call the Romantic symbol, the *locus classicus* of which in English is in Coleridge, occurs explicitly in Lowth's *Lectures,* sixty-three years earlier, under the heading "mystical allegory."

Finally, the attitude that biblical poetry alone supplies ideas commensurate with the subject of God, as well as Lowth's comparative judgment of Greek and Hebrew poets, is reinforced by Coleridge. In 1802, Coleridge writes to Sotheby that in Greece, "All natural Objects were *dead,*—mere hollow Statues—but there was a Godkin or Goddessling *included* in each. . . . At best, it is but Fancy, or the aggregating Faculty of the mind—not *Imagination,* or the *modifying* and *coadunating* Faculty. This the Hebrew Poets appear to me to have possessed beyond all others & next to them the English. In the Hebrew Poets each Thing has a Life of it's own, & yet they are all one life." This, Coleridge's first formulated distinction between fancy and imagination, is never quoted in the context from which it springs, the Hebrew poets.[29]

Lowth explores in depth several crucial issues: parallelism and therefore the characteristics of poetry in general as distinguished from prose, not by metrical composition or vocabulary (poetic diction) but by emotional elevation and syntactic function (Jakobson's "poetic function"); a reassessment and elevation—based on "imagination" and "personification"—of lyric forms and genres; a stress on the vital use of personification as nature humanized; a recognition of the origin of poetry and poetic forms in the daily practices, beliefs, and *mentalitié* of a culture; a keen sense of the oral nature of early impassioned poetry; a link between poetry and the prophetic mode; an analytic of the sublime that goes well beyond Longinus and has affinities with Burke and Kant; and, a definition of "mystical allegory" that embodies the qualities of Coleridge's "tautegorical" and prophetic symbol, and one that draws these qualities, as will Coleridge, from Scriptures relating the narrative history of the Hebrew people. Lowth presents in his *Lectures* ideas of utmost importance and centrality for Western poetics, aesthetics, and culture, as well as for a renegotiation of what the Bible means in religious and secular contexts.

4

Lowth reminds us, too, that we may study religion as a human phenomenon, and that insights into religious texts are not limited to them alone. Spiritual life, like mythology, may not be in any one of its particular forms universally true, but it is universal. As such, it inevitably becomes a factor in the way we read and interpret literature, more so, obviously, in some cases than in others, but not something devoutly to be ignored. Schleiermacher is often credited with establishing the study of religion in this intellectual sense, and it is no accident that he is also credited as the founder of modern hermeneutics, though his approach has roots as early as Shaftesbury, and he knew Lowth, too. Regarding the inclusion of the study of religion and the examination of religious values and texts in literary and critical circles in the secular academy, I want to suggest a view different from many often expressed. To those convinced that a wall must separate even the *study* (not the advocacy or practice) of religion from the study of what is literary, I would suggest closing Empson for a while and opening Lowth or Schleiermacher. The freer and more liberal study of literature requires not adherence to, but the careful study of, and attention to, all varieties of religious experience and faith—in the sense that William James calls any such faith or belief, wherever it occurs, a "human fact." In like manner, the study of religion, whether doctrinal, theological, historical, or comparative, requires the different analyses of language and culture that Lowth and others, such as Frye and Eliade, perform. Lowth does this without proselytizing and without prejudice. As Thomas Preston notes, while widely popular and generating "an almost astonishing interest," the phenomenon of "eighteenth-century biblical criticism enjoyed a remarkable ecumenicism free of sectarian controversy."[30] Language and the forms of language—narration, genre, figuration, structures, and combinations of words—are of utmost importance, not just for hermeneutical or doctrinal examination of scriptures in individual religious traditions, but for fuller knowledge of the history of writing, oral practices, and cultures. Although different perspectives accompany particularly held beliefs, none of this requires belief or the valorization of belief, anymore than Leslie Stephen felt compelled to believe the arguments he summarized in his treatment of eighteenth-century religious issues. An admitted agnostic, Virginia Woolf's father certainly did not. Yet he knew that if literary and critical study—and if cultural study seen through the lens of criticism—embraces philosophy, anthropology, linguistics, law, and sociology, but rejects religion, or, put more acutely, rejects even the study of religion, religious texts, and religious values, then we are left with a parochial, secular, and frightened "liberalism" whose exclusion strives with hypocritical displays of religious condemnations, registered brilliantly, for example, in Burns's "Holy Willie's Prayer." It makes little sense to invoke the ghost of the Enlightenment or any other intellectual movement to expunge the vapors of what might be considered modern superstition and elitism, based on religious values, seeping into Helicon's pure stream of literary theory or aesthetics to pollute its academic discourse. Hume condescends to examine in detail, rather than to dismiss, religious issues. Even for the author of "What Is Enlightenment?" the study of religion is worthy as a subject of investigation. When Fichte publishes his first major work, the anonymous *Kritik aller Offenbarung,* or *Critique of all Revelation,* many assume Kant is the author, a verdict not displeasing to the older master. Lowth, a profoundly important thinker, links language with history, belief, everyday life, and the cultural practices of a particular people. It seems right to recall the continued relevance of his insights, and right for us to credit and use them.

9

Lincoln's Language, and Ours

Lincoln may be considered the last great figure of the Enlightenment. And, in a larger sense, he rekindles a continuing American Enlightenment, one started before his birth. Although he had little formal schooling, he was by his own reckoning educated in the spirit and by the letter of eighteenth-century literature and political ideals. Finally, he faces the Civil War, the culminating, violent crisis of the single greatest issue of government and humanity left unresolved by the Enlightenment framers of the Constitution, slavery. And, as Allan Nevins has remarked, that war was not only about slavery, it was about the future of race in America, too. So, to the extent that race and justice remain great, unresolved issues, we continue the legacy imperfectly bequeathed by the founding fathers and extended by figures such as Lincoln, Douglass, Stanton, Kennedy, and King. Such an Enlightenment is never completed, for it holds the prospect of continually making "more perfect" a union first ideally conceived in words but flawed in practice. This Enlightenment is no historical span or period but a continual process of intellectual and practical achievement. We suspect the idea of progress. But without conviction in a continuing moral and civil improvement that aims to achieve the hopes of *all* people in the nation, and even of the world, we invite cynicism and condone injustice.

By his own account, delivered February 21, 1861, Lincoln first understood this principle of an extended Enlightenment operating "for all time to come" in America—and in world affairs—when, "away back in my childhood, the earliest days of my being able to read, I got hold of a small book, 'Weem[s]'s Life of Washington.'" Lincoln tells the New Jersey Senate that after reading Weems's account of Washington and his army crossing the Delaware amid ice floes to attack the British at Trenton (where Lincoln was addressing the state senate), "I recollect then, boy even though I was, that there must have been something more than common that those men struggled for . . . something that held out a great promise to all the people of the world for all time to come." The next day at Independence Hall, February 22, Washington's birthday, he remarks that such a struggle—a struggle we have yet to complete—with the Declaration of liberty initiating its long course, gave hope "not alone to the people of this country, but hope to the world for all future time. It was that which gave promise that in due time the weights should be lifted from the shoulders of all men, and that *all* should have an equal chance" (2: 209, 213).[1]

Shelby Foote says that Lincoln's language is the language of Mark Twain, that he "wrote American—same kind of American that Mark Twain was to write later on."[2] I do not mean to deny this view; it can be defended. But it is incomplete. It misses a more important aspect of Lincoln's language, especially of his prepared speeches and writing, one that has eluded historians, critics, and biographers. In his correspondence, addresses, and formal documents, in political action and applied wisdom, Lincoln's prose carries the defining marks of eighteenth-century English letters and criticism. This view goes against the grain. Lincoln's language, many accounts affirm, draws on the homey metaphors and parables of his native land, first experienced as a boy and young man attuned to the rhythms of field, forest, river, and town. This accurately marks Lincoln's informal conversation and many oral remarks. But when Roy Basler's authoritative edition appears in the early 1950s, Edmund Wilson notes the dominant tone: "To read Lincoln thus in bulk is to meet a being very different from the Lincoln of humorous folklore and sentimental legend. Except in the debates with Douglas and some of his early productions, there is little humor in these volumes, and only the gravest sentiment." Especially after the repeal of the Missouri Compromise in 1854, which in Lincoln's third-person account of himself "aroused him as he had never been before," his language sharpens. His writing and formal speech spring most directly from eighteenth-century literature and rhetoric.[3]

What did Lincoln read as a boy and young man besides Parson Mason L. Weems's *Life of Washington?* I would like to linger on his early literary and critical experiences because they establish the foundation of his later achievement in writing. This reading also helps to determine, by his own admission, his life-long political principles.[4] The books on his young shelf, those we know of, include these: first, biographies—the part of literature Johnson loves most because, as he says, it can be put to use. Biography as a genre in English, though practiced for several centuries, is chiefly set in its modern form by Johnson and by James Boswell's *Life of Johnson.* Lincoln, among the few books we know he reads as a youth, has the biography of Washington by Weems and probably a second, according to Roy Basler, by David Ramsay. (It is significant that some of the best, most widely read Lincoln and Johnson scholars—Joseph Wood Krutch, John Wain, David H. Donald, W. J. Bate, James Clifford, Carl Sandburg, and Douglas L. Wilson—have all written biographies of their subjects.) As Harry Truman remarked a century after Lincoln died, "No one ever loses by reading history, great literature. . . . Readers of good books, particularly books of biography and history, are preparing themselves for leadership."[5] Lincoln extends his early biographical and historical reading with Franklin's *Autobiographical Sketches,* which recommends, as Johnson himself recommends, the study of Addison and Steele to help form a prose style worthy of public discourse. Franklin and Johnson follow their own advice; Jefferson, too, reads and studies *The Spectator.* So does Lincoln. Addison and Steele he reads in his youth, and later we find Lincoln quoting Jefferson's *Autobiography* (2: 124).

Almost always overlooked, but significant, are two other books Lincoln has. One is William Scott's *Lessons in Elocution* (1779), which owes much to Thomas Sheridan's famous work *Elocution* (1762). Sheridan, an Irish actor and theater manager, and his wife, Frances Sheridan, an accomplished writer of fiction, were parents of the brilliant playwright and gifted parliamentary orator Richard Brinsley Sheridan, an associate of Johnson, Burke, and Charles James Fox. The younger Sheridan's speech on Catholic emancipation inspired Frederick Douglass (see Chapter 1). It is in Scott's *Elocution* that Lincoln first reads Shakespeare, and Shakespeare, providing more allusions in his letters and papers than any

Autograph fragment of Lincoln's speech beginning "Why, Kansas is neither the whole, nor a tithe of the real question" (ca. December 1857). This became part of the "House Divided" speech (June 16, 1858). The Gilder Lehrman Collection, on deposit at The Pierpont Morgan Library, New York. GLC 2533. Reproduced by permission.

Why, Kansas is neither the *whole,* nor a *tithe* of the real question.

"A house divided against itself can not stand"

I believe this government can not endure permanently, half slave, and half free.

I expressed this belief a year ago; and subsequent developments have but confirmed me.

I do not expect the Union to be dissolved. I do not expect the house to fall; but I *do* expect it will cease to be divided. It will become *all* one thing, or *all* the other. Either the opponents of slavery will arrest the further spread of it, and put it in course of ultimate extinction; or its advocates will push it forward till it shall become alike lawfull in *all* the states, old, as well as new. Do you doubt it? Study the Dred Scott decision, and then see, how little, even now, remains to be done.

other writer, becomes Lincoln's favorite poet, exceeding even Burns. Scott (1750–1804) was British. All American publications of his *Elocution,* virtually one every year for the first two decades of the nineteenth century, derive from the fourth or later British editions. His work draws from the Scottish New Rhetoricians,[6] and he writes the preface to his first edition in 1786, in Edinburgh. Lincoln copied out, repeated, and memorized sections from Scott. There is something else about Scott's *Elocution* and its connection to Sheridan's *Elocution.* Almost fifty years after the Civil War, Chauncey Depew notes, "In speaking Mr. Lincoln had a peculiar cadence in his voice, caused by laying emphasis upon the key-word of the sentence."[7] In *Elocution,* Thomas Sheridan is at pains to teach orators that in their delivery, they should stress one and only one word of each complete sentence: that one word should best convey the vital rhetorical or logical point of the sentence. This advice is passed on by Scott. Mark Twain later calls these the "crash words."

The second neglected book of Lincoln's youth is Lindley Murray's (1745–1816?) *English Reader.*[8] This popular, substantial school text offers poetry and prose "selected from the best writers," nearly all drawn from the English eighteenth century, a few from the seventeenth. Selections are designed "to inculcate some of the most important principles of piety and virtue," a statement that echoes Johnson's avowed purpose in his moral essays, and in his dedication of the *Lives of the Poets* to the promotion of piety—meaning not exclusively religious faith, but a sense of political, social, and national connections and bonds, a faith colored by a recognition of the terrible forces of history and grounding itself ultimately in Providence (see Chapters 2 and 6). This tone, this *pietas,* is in keeping with Lincoln's formal deliveries such as the Second Inaugural and Gettysburg Addresses. Like Coleridge's praise of Burke as a statesman relying on *principles,* Lincoln repeatedly uses this sense of *principle,* for him certainly a principle of "piety and virtue." One prominent instance is his speech on the Kansas-Nebraska Act, another his remarks at Independence Hall in Philadelphia shortly before his First Inaugural.

Many of Murray's *English Reader* extracts come from the Scottish New Rhetoricians James Harris, James Beattie, and Hugh Blair. The last two, among others Lincoln reads in excerpted form, advocate plainer, straightforward prose without relinquishing powerful phrasing or bold, simple metaphors. Those the New Rhetoricians elevate above complex, long-drawn out conceits. The New Rhetoricians, with the exception of Adam Smith, who distrusts imagery, consider reasoned prose with striking but plain images as the highest form of delivery. Murray's *Reader* also includes Addison, Pope's "Essay on Criticism"—which Lincoln, along with the "Essay on Man," later quotes in his writing—Oliver Goldsmith—also quoted by Lincoln—David Hume, the historian William Robertson, who produced his *History of America* in 1777, and extracts from Johnson's moral tales of "eastern" origin and lines on "The Vanity of Wealth." Other eighteenth-century poets, among them Prior, Gay, Akenside, Gray, Thomson, and Cowper, are included by Murray. Thomson and Cowper are notable for detailed images of nature and rural life, their appreciation of the commonplace, a relaxed, often informal diction, and, along with Gray, a deeply held belief in the bond between poetic genius and political liberty. Later in life, to a writer planning a biography of him and seeking information about his early years, Lincoln quotes from the most popular of eighteenth-century poems, Gray's "Elegy in a Country Churchyard." His own early life, explains Lincoln, would best be recorded in "the short and simple annals of the poor."

David C. Mearns refers obliquely to the Murray and Scott readers as "a few textbooks, anthologies, and half-forgotten miscellanies, which biographers have grimly resurrected from a comfortable oblivion."[9] But Mearns does not appear to have consulted the volumes and perhaps did not have access to them. If he had, he would have recognized the connections with Lincoln's prose, both in style and as a source or prompting for several of Lincoln's quotations, later in life, from other writers, a topic we will explore. Lincoln studied Thomas Dilworth's *New Guide to the English Tongue* (at times cited as Dilworth's *Spelling-Book*), a text that, like Scott's *Elocution,* contains selected pieces of prose and verse from eighteenth-century British writers. Dilworth (d. 1780) was a schoolmaster in Wapping, now part of the Port of London, and his *New Guide* first appears in 1754. Lincoln also reads Samuel Kirkham's *Grammar,* an American publication, but drawing heavily from the late eighteenth-century British study of language and rhetoric.

Lincoln's copy of *The Oriental Moralist* or *Beauties of the Arabian Nights* has a further English connection, and a Johnsonian one, too, if we accept Geoffrey Tillotson's argument that the *Thousand and One Arabian Nights,* first popular in the eighteenth century, contributed to the source material for *Rasselas* (1759). At any rate, the Reverend Mr. Cooper, who drew up the 1797 edition of *The Oriental Moralist* read by Lincoln, gave the *Thousand and One Nights* an ethical treatment dovetailing nicely with the intentions of Johnson's extended "eastern tale." In a different genre, insofar as we can speak of Lincoln's familiarity with hymns and that kind of religious poetry, he seems to have learned hymns by the great English hymnist Isaac Watts (1674–1748), and later quotes Watts at least once. Watts, remarks Johnson, "was one of the first authors that taught the Dissenters to court attention by the graces of language." John Wesley (1703–91), associated with Watts, is also one of the two dozen or so writers Lincoln later quotes with his pen, probably from memory. For poetry, besides what he finds in Murray's reader and the Shakespeare printed in Scott's *Elocution,* Lincoln becomes a lover of Burns and recites much of his verse by heart. Early in adult life he indulges a liking for the humorous poems of Thomas Hood the elder, an English writer, and William Knox (1789–1825), a Scottish poet whose "Mortality" Lincoln quotes twice in his correspondence.

Lincoln also reads other books prized by the English and American eighteenth-century common reader and by Johnson himself. The titles are often identical. Among the scant dozen or so books that make up Lincoln's young library we find *Robinson Crusoe, Pilgrim's Progress,* and Æsop's *Fables,* along with the version of the *Thousand and One Nights.* Now, the three books of which Johnson never tired, said Mrs. Thrale, were *Robinson Crusoe, Pilgrim's Progress,* and *Don Quixote.* The first two of these, and Æsop's *Fables,* Johnson and Lincoln share. Each man seems to identify with the protagonists of the two spiritual autobiographies, a castaway and a pilgrim, lonely individuals facing great odds and suffering.

Lincoln's formative reading and learning are drawn from the time of Johnson and the younger Jefferson. What Johnson read and specifically valued—or actually wrote—comprises a significant part of Lincoln's early reading and overlaps with Jefferson's. The authors Lincoln and Jefferson share include Addison, Pope, and Shakespeare. From 1847 to 1849, Lincoln read books in the congressional library, itself generously donated by the second president in order to reestablish it the year after the British had sacked Washington, D.C., and destroyed the original library in 1814, when Lincoln was five. In Illinois, Lincoln joined local debate and literary clubs. He cultivated his attachment to poetry, too, and owned the works of Cowper, Gray, and Burns. Dennis Hanks reported, "Lincoln was lazy—a very lazy man—He was always reading—scribbling—writing—Ciphering—writing Poetry &c. &c." Henry McHenry told William Herndon that Lincoln "read so much—was so studious—took so little physical exercise—was so laborious in his studies that he became Emaciated & his best friends were afraid that he would craze himself—make himself derange [*sic*] from his habits of study which were incessant."[10]

As an American provincial, Lincoln receives new literary modes and fashions later than readers in Boston, New York, Philadelphia, or Charleston. Aside from the often mentioned King James Bible and Shakespeare, whose language is characterized throughout the eighteenth and nineteenth centuries in the United States as well as Great Britain with Johnson's phrase, "the well of English undefiled," the works that influence Lincoln most in style, morals, and content are produced either by the English eighteenth century or by American authors of the Declaration of Independence, the Constitution, and the Northwest Ordinance. Those Americans, born and bred as British, are themselves educated in eighteenth-century English prose and write accordingly: Jefferson, Washington, Madison. Two American Whigs whose speeches Lincoln admires and consults, Henry Clay and Daniel Webster, also write with later eighteenth-century rhetoric and delivery in mind. In his eulogy for Clay, Lincoln identifies the life of his older political ally, born in 1777, with the life of the nation itself. Then, after remarking that Clay had little formal education, Lincoln says this about his language: "Mr. Clay's eloquence did not consist, as many fine specimens of eloquence does, of types and figures—of antithesis, and elegant arrangement of words and sentences; but rather of that deeply earnest and impassioned tone, and manner, which can proceed only from great sincerity and a thorough conviction, in the speaker of the justice and importance of his cause. This it is, that truly touches the chords of human sympathy. . . . All his efforts were made for practical effect. He never spoke merely to be heard" (1: 264). These remarks effectively repeat the emphasis of the Scottish New Rhetoricians on passion, sentiment, sympathy, and direct, heartfelt expression.

Burke warned Parliament in *On Conciliation with the Colonies* (1775; see Chapter 2)—trying to persuade his colleagues of American tenacity and intelligence—that twice as many copies of Blackstone's *Commentaries* had sold in the rebellious and litigious colonies as in the mother country, despite a colonial population half her size. Some accounts suggest that the first law book Lincoln studies are the *Commentaries*[11] by Sir William Blackstone (1723–80), English jurist. This work derives from the first Vinerian law lectures at Oxford; the second series was composed by Robert Chambers and Samuel Johnson. In 1860, J. M. Brockman asks Lincoln "the best mode of obtaining a thorough knowledge of the law." The presidential candidate, reflecting on his own method, replies, "The mode is very simple, though laborious, and tedious. It is only to get the books, and read, and study them carefully. Begin with Blackstone's Commentaries, and after reading it carefully through, say twice . . . Work, work, work, is the main thing" (2: 180).

Much has been made of the fact that Lincoln, as part of his legal education, reads *The Revised Laws of Indiana,* perhaps prior to Blackstone's *Commentaries.* But what is important about it? Its prefatory matter includes texts of the Declaration of Independence, the Constitution, and the Northwest or "Great" Ordinance of 1787. (Acts of the Congress convened under the Articles of Confederation are called Ordinances.) These documents epitomize later eighteenth-century intellectual prose honed by study and practical application of previous models drawn from English literature. And Lincoln often states that his political principles stem exclusively from the Declaration of Independence, the Constitution, and the Ordinance of 1787, all approved, as he notes, by bodies with memberships that overlap significantly. Shortly before his First Inaugural, Lincoln speaks at Independence Hall. Rarely is he more direct and personal about his feelings: "I am filled with deep emotion at finding myself standing here in the place where were collected together the wisdom, the patriotism, the devotion to principle, from which sprang the institutions under which we live." And nowhere is he more direct about the origin of his principles: "[A]ll the political sentiments I entertain have been drawn, so far as I have been able to draw them, from the sentiments which originated, and were given to the world from this hall in which we stand. I have never had a feeling politically that did not spring from the sentiments embodied in the Declaration of Independence" (2: 213).

This is no down-home anecdote or folksy rejoinder. The speech contains a carefully constructed, rhetorical statement closing with an amplified triad ("the wisdom, the patriotism, the devotion to principle"), lengthening and building. He shifts his "I" to the audience's—and the nation's—"we," echoed by the next sentence also moving from "I" to "we." Then he strikes a crescendo with his final, declarative statement in the absolute: "I have never. . . ." Throughout, Lincoln keeps an emotional pitch by appealing to "sentiments" and "feeling." The language is not typical of Shakespeare's, nor of the Bible, nor is it characteristic of ornate American rhetoric of the day, what Lincoln elsewhere calls "bombastic parades"—for example, the grandiose manifest destiny pose Douglas strikes in their sixth debate. Lincoln's language assimilates the formal yet flexible, the strong, direct, chaste, style prized by the later eighteenth century and exemplified in the Declaration itself. Time after time when we hear Lincoln's clauses or phrases, Edmund Wilson's brief remark is apt: "he is working for the balance of eighteenth-century rhythms." And Lincoln's recourse to "sentiments," "feelings," and "sympathy," here and in his praise of Clay's language cited earlier, is a hallmark of British moral and rhetorical training.

In a terrible, deeply felt—and prophetic—continuation of his public credo concerning the origin of his principles, a credo that begins as early as his 1838 Lyceum Address, Lincoln, to take the presidential oath in a matter of days and now speaking as the nation's chief executive, essentially paraphrases Patrick Henry: "But, if this country cannot be saved without giving up that principle [the principle of liberty for all]—I was about to say I would rather be assassinated on this spot than to surrender it." The end of this speech he punctuates by another affirmation in cadenced, rhythmic clauses, each leading to the next and closing with his submission to the will of Providence: "I may . . . have said something indiscreet, (cries of 'no, no'), but I have said nothing but what I am willing to live by, and, in the pleasure of Almighty God, die by" (2: 213–14). These remarks at Independence Hall he delivers on Washington's Birthday. At Ford's Theater four years later, he will be assassinated in a box adorned for the night with an engraved portrait of Washington facing toward the audience, a kind of presidential seal used before such a device had been designed.

Lincoln had already given a preamble to his 1861 Philadelphia visit by responding to Mayor Alexander Henry in formal but felt phrasing: "[I]f it were convenient for me to remain with you in your city long enough to consult, or, as it were, to listen to those breathings rising within the consecrated walls where the Constitution of the United States, and I will add, the Declaration of American Independence was originally framed, I would do so." The "consecrated walls" resonates with later wording in the Gettysburg Address. Aside from a technical lack of agreement in the penultimate clause, this statement is rhetorically poised and based on sincerity, the quality he praised as the pith of Clay's eloquence. Lincoln says in a striking repetition: "I promise you in all sincerity, that I bring to the work [the presidency] a sincere heart" (2: 212).

Many politicians and citizens avow a deep, unshakable faith in the Declaration of Independence and the Constitution. But, more that any other president, Lincoln holds emphatically to the sheet anchor of these documents, avows them publicly, and, as he understands them, follows stringently their principles in practice. He begins those avowals as early as the Lyceum Address in Springfield, when he is twenty-eight. They are heightened after the *Dred Scott* case. And if interpretation of those documents differs, we can recognize in Lincoln's principles a view utterly at odds with that set down by Chief Justice Roger B. Taney in the *Dred Scott* opinion.[12] Few mention the Northwest Ordinance of 1787, yet it, too, is instrumental to Lincoln because, as he points out, it prohibits slavery in those territories; and he also notes that Jefferson, though a slave owner, played a key role in securing its passage.

Johnson, Jefferson, Burke, Paine, and Lincoln unite practical imagination with a moral stance, creating that perspective through powerful language attuned to ethical predicaments and human motives. The similarities between Lincoln's formative reading, his later prose style, and his political principles point to more than accident or chronological coincidence. Others may have read what Lincoln did—his reading is not idiosyncratic and includes common texts—but he culls, studies, distills, and *applies* the reading and language dear to him. His applications shape an imaginative vision that works through gathering crises to secure a new birth of freedom.

We have noted a few instances when Lincoln quotes others. He is not a highly allusive writer, yet from time to time he cites literary works, and it is interesting to tally the results. Of forty-eight quotations or allusions identified in his *Speeches and Writings 1838–1865,* twenty-five are from the Bible (many are paraphrases), five from Shakespeare. This fact, long known, has established the importance of those works for him. Of the remaining instances, though, the results are equally striking, even if overlooked. Seventeen of the remaining nineteen are either from British writers of the seventeenth (1), eighteenth (9), and early nineteenth (4) centuries, or from Jefferson (3). For example, as Lincoln quotes Pope's "Essay on Man," so, too, did John Dickinson in his influential *Letters From a Farmer in Pennsylvania* (1768). Among the thirty-nine signers Lincoln so admires, Dickinson served as one of Delaware's five delegates to the Constitutional Convention. The earliest text Lincoln quotes, aside from Shakespeare or the Bible, is from the English poet Robert Herrick (1591–1674), whom he encounters first in Lindley Murray's anthology. What, then, of the remaining two quotations? These are the only ones from American writers other than Jefferson. The first is from a 1775 poem by John Trumbull (1750–1831), an imitator of Pope. Trumbull is a name bandied in the Lincoln-Douglas debates. Lyman Trumbull, Lincoln's friend and political associate, born and raised in "old Connecticut," as Douglas derisively calls it, is related by blood to John Trumbull, one of the Hartford Wits who wrote *The Anarchiad,* published again in 1861, in an attempt to recall the dangers of abandoning the Union in favor of individual states and factions (see Chapter 3). Lyman Trumbull helps Lincoln, Frederick Douglass, and others form what Stephen H. Douglas scorns as the "Black Republican" party. There is, it turns out, a sort of personal connection between the leader of the old Connecticut Wits and the new man from Illinois. As John Trumbull worked to further the cause of Washington, so Lyman Trumbull, descended from the same Connecticut family, works with Lincoln, who in turn quotes the ancestor of his political ally.

The second and only other American writer Lincoln quotes aside from

Jefferson is Fitz-Greene Halleck, from his popular poem *Marco Bozzaris*. And if Halleck's name, like Trumbull's, sounds familiar for reasons other than literary ones—though his name was once a household word and his disappearance from the canon a fascinating story—it is because in 1862 Lincoln names Henry W. Halleck, Fitz-Greene's kinsman, commander-in-chief of the Union armies. Both men descend from Peter Halleck (or Hallock) of Long Island. General Halleck later contributes to the erection of a monument in Connecticut honoring his relation Fitz-Greene (1790–1867), the first public monument to celebrate an American writer. A statue of Fitz-Greene stands in Central Park on Literary Walk, near Shakespeare's and that of the other English writer whom Halleck and Lincoln mutually admire, Burns. So, aside from Jefferson, Lincoln quotes but two American writers, Trumbull and Halleck, and they both enjoy family connections with men whom Lincoln works with regularly. And both are by their contemporaries explicitly identified with British literature. Halleck writes a well-known poem about Burns, as well as others avowedly indebted to Byron, Campbell, Scott, and Southey. The first study of Halleck, published in 1869, is written by another Union general, James Grant Wilson, who serves under Henry W. Halleck and participates in the siege of Vicksburg.[13]

To account more exactly for Lincoln's remaining references taken from the nineteenth century—all written before 1825—he cites two early nineteenth-century British writers, William Knox and Charles Phillips. At least seven of the English writers Lincoln quotes he encounters first in Murray's *English Reader*. And, to repeat, his first reading of Shakespeare comes from Scott's *Lessons in Elocution*, indebted to Thomas Sheridan's *Elocution*. Citation tallies are hardly the way to characterize Lincoln's style, but they indicate clearly what forms his literary foundation: predominantly British rhetoric and poetry from 1750 to 1825, and Jefferson.

2

There is no substitute for taking Lincoln's own advice about books: "study them carefully." We have the space to look at a few examples and can start with a familiar one. Using the emphatic *shall*, the close of the Gettysburg Address builds on a string of relative pronouns and independent clauses:

> *that* from these honored dead we take increased devotion . . .
> *that* we here highly resolve
> *that* these dead *shall* not have died in vain—
> *that* this nation, under God, *shall* have a new birth of freedom—
> and *that* government of the people,
>> by the people,
>> for the people,
> *shall* not perish from the earth. (2: 536)

Here is the analogous pattern in Jefferson, quintuple relative pronouns at the start of the Declaration of Independence, also using the verb *to be* and ending with an avowal that government is of the people. It begins with the clause that Lincoln quotes to end the first sentence of his address:

> *that* all men *are* created equal,
> *that* they *are* endowed by their Creator with certain unalienable Rights,
> *that* among these *are* Life, Liberty and the pursuit of Happiness.
> *That* to secure these rights Governments *are* instituted . . .
> *That* whenever any Form of Government becomes destructive of these
>> ends, it *is* the Right of the People to alter or to abolish it.

Lincoln's "of the people, by the people, for the people" echoes phrases by Theodore Parker, the American transcendentalist, but is more likely harkening to Daniel Webster's "Second Speech on Foote's Resolution" (1830), a speech that expresses fear of civil war and of "a land . . . drenched, it may be, in fraternal blood," words haunting Lincoln and anyone else at Gettysburg who knew them. Webster in his speech called on "Liberty and Union, now and forever . . . The People's government, made for the people, made by the people, and answerable to the people."

   Simple, effective repetitions also characterize the close of Lincoln's Second Inaugural Address—"With . . . with . . . with . . . to see . . . to finish . . . to bind up . . . to care . . . to do" (2: 687); earlier, similar repetitions mark his speech on the Kansas-Nebraska Act, where he invokes "Let us" five times, followed by, "If we do this, we shall . . . we shall . . . we shall" (2: 339–40). The Gettysburg Address and other speeches are frequently contrasted to the "bombastic parades" of American oratory. But not all American public composition was flowery. The tone, vocabulary, and level of diction in Lincoln's address reflect—it is remarkable how closely they reflect—the tone, vocabulary, diction, and level of decorum found in the personal invitation written to him to make "a few appropriate remarks" in the first place ("it is altogether fitting and proper that we should do this"). The invitation, about equal in length to the address itself, is preserved on a plaque at the Gettysburg National Cemetery a short walk from the place Lincoln spoke.

It is not surprising that Lincoln can sound like a student of the Enlightenment. He is one. Criticizing Douglas: "When he says he 'cares not whether slavery is voted down or voted up,'—that it is a sacred right of self-government—he is in my judgment penetrating the human soul and eradicating the light of reason and the love of liberty" (1: 527). Or, again, when Lincoln renders judgment in his First Inaugural Address, his words and principles recall Burke's organic constitutional vision, as well as restate what was known as "Union Theology":

> I hold, that in contemplation of universal law, and of the Constitution, the Union of these States is perpetual. Perpetuity is implied, if not expressed, in the fundamental law of all national governments. It is safe to assert that no government proper, ever had a provision in its organic law for its own termination. Continue to execute all the express provisions of our national Constitution, and the Union will endure forever—it being impossible to destroy it, except by some action not provided for in the instrument itself. (2: 217)

Late in the war, Lincoln writes a now famous letter to Lydia Bixby on the death of her five sons who served in the Union army (it does not matter that Lincoln was misinformed; "only" two of her sons died in battle and one may have perished in a Confederate prison camp). The letter includes this sentence of tenderness and respect: "I feel how weak and fruitless must be any words of mine which should attempt to beguile you from the grief of a loss so overwhelming" (2: 644, 755n). To state how "weak" it is to use words to "beguile" a mourner from "grief" or "sorrow" is a common phrase in the eighteenth-century etiquette of consolation. It derives from a sentimental, sincere tradition. Though Lincoln is no novel reader—he apparently tried *Ivanhoe* once but put it down—it is interesting to note that the same elocution he appropriates with such effect in writing Mrs. Bixby is found in the last sentence of Ann Radcliffe's popular English novel *The Mysteries of Udolpho* (1794): "And if the weak hand that has recorded this tale, has by its scenes, beguiled the mourner of one hour of sorrow . . . the effort . . . has not been vain." In Lincoln's letter, it is as if he recognizes and feels responsible for a situation that not only meets the strength of the phrase but exceeds it: here is a fearful case in which he employs it as no fiction. He ends his letters variously, often "Yours truly" or "Yours very truly," occasionally "Yours as ever" or "Your obedient servant," rarely "Your friend" or "Respectfully." The letter to Mrs. Bixby ("Yours, very sincerely, and respectfully") is the *only* letter that I have been able to locate that Lincoln closes with the word "sincerely."

Lincoln's rhythms and interplay of sounds are sophisticated yet not stiff. Alerting the ear and intellect, they have the flexible order of persuasive public speech. From early in his career comes this arresting sentence:

- / - / (X)- - / - (x) - / -‖ - - (x)/ - /- (X)/(-) - /
We find ourselves in the peaceful possession of the fairest portion of the earth. (1: 28)

Alliteration (*p, f, s*), assonance (*e, e, a*), and consonance (*th*), along with simple repetitions and a balance of rhythm, stress, and pauses, ordered but without rigid antitheses, form a memorable phrasing. As often in excellent public rhetoric, we get an *approximation* of the poetic iambic pentameter (or heroic) line, but rarely that line precisely. The result, frequently a "line" of nine or eleven syllables, not ten, with varied stress patterns and usually with four, not five, strong beats, especially if there are nine syllables, is what Edmund Wilson had in mind when he said Lincoln often writes "a kind of constricted blank verse." This pattern is based on iambic stress but diverges from its strict rule, though occasionally keeping it as a sentence ends or a clause reaches its climax, as in the later example below, ending with "can long endure." A more recent instance is the following:

- / - - / - - / - /
Ask not what your country can do for you,
/ - / - / - - / -
Ask what you can do for your country.

F.D.R. is a master of this kind of "line":

    -    - / - - / - / - /
We have nothing to fear but fear itself.
      - / -   - / - / - /
. . . a date which will live in infamy.

Quoting Carlyle, Martin Luther King, Jr. uses it effectively:

    - / - / - / - / -
Because no lie can live forever . . .

So does Ronald Reagan, in words inscribed where he will rest:

    / - / - - /   - / - /
I believe in my heart that man is good.

Perhaps best known is Patrick Henry's cry:

    /   -   / - / - / - /
Give me liberty or give me death.

Lincoln knew these strong rhythms from Jefferson, too:

    - / - / -   - / - - /   /
Almighty God hath created the mind free.
    /   - / - / / - / - /
God who gave us life gave us liberty.

Lincoln's rhythms often follow the kind of pattern we have been noting, in this next example complemented by repetitions of "nation," "conceived," and "dedicated" that flank his central claim from the Declaration, the "proposition that all men are created equal":

Four score and seven years ago   / / - / - / - /
our fathers brought forth on this continent,   - / - - / - - / - /

a new nation, conceived in Liberty,	- / / - - / - / - /
and dedicated to the proposition	- / - / - - - / - / -
that all men are created equal.	- / / - - / - / -
Now we are engaged in a great civil war,	/ - - - / - - / / - /
testing whether that nation, or any	/ - / - / / - - / -
nation so conceived and so dedicated,	/ - / - / - / / - / -
can long endure.	- / - / (2: 536)

To achieve emphasis, his length of phrasing often shortens then lengthens to a longer "line." Here is that effect in balanced clauses and phrases, with key junctures in a triple stress ("*we here*—hold"; "the last best, hope"):

The fiery trial through which we pass,	- / - / - / - /
will light us down, in honor or dishonor,	- / - / - / - / - / -
to the latest generation.	- - / - / - / -
We *say* we are for **the Union.**	- / - - / - / -
The world will not forget that we say this.	- / - / - / - - / -
We know how to save **the Union.**	- / - - / - / -
The world knows we do know how to save it.	- / / - / - / - / -
We—even *we here*—hold the power,	/ - - / / / - /
and bear the responsibility.	- / - - / - / - /
In *giving* freedom to the *slave*,	- / - / - - (or/) - /
we *assure* freedom to the *free*. . . .	/ - / / - - (or/) - /
We shall nobly save, or meanly lose,	/ - / - / - / - /
the last best, hope of earth.	- / / / - /
Other means may succeed; this could not fail.	/ - / / - / - / - /
	(2: 415)

Incidentally, the phrase "last best, hope" (Lincoln punctuates it unusually) is found in English verse beginning with William Lisle Bowles. Lincoln may have encountered it in James Percival's *Hellas,* an American poem. At times Lincoln's phrasing alternates between six and eight syllables, a variation of the ballad stanza:

Let no one be deceived.	- / - / - /
The spirit of seventy-six	- / - - / - - /
and the spirit of Nebraska	- - / - / - / -
are utter antagonisms	- / - - / - / - (2: 339)

In 1846–47, Lincoln writes two poems, both in ballad form, one comic, "The Bear Hunt," one an elegy of twenty-four stanzas, "My Childhood-Home I see Again" (1: 120–22). Nearly flawless in its rhythm, the latter is striking and closes,

> The very spot where grew the bread
> That formed my bones, I see.
> How strange, old field, on thee to tread,
> And feel I'm part of thee!

In his prose, another alternation of trimeter and tetrameter phrasing incorporates balance and personification, reminiscent of eighteenth-century usage, to establish closure for the "House Divided" speech. We hear eight syllables, then six and six, then eight again, the last read as iambic tetrameter, especially since Lincoln spoke slowly and emphatically:

Wise councils may accelerate	/ / - - - / - /
or *mistakes delay* it,	- - / - / /
but, sooner or later	/ / - - / -
the victory is *sure* to come	- / - / - / - / (1: 434)

There's no doubt that Lincoln's oral remarks and a few passages in his writing convey a colloquial American flavor. Regarding General Meade's pursuit of Lee after Gettysburg, Lincoln says it reminds him "of an old woman trying to shoo her geese across a creek." But such imagery and pith do not fully or generally characterize the prose and more formal speech. Lincoln himself seems to have been aware of this, and of the nature of his writing when, almost in self-parody and with wry humor, he consoles one advisor, worried that the presidential candidate of 1860 would state too much before the general election takes place: "Allow me to beg that you will not live in much apprehension of my precipitating a letter upon the public." Douglas Wilson remarks that "Telling stories and reading the works of humorists to his Cabinet are part of the Lincoln legend, and yet one of the truly remarkable things about Lincoln as President is the extent to which he resorted to literature. Perhaps no President turned to English poetry while in office with the frequency that Lincoln did."[14]

The power, cadence, organization, and moral tone of Lincoln's language derive from a tradition that goes back to Addison and Steele and extends up

Abraham Lincoln and his son Tad on a *carte de visite* based on Anthony Berger's photograph taken at Matthew Brady's studio in February 1864. This is the only known photograph of Lincoln with his reading glasses. The Gilder Lehrman Collection, on deposit at The Pierpont Morgan Library, New York, New York. GLC 242.13. Reproduced by permission.

through important moralists, essayists, critics, rhetoricians, politicians, philosophers, and historians—almost exclusively British—of the eighteenth century. In the colonies and the young Republic, Jefferson, Adams, Madison, and Monroe cultivate styles built on these British writers. Soon afterwards, so do Webster and Clay. This conscious cultivation touched the politicians Lincoln most admires: the signers of the Declaration, the framers of the Constitution, the members of the Congress who in 1787 passed the Northwest Ordinance. As he remarks about his own opposition to the Nebraska Bill, replying to Douglas in their first debate: "I am fighting it . . . in the Jeffersonian, Washingtonian, and Madisonian fashion" (2: 516).

Garry Wills's important book, *Lincoln at Gettysburg: The Words That Remade America,* connects Lincoln's address to intellectual patterns and literary predecessors: ancient Greek funeral orations, the modern revival of Greek taste, the cemetery movement, transcendentalism, romanticism, and the writings of the founding fathers. Many of these connections are more important for understanding the occasion of the address and the dedication of the National Cemetery than Lincoln's words themselves. But late in the book, Wills analyzes Lincoln's style. In five or six pages he hits at the heart of the matter all along: Lincoln's address, argues Wills, reflects basic principles prevalent in one school of American oratory established by Hugh Blair: "Lincoln may have known Blair directly; he certainly knew his principles from derivative texts. . . . His work seems the very embodiment of Blair's ideal." What Wills does not state, however—it runs counter to his point about Lincoln's distinctively American style and Blair's "American" School—is that Hugh Blair, certainly one of the authorities of American rhetoric, was not an American but the Scottish New Rhetorician who delivered his *Lectures* from 1759 to 1783 in Edinburgh. His influence had been felt in America eighty years before Gettysburg. As we have noted above, when Lincoln first studies Murray's *English Reader,* he reads excerpts from Blair's work. Early in the twentieth century, Lord Curzon, diplomat and chancellor of Oxford, speaking on "Modern Parliamentary Eloquence," suddenly turns from his countrymen to speak about the Gettysburg Address and the Second Inaugural, "among the glories and treasures of mankind. I escape the task of deciding which is the masterpiece of modern English eloquence by awarding the prize to an American."[15] He was an American who had gone to school with the British all along.

The legend that Lincoln's language is untutored, "natural," and uniquely American neatly plays into the notion that it is not necessary in a democracy to sharpen skills of composition, and that an egalitarian attitude to language will not only suffice, it will produce the best results: the greatest prose written by a president and written, moreover, by perhaps the greatest president. But the legend is not true. Lincoln learns the language by the same means he recommends acquiring knowledge of the law, in his own words: "It is only to get the books, and read, and study them carefully. . . . work, work, work, is the main thing." Steady application, mastery of the principles of grammar, close attention to details until they become second nature, then redrafting and—constantly, from his earliest reading—setting before himself models of excellent English prose and poetry attuned to biography, history, the moral life, and public values; then, as dictated by the situation in which he found himself and his country, and as guided by those statesmen and writers who established the Union he stood to preserve, he places on this foundation the conviction of his own principles and the stamp of his own sincerity. This is the power of Lincoln's language.

10

Recommitment

For two hundred years, from the Hanoverian settlement of 1714 in Great Britain to the outbreak of World War I, democratic societies—and societies struggling to become democratic—establish in the English-speaking world a modern practice of language and rhetoric devoted to the deliberation of public values. Its mature students, some of whom we have followed in this volume, set political policies, forge compromises, criticize authority, exert pulpit oratory, and shape cultural life. They understood their activities to come under the heading of "literature" or "rhetoric." Beginning in the late nineteenth century and accelerating in the twentieth, this capacious study waned and its practice narrowed. In schools and universities, a focus on fictive works and literary theory supplanted it in bulk and prestige. What can be done to redirect energy to all broader uses of literary expression, including those that inform public life?

A premium on persuasive language and on the literary dimensions used to express public issues affects the course of events. It makes history. At one time it helped deliberative bodies establish a new nation conceived in liberty. Delegates from the colonies ask Jefferson to draft the Declaration because they consider him a superior stylist. How had he acquired that skill? He had studied the British New Rhetoricians—Kames, Blair, Sheridan—with care. He studied one of their practical exponents, Patrick Henry, seven years his senior. Jefferson even marked the written Declaration with pauses for oral delivery. His cadences owe something to James Macpherson, who attended Lowth's lectures: Jefferson wrote to Macpherson's brother asking for manuscripts of the *Ossian* "poems," their rhythm heavily influenced by Lowth's analysis of biblical parallelism. In Great Britain and its dominions, across decades of debate, eloquence aids the peaceful abolition of slavery. Lincoln keeps the Union whole thanks in part to the power of his words. He remarks that the names of those in Great Britain who spoke and wrote against the slave trade, such as Wilberforce, are known to "School-boys," while opponents of abolition "like tallow-candles . . . at last . . . flickered in the socket, died out, stank in the dark for a brief season, and were remembered no more, even by the smell."[1] Each new enfranchisement and reform in a democratic society, each defense of a right under threat, depends on public persuasion through language. One can make a cogent case that twentieth-century speakers such as Churchill, the two Roosevelts, and King train themselves in rhetorical traditions springing directly from the previous two centuries.

In Great Britain and soon after in the United States, a long series of books and textbooks dedicated to rhetoric, persuasion, oratory, and language flourish from the 1740s until after the Civil War. Their study enables deliberation of public values. Almost every school and university in America and Great Britain requires students to read one or several of these books in a planned course of study lasting three or four years. This concluding chapter is not the place to give a history of their enormous impact on political life and cultural values.[2] A mere list of editions of these works, one line for each publication, would run longer than this chapter. To the many advocates of this study mentioned in earlier chapters, among them Hugh Blair, George Campbell, the Sheridans, and John Quincy Adams, we should add John Witherspoon. Born a Scot but later president of Princeton from 1768 to 1794, Witherspoon invokes "the great rule of sincerity" that Lincoln later sees epitomized by Clay, who had little formal schooling but studied oratory and read diligently. We could also add Thomas Whatley, Caleb Bingham—he compiled the *Columbian Orator,* the book that inspired Douglass—as well as Henry N. Day, W. G. T. Shedd, and Edward T.

Channing. Channing taught Emerson, Holmes, Dana, Parkman, and Thoreau. While this educational tradition has its own internal differences and evolution—for example, some emphasize writing over delivery or oratory, some stress poetry over practical debate—its main outlines clearly aim at an infusion of powerful language into everyday activities and decisions, what Emerson calls "the conduct of life." One key is the application of earlier writers as models that may be drawn upon for present purposes. That is what Emerson has in mind when, in the section of *English Traits* entitled "Literature," he ventures, thinking not just of England, "Every new writer is only a new crater of an old volcano." We have seen how Pope uses Horace, the Connecticut Wits use Pope, Burke uses Pope and Milton, Lincoln uses Jefferson and Clay, Lowth uses ancient Hebrew poetry, and Vico uses all narratives to depict the nature of civil societies. These applications follow no formulas. Later generations transform Lowth's work into a secularized aesthetic, its credo put economically by Ruskin in *Modern Painters*: "To see clearly is poetry, prophecy and religion—all in one." But in 1895, John Vance Cheney in his study *That Dome in Air* lists Lowth's *Lectures* in the table of contents as "a forgotten volume." The original may be forgotten because it is so thoroughly assimilated. Or, newer applications may simply outshine the old. Emerson remarks, "When Shakespeare is charged with debts to his authors, Landor replies, 'Yet he was more original than his originals. He breathed upon dead bodies and brought them into life.' "

We have seen, too, that attention to the literary qualities of public deliberation and cultural life is not specifically ideological in origin. As early as ancient Greece, its origin and practice is broadly democratic. It crosses party lines. It is not sectarian. It admits the formation of plural, diverse tastes. It is an instrumentality that serves many masters, which makes it essential training for politics and law. Solon wrote his legal code in verse. And as William Dean Howells reports, William Blackstone left off the study of literature only because he said law was "a jealous mistress" who would suffer no rival. We have also seen—to state explicitly what throughout this book has often been implied—that a tradition of committed literature connects British and American letters profoundly. Their intertwining is manifold. Another diligent student of the new British rhetoric of the mid-eighteenth century, Thomas Paine, like Jefferson, turns it against the mother country and urges the creation of a new nation. In January 1776, he writes, "In the following pages I offer nothing more than simple facts, plain arguments, and common sense. . . . [N]othing can settle our affairs so expeditiously as an open and determined declaration for Independence." Burke, with

both admiration and pungent humor, calls him "the great Paine." But the genesis of American studies since 1930, while producing incalculably positive effects,
including recently even a chair of American literature at Oxford, has overlooked
the enormous comity—the sharing and connection—between British and
American writing, now oddly a relatively neglected area of comparative literature.

What the case studies and profiles in this book have shown, then, I hope,
is that the study of language and rhetoric need not be an isolated profession or
discipline but must be studied with intense focus. It is an activity essential to
cultural developments, wise political deliberation, and ethical reflection. When
young, Sam Johnson and Abe Lincoln each study and argue both sides of a
question, Lincoln as a lawyer and Johnson "talking for victory" at the home of
Gilbert Walmesley. This kind of language one might later hear in Johnson's
Literary Club or Emerson's Saturday Club. The point is, in each, individuals of
varied professional interests meet. The previous chapter spoke about the sources
of Lincoln's literary and rhetorical education. Seeming at first scant, they are
actually impressive. On this point, Edmund Wilson quotes Roy Basler, Lincoln's editor: "A careful examination" of books Lincoln had on elocution and
grammar, "which Lincoln studied both in and out of school will not impress
anyone with Lincoln's poverty of opportunity for the study of grammar and
rhetoric. It is safe to say that few children today learn as much through twelve
years of formal schooling in these two subjects as one finds in the several textbooks Lincoln apparently read." Wilson remarks that rhetoric then was taught
thoroughly.[3]

That is not the case now. The loss began before World War I and later
intensified. Even an institution once renowned for leadership in this area, Harvard, has, in the words of one well-informed commentator, "destroyed rhetoric."[4] While programs at a few schools unite rhetoric with other forms of literary
study on an equal footing, it is far more usual to see a split between "literature"
on one plane and "rhetoric" or "composition" on another, usually with the
latter accorded less prestige, lower teaching salaries, and heavier teaching loads.[5]
Daily recitation in complete sentences, either memorized or ex tempore, is uncommon, usually restricted to a few oral reports scattered through the school
year. In debate clubs and societies, while attention is given to effective presentation, there still is little study of past models, little conscious investigation of the
verbal structures of logic and argumentation. In business, civic organizations,
and political associations, people frequently identify the school course they wish

they had taken, or could have taken, as one in public speaking. The situation is mixed but, in the main, divisions of American schools responsible for rhetoric have abdicated their duty, often limiting it to the correction of rudimentary faults in grammar and style. One course in composition at the college level is hardly sufficient to establish sharp skills in communication and persuasion. "Writing Across the Curriculum" may revitalize the literary, rhetorical bent to the expression of public values and deliberations, but this will be achieved only if excellent models are available to emulate.

A relevant study of rhetoric of the kind once cultivated is still available to us if we reach out for it. The models are there, even contemporary ones. Its earlier practice has been loosely associated, following Jürgen Habermas, with "the public sphere," a practice open in the eighteenth century for the first time to a significant part of society not born to privilege. But my analysis is not derived from Habermas; rather, it is derived from the instances included in this book as well as others, and is aimed at what the study of public rhetoric and the literary exercise of deliberative language can teach us now—as it taught Lincoln—when we turn to our own political and cultural agendas. What attitude is necessary for this to happen?

The best minds in the century immediately preceding Lincoln study language, public literary expression, and rhetoric: in their estimate these constitute a central enterprise. Many distinguish themselves in other fields, but they begin with rhetoric and criticism as a deep foundation. For example, beyond Adam Smith's *Wealth of Nations* (1776) and his earlier, undervalued *Theory of Moral Sentiments* (1759), a powerful answer to Hobbes and influential in developing a literary and social theory based on the principle of "fellow-feeling" or sympathy, we find yet earlier, probably in 1748, that Smith delivers *Lectures on Rhetoric and Belles Lettres,* later rescued from auditors' notes and published in 1963. In science, Joseph Priestley, discoverer of oxygen and a founder of modern chemistry, expresses radical political principles and eventually emigrates to America, settling on the banks of the Susquehanna, much as Coleridge and Southey, influenced by Priestley, envisioned doing to establish their utopian Pantisocracy. Yet Priestley, teaching at a Unitarian college and influencing William Hazlitt, who spent his own childhood in North America, first writes two books, *Lectures on Oratory and Criticism* and *A Course of Lectures on the Theory of Language and Universal Grammar,* both taught to students in the early 1760s. Priestley and Smith are two of the New Rhetoricians who from 1760 to 1790 redefine figures of speech, oratory, and poetics. Many are political economists, social reformers, divines, and moralists. We have seen that they write some of the first things Lincoln reads, and that their rhetorical principles inform his prose.

Women writers and scholars, among them Frances Burney, Anna Laetitia Barbauld, Maria Edgeworth, Hannah More, Elizabeth Carter, Charlotte Lennox, Sophia Lee, and Mary Wollstonecraft, they all acquire acute literary educations and exercise their social commentary through literary achievement. Several receive rhetorical training from family members. Jane Austen, supreme observer and satirist of personal morality and social mores, steeps herself in intellectual prose as well as novels. Reading her fiction reminds us that Johnson's essays on domestic and public topics rank first among her favorite nonfiction. Wollstonecraft's reasoned rhetoric in her *Vindication of the Rights of Woman* is performative; that is, her writing itself demonstrates that she can think and argue with exceptional force, a skill then presumed to be the province of men. So, wielding the great instrumentality of literate persuasion, her work thus argues, performatively as well as explicitly, to open all learned professions to women, for those professions depend on that very skill in language. This reform she does not demand happen immediately, but implies it will occur in due course, a tactic itself part of her brilliant rhetorical strategy.

In law, Henry Home practices for years before becoming a member of the Scottish bench. Yet later he writes the three volumes of *Elements of Criticism* (1762), influential for decades on both sides of the Atlantic. Sir Joshua Reynolds, famous portraitist and first president of the Royal Academy of Art, produces *Discourses* on art that are important works of cultural criticism. Even in horticulture and landscape professions we see an interest in the critical occupation. Thomas Whately turns to his magnum opus, *Observations on Modern Gardening* (1785), only by interrupting work on his *Remarks on Some of the Characters of Shakespeare*. Burke recommends the Shakespearean character criticism of another writer, William Richardson, as an invaluable aid in reading the motives of political behavior. Lincoln applies this intuitively, studying Shakespeare as much, he says, as any unprofessional reader.

The point of the preceding three paragraphs is not to give a potted history familiar to a few, but to recall that the individuals we have glanced at, and more as well—while associated with politics, science, philosophy, landscape art, religion, painting, law, women's rights, and economics—attain their eminence first through the study of writing and speaking. They assume such training to be essential. In each case, one of their first and lasting interests is the practice and criticism of humane letters, the constellation of words and texts expressing complex relationships between and among ideas, aesthetics, culture, spiritual values, ethics, and political action. These individuals commit to an intensive study of rhetoric and humane letters as a core activity, one as basic as economics, history, or science in helping us to understand and govern. Equally committed is Colonel Joshua Lawrence Chamberlain, later major general, commander of the Twentieth Maine Infantry at Gettysburg. His regiment effectively repelled the Confederate attack on the Union left flank at Little Round Top, a key fight in the three-day battle. Wounded six times in the war, Chamberlain receives the Congressional Medal of Honor and is selected by Grant to receive the Southern surrender at Appomattox. He becomes prominent in Maine politics, serves as governor, and then as president of Bowdoin College (1873–81), where he participates in debates over the Reserve Officers Training Corps (ROTC). His training? Until 1862, Chamberlain was professor of rhetoric and oratory and of modern languages at Bowdoin, and also professor of natural and revealed religion. In that last position he succeeded his colleague Calvin Stowe, husband of Harriet Beecher, and the American editor and proponent of Robert Lowth.

Significantly—it's part of what makes him a great literary figure—Samuel Johnson subsumes many of these professional interests: with Robert Chambers he writes the Vinerian law lectures at Oxford; he mentions law as his prime object when he enters that university; he composes sermons, practices moral philosophy, keeps up a serious interest in chemistry, knows navigation, publishes political tracts, and sets down close to half a million words—a *thousand* pages—of parliamentary debates early in his career, writing speeches whose style and force even now some editors of political orations mistakenly attribute to members of Parliament.

Johnson depicts the critical study of language and literature in *Rambler* 3 as originally bearing a torch, of which it was "the particular quality immediately to shew every thing in its true form, however it might be disguised to common eyes." In *Rambler* 208 he says such "criticism . . . is . . . ranked among the subordinate and instrumental arts": it is a means or instrument for use in other professions, activities, and arts, one necessary for their best exercise. This is also what Lincoln conveys about the study of language in his "Lecture on Discoveries and Inventions." He states that to carry on "communication, some *instrumentality* is indispensable"; this instrumentality is speech and writing, which "greatly facilitates" all other forms of knowledge, all "discoveries and inventions." It is the study and perfecting specifically of language in written and printed form that Lincoln links with every advance in human knowledge, morals, and government.[6]

2

But, to return, what about language and rhetoric now? There are healthy signs, at least in quantity; several journalists, scholars, and civil servants address the subject.[7] But disturbing trends exist, too, one of which is the self-enclosed, hermetically sealed nature of much academic writing on the subject of literature. It has perfected what Matthew Arnold calls "the jargon of modern criticism." David Lodge notes that in today's literary studies, specialists "at the coal-face are unintelligible to the general public," and those "who are intelligible often have nothing valuable to say." There is nothing new here; this trend infects the academy periodically. Sir Philip Sidney, more than four hundred years ago in his *Apology for Poetry,* speaks of courtiers (politicians), who, despite relatively little academic learning, nevertheless put to good use what they have learned, while ostentatious, insecure professors become opaque and lose their audiences: "I have found in divers small-learned courtiers a more sound style than in some professors of learning . . . the courtier, following that which by practice he findeth fittest to nature, therein (though he know it not) doth [perform] according to art, though not by art: where the other, using art to show art . . . flieth from nature, and indeed abuseth art."

But beyond specialization and the frequent failure of the academy to find an exterior point of reference, here is a critical assessment of another trend, this one outside the college and university world. We are not exactly developing Sidney's ideal courtier: Instead, "We are losing our ability to manage ideas; to contemplate, to think. We are in a constant race to be first with the obvious. We are becoming a nation of electronic voyeurs whose capacity for dialogue is a fading memory. . . . Consider this paradox: Almost everything that is publicly said these days is recorded. Almost nothing of what is said is worth remembering. And what do we remember? Thoughts that were expressed hundreds or even thousands of years ago by philosophers, thinkers, and prophets whose ideas and principles . . . endured without videotape or film. . . . We have become so obsessed with facts that we have lost all touch with truth." This jeremiad is not any academic's. And it is not from a poet and soldier like Sidney. Ted Koppel, popular and respected media news figure, made these remarks as he accepted the 1985 Broadcaster of the Year Award from the International Radio and Television Society. In other words, our inherited gift of language is in new jeopardy, our grasp of it slipping from uses that subtly denigrate thought and value.

Book reviews tumble off the presses; academic and commercial publishers release volumes of criticism advertised by dedicated mailings; submissions flood specialized journals. But this refined activity takes place in an American society in which one-fifth of the population is functionally illiterate, the highest rate among developed nations, and it takes place in a culture with growing, complex problems in ethics, where political rhetoric is often degraded to ten-second spots, "photo ops," and "factoids." One study reveals that the average time of a television news sound bite in 1968 was 42.3 seconds; by 1988, despite twenty-four-hour newscasts, the average time had plunged to 9.8 seconds—about thirty words, fewer than one bumper full of bumper stickers.[8] We can assume it is even shorter now. We live in a democratic society in which literary study of the most sophisticated stamp rests side by side with adult illiteracy and superficial public discourse.

Examples of incoherent "rhetoric" might be plucked from the remarks of many public servants and presidents. In citing George Bush, I imply no partisan monopoly on skewed speech. Replying to a student's question whether the federal government would seek ideas abroad to improve American schools, Bush replies,

> "Well, I'm going to kick that one right into the end zone of the Secretary of Education. But, yes, we all have—he travels a good deal, goes abroad. We have a lot of people in the department that does that. We're having an international—this is not as much education as dealing with the environment—a big international conference coming up. And we get it all the time—exchanges of ideas.
>
> "But I think we've got—we set out there—and I want to give credit to your Governor McWherter and to your former Governor Lamar Alexander—we've gotten great ideas for a national goals program from—in this country—from the governors who were responding to, maybe, the principal of your high school, for heaven's sake."

Speaking at a school commencement, Bush reports on a tour of the Lincoln Bedroom in the White House that he conducted for Vaclav Havel, playwright, president of Czechoslovakia, and later president of the Czech Republic. Havel studied to master impeccable English and soon delivered polished speeches in it. Bush remarks, "And the look on his face, as the man who was in jail and dying, or living—whatever—for freedom, stood out there, hoping against hope for freedom."[9] At least Bush did not sell mini-time-shares in the Lincoln Bedroom (a room where Lincoln never slept, unless he dozed off during cabinet meetings then held there).

In magazines, young people read hundreds of items similar to the one that claims clothing designers make "courageous *statements*" by lowering hemlines four centimeters, or by mixing plaid with houndstooth. As for belief, diet drinks appeal because "I believe in me." Faith is something to have in brokerages. One may expound a "philosophy" of anything, including the length of collar points; eventually, a philosophy of wisdom sounds odd. "Aesthetic Institutes" in Switzerland or Palm Beach are places to get a face-lift. Ethical terms are brought to bear in electronic and commercial voyeurism. Here is Christian Dior's confused mouthful: "Fashion defends the rights of imagination and endows frivolity with a moral code." Oscar Wilde comes closer to the mark when he says that fashion is something so hideous that it needs to be changed every six months. If a product costs a lot, one can try the ultimate comparison—consumption is so much like imaginative art that it is hard to distinguish the two: "Like poets or magicians," proclaims one ad, "Cartier creators know the wonder of dreams and the mystery of desire. And like those masters of imagination, the Cartier artists interpret those dreams and desires for a clientele which, like Cartier, is unique in all the world." The clientele will own the interpretation of dreams, not what Freud had in mind, and will place in safety deposit boxes the mastery of imagination, not what Coleridge envisioned either. With a message similar to Cartier's, yet more bold, another company takes the second-person gambit: "You could spend more for an equally beautiful piece of art. But Rembrandts have lousy pickup. Michelangelo. Cézanne. Van Gogh. Mercedes. . . . only one can be admired from within . . . you drive your masterpiece. And you realize . . . this just may be the most powerful work of art you've ever experienced."

Wayne Booth has proposed that states wage an education tax on what he calls this "cultural garbage" of advertising. But many literary critics express a tame attitude toward the debasement of language found in consumer "culture." It is accepted as an inescapable element of postmodernism, perhaps because, as it exploits, so can it be exploited. Take words and language with deep, historically layered significations; take well-written sentences implying profound, complex values and ethical choices: then apply those same words and sentences to mass marketing or to political slogans. It sells; it wins campaigns. One televised commercial for DeBeers, shown while apartheid still was law in South Africa, put it this way—the narrator's voice accompanied by two white, well-to-do hands clasping each other inside a fabulously expensive necklace originating in the mines—"More profound than words [telling pause to fade out] . . . diamonds." The vocabulary of consumer material culture has, with sly ingenuity, adopted and adapted a vocabulary originated by rhetoric and literary criticism, words that carry the weight of judgment, worth, and value. And, not wanting to miss a bandwagon, even one going in reverse, academic literary criticism has reciprocated by adopting many earlier, now shopworn, tags of fashionable commercialism: ideas or theories are "hot tickets" or "properties." They gain "cachet," develop "market strategies," stay "in vogue," then grow "passé." Prose styles are "sexy." Books are "packaged." You cannot get away in the academic world any longer with calling something a "masterpiece" or "work of art." That language, we have just seen, is for selling cars. A great literary work is instead a "monument" or an "intertext." The language of criticism and the language of advertising, each in its own self-doubt, self-promotion, and scramble for attention, have engaged in a kind of pathetic flip-flop. In graduate schools, even in colleges, the study of language and literature, itself often mercilessly commodified, frequently fails to ask questions about public values or private ethics.

Aldous Huxley was prescient about the temptation to pervert literate language when selling either objects or pushing political tyranny. In his novel *Antic Hay* (1923), published nine years before *Brave New World,* the public relations specialist Mr. Boldero tells the unlikely protagonist of the story, an Oxford graduate identified in the first words of the book as "Gumbril, Theodore Junior, B.A. Oxon": "There is no better training for modern commerce than a literary education. As a practical business man, I always uphold the ancient universities, especially in their teaching of the Humanities." In one sense, the humanities are an excellent preparation for the world of affairs, but Huxley's point is that if their study is used exclusively to sell goods rather than to deliberate values, we constrict the range of culture and damage the vitality of democracy.

Prophesied by Huxley, the trends and uses of language just mentioned, from Koppel's warning to the claim that a Mercedes is superior to a Michelangelo, are corrosive because one goal of literature and rhetoric has been to produce liberated minds free to make autonomous choices, yet to do so while respecting the liberties, choices, and histories of others who may disagree. Every rhetorical act is social and political, at least it can be, for it requires nothing less than an informed, scrupulous use of language and—through language—an imaginative vision of human experience, communication, and institutions. The most troubling, irreducible problems in public and private sectors are those that cannot be quantified or solved by technical means alone, especially if those means cause serious objection. Problems of policy, ethics, and power, often moral in nature—hence the older title "professor of rhetoric and moral philosophy"—must be expressed and analyzed in language that involves the fluidities and crosscurrents of value judgments, different types of knowledge, even aesthetic preferences. The goal of critical thinking in literate, forceful language—literary language, in its widest signification—embraces social rhetoric and expression. The goal of such thinking is not to uphold one given power structure, cultural point of view, or ideology, but to produce independent minds, which in self-awareness and self-criticism think and judge on their own. This education, from *e* + *ducere,* to lead out, is the opposite of indoctrination.

The study of literary language and rhetoric in a wider public sphere can be revitalized. But it is endangered on the one hand by specialized academic atrophy and, on the other, by marketplace hype and the instantaneous media. Writers examined in this book, including Lincoln and his admired framers of congressional and parliamentary democracy, remind us in our formative and continuing educations as professionals, and even more importantly as citizens, that if we lose touch with their eloquence and practice of language, we do so at our peril. We may not at first pay a price in our private or public lives. Ironically, to lose sight of—or to divert—the larger aims of language, literature, and public rhetoric may temporarily further the standing of some if they know how to package the diversion and make it new. But we eventually pay a price nationally. The result, as we saw Pope reveal it at the birth of modern parliamentary government, is the triple curse of corrupted language, corrupting money, and corrupt politics. The study of language and rhetoric can erode further, becoming a profession solely unto itself rather than one that fosters an instrumental skill to inform other professions, including politics, and to promote civic virtue—what Lincoln identifies, with his emphasis, as "the *political religion* of the nation." If such erosion continues, we will seal ourselves in debased forms of deliberation that restrain us from what Lincoln calls our "unfinished work." His example, and Swift's, and so many others', call on us to use language to serve human liberty, without which all culture and art exist in chains.

Notes

Abbreviations of publications frequently cited

CL	*College Literature*
DAB	*Dictionary of American Biography*
EAL	*Early American Literature*
EC	*The Eighteenth Century*
ECL	*Eighteenth-Century Life*
ECS	*Eighteenth-Century Studies*
ELH	*English Literary History*
JEGP	*Journal of English and Germanic Philology*
JHI	*Journal of the History of Ideas*
HLQ	*Huntington Library Quarterly*
MLQ	*Modern Language Quarterly*
MLR	*Modern Language Review*
MP	*Modern Philology*
N&Q	*Notes and Queries*
NLH	*New Literary History*
PLL	*Papers on Language and Literature*
PMLA	*Publication of the Modern Language Association*
PQ	*Philological Quarterly*
SECC	*Studies in Eighteenth-Century Culture*
SEL	*Studies in English Literature*
SiR	*Studies in Romanticism*
SP	*Studies in Philology*

Notes to Chapter 1: The Committed Word

1. *Abraham Lincoln, Speeches and Writings 1859–1865,* ed. Don E. Fehrenbacher (New York: Library of America, 1989), 6–7.

2. See Kenneth Cmiel, *Democratic Eloquence: The Fight Over Popular Speech in Nineteenth-Century*

America (New York: William Morrow, 1990). In *Democracy in America* (vol. 1, chap. 11; vol. 2, ɪ, chaps. 14–15; vol. 2, ɪɪ, chap. 6), Tocqueville examines newspapers and literature in national life.

3. *Abraham Lincoln*, 493. Like many reports of Lincoln's oral remarks, this one has been challenged. See Garry Wills, *Lincoln at Gettysburg: The Words That Remade America* (New York: Simon & Schuster, 1992), 36, 269 n. 27. Wills cites Frank L. Klement. Complete appraisals of Lincoln's remarks are in Don E. Fehrenbacher and Virginia Fehrenbacher, *Recollected Words of Abraham Lincoln* (Stanford: Stanford University Press, 1996).

4. "History versus Criticism in the Study of Literature" (1935), in R. S. Crane, *Idea of the Humanities and Other Essays Critical and Historical*, 2 vols. (Chicago: University of Chicago Press, 1967), 2: 13. For discussion of these issues, see Howard D. Weinbrot, "Historical Criticism, Hypotheses, and Eighteenth-Century Studies: The Case for Induction and Neutral Knowledge," in *Theory and Tradition in Eighteenth-Century Studies*, ed. Richard B. Schwartz (Carbondale: Southern Illinois University Press, 1990), 66–92.

5. Frederick Douglass, *Narrative of the Life of Frederick Douglass, An American Slave, Written by Himself*, ed. Benjamin Quarles (Cambridge: Harvard University Press, 1960), 58–59, 66–67. Other authors of slave narratives who link literacy, rhetoric, freedom, and power include William Wells Brown, Moses Grandy, James Pennington, and Thomas Smallwood.

Notes to Chapter 2: Burke's Poetry and Prophecy

1. I owe debts to Gerald Chapman's *Edmund Burke: The Practical Imagination* (Cambridge: Harvard University Press, 1967), and to his "Burke's American Tragedy," in *Johnson and His Age*, ed. James Engell (Cambridge: Harvard University Press, 1984), 387–423, esp. 392–94, which drew my attention to quotations and sources, particularly where Burke addresses American affairs. For example, Robert DeMaria, ed., *British Literature 1640–1789* (Oxford: Blackwell, 1996), contains only parts of the *Inquiry* and a dozen pages from the *Reflections*.

2. For a compressed antidote to such misreadings and a wise assessment of "Burke the Perennial Political Philosopher," see Peter J. Stanlis, *Edmund Burke, The Enlightenment and Revolution* (New Brunswick: Transaction Publishers, 1991), 104–11, esp. 107, 111. Conor Cruise O'Brien, *The Great Melody, A Thematic Biography and Commented Anthology of Edmund Burke* (Chicago: University of Chicago Press, 1992), may be fruitfully paired with Chapman's *Practical Imagination*. However, O'Brien is often speculative and his conclusions sometimes shaky, as Stanlis points out in his review essay in *The Modern Age* (Winter 1994): n.p. See also Harvey Mansfield, Jr., preface and introduction to *Selected Letters of Edmund Burke* (Chicago: University of Chicago Press, 1984); A. C. Goodson, "Burke's Orphics and Coleridge's Contrary Understanding," *The Wordsworth Circle* (Summer 1991); and, as correcting the introduction to the volume of the Oxford edition of the *Reflections* by L. G. Mitchell, the review essay of that volume by John Faulkner in *ECS* 24 (Summer 1991): 537–46. On the vacillating fortunes of the label "Tory" and the fact that Burke was associated with Whig and Tory views, see James Sack, *From Jacobite to Conservative: Reaction and Orthodoxy in Britain, c. 1760–1832* (Cambridge: Cambridge University Press, 1993), chap. 4, "Toryism redivivus," 64–111, esp. 64–66, 90–99; Faulkner's unpublished "Burke's Perception of Richard Price" shows Burke in something other than a stereotypical "conservative" light. In a well-informed but inflexible interpretation centering on the *Reflections*, Jürgen Klein sees Burke's error as an overreliance on traditional values: he fails to register changing economic and social conditions. But Mansfield's comment about Burke and the French Revolution is more accurate: "He loses credit for his foresight because he acted on it." In his introduction to *England zwischen Aufklärung und Romantik: Studien zur Literatur und Gesellschaft einer übergangsepoche* (Tübingen: Narr, 1983), 14–15, and in "Ethik und Politik bei Edmund Burke," 51–81, esp. 58, 62, 73, Klein downplays Burke's prophetic powers. Yet Klein's work deserves recognition among English-speaking scholars. For

the Graubard quotation, see *Burke, Disraeli, and Churchill: The Politics of Perseverance* (Cambridge: Harvard University Press, 1961), preface.

3. Steven Blakemore, "Burke and the Fall of Language: The French Revolution as Linguistic Event," *ECS* 17 (Spring 1984): 284–307, remarks on Burke's feeling that the insanity of the Revolution "is part of the new and pernicious power of the written word to pervert human nature" (302), and quotes Burke on the effect of French revolutionary writings: "These writings and sermons have filled the populace with a black and savage atrocity of mind, which supersedes in them the common feelings of Nature, as well as all sentiments of morality and religion . . ." (3: 435). However, Burke would not have thought such a potentially perverse power of the written word in any sense new. Blakemore, providing a helpful angle (286, 306), occasionally falls into categorical statements, for example, asserting that for Burke, language is "unchanging" (300); see also Blakemore's *Burke and the Fall of Language* (Hanover: University Press of New England, 1988). He adumbrates well the complexity of Burke's thought in "Burke and the Revolution: Bicentennial Reflections," in *Burke and the French Revolution: Bicentennial Essays,* ed. Steven Blakemore (University of Georgia Press, 1992), 144–67, esp. 144–45, 155–56.

4. For the "origin" and nature of Burke's political views, see the standard studies, Ross J. S. Hoffman and Paul Levack, eds., *Burke's Politics: Selected Writings and Speeches of Edmund Burke on Reform, Revolution, and War* (New York: Alfred A. Knopf, 1949), introduction, xi–xxxvii; Peter Stanlis, *Edmund Burke and the Natural Law* (Ann Arbor: University of Michigan Press, 1958); Alfred Cobban, *Edmund Burke and the Revolt against the Eighteenth Century: A Study of the Political and Social Thinking of Burke, Wordsworth, Coleridge, and Southey,* 2d ed. (London: G. Allen & Unwin, 1960); Chapman, *Practical Imagination*; and Francis P. Canavan, *The Political Reason of Edmund Burke* (Durham: Duke University Press, 1960). Those first approaching Burke's writing should consult W. J. Bate's still compelling introduction to *Edmund Burke: Selected Works* (New York: Modern Library, Random House, 1960), 3–39; Frank O'Gorman, *Edmund Burke: His Political Philosophy* (Bloomington: Indiana University Press, 1973); and Reed Browning, "The Origin of Burke's Ideas Revisited," *ECS* 18 (Fall 1984): 57–71. Browning's first three notes provide general references. His conclusion, that Burke draws directly on Cicero, the court Whigs, and Robert Walpole, is anticipated in part by others, including Graubard, *Burke, Disraeli, and Churchill: The Politics of Perseverance,* 78–79. Daniel E. Ritchie, ed., *Edmund Burke: Appraisals and Applications* (New Brunswick: Transaction, 1990), is an excellent compilation of views from Coleridge through Raymond Williams and Robert Nisbet.

5. Browning ends his study by calling "Burke's rhetorical gift" his "greatest contribution" (71). Yet Burke is not simply "garbing" what Browning terms "a body of received doctrine." This could hardly be said, for instance, of his writings on India. Claude Rawson, in "Revolution in the Moral Wardrobe: Mutations of an Image from Dryden to Burke," in *Satire and Sentiment 1660–1830* (Cambridge: Cambridge University Press, 1994), 133–96, shows how the image of dress, drapery, and ornament is related to the fundamental movement of Burke's thought and his view of human nature and societies: the power and method of his language and of his intellect are inseparable. Burke's use of literary models is well explored by Frans De Bruyn, *The Literary Genres of Edmund Burke: The Political Uses of Literary Form* (Oxford: Clarendon, 1996). De Bruyn is best on Burke's use of satire, the pastoral, and drama, but devotes an epilogue to "The Prophetic Burke" (283–97), where he highlights Burke's use of the jeremiad.

6. *The Parliamentary History of England from the earliest period to the year 1803,* ed. W. Cobbett, 36 vols. (London, 1806–1820), 23: 613 (March 7, 1783), hereafter cited as *PH.* This and the three following quotations are cited from Chapman's "Burke's American Tragedy," 391, 390 n, 415, 417.

7. *PH,* 28: 361 (February 5, 1790); see Blakemore, "Burke and the Fall of Language," 284. For Burke's view of the Revolution of 1688, see also *Reflections* in *The Works of the Right Honorable Edmund Burke,* 12 vols. (Boston: Little, Brown, 1865–67), 3: 252–54, 270–71. This is a standard American edition. Some later Little, Brown editions have different pagination. Hereafter citations from *Works* are given in the text by volume and page.

8. To the Duke of Richmond, *The Correspondence of Edmund Burke,* ed. Thomas W. Copeland et

al., 10 vols. (Chicago: University of Chicago Press, 1958–78), 3: 217 (September 26, 1775). Hereafter cited as *C.*

9. To the marquess of Rockingham, *C,* 3: 278.

10. Thomas Somerville, *My Own Life and Times, 1741–1814* (Edinburgh, 1861), 222; quoted by Chapman, "Burke's American Tragedy," 417.

11. To Richard Shackleton, March 3, 1783, Wentworth House Papers.

12. Northhampton MSS, A.xxvii.87; quoted by Chapman, "Burke's American Tragedy," 422.

13. *The Letters of David Hume,* ed. J. Y. T. Greig, 2 vols. (Oxford: Clarendon, 1932), 1: 126.

14. *Biographia Literaria,* eds. James Engell and W. J. Bate, 2 vols. (Princeton and London: Princeton University Press and Routledge & Kegan Paul, 1983), 1: 217, 190–92. Notes give additional information and references for Coleridge on Burke.

15. See Coleridge's tart remarks on Wordsworth's lines, *Biographia,* 2: 138. There the image of the eye and its surview are connected with prophecy. For Burke's profound impact on Wordsworth, see James K. Chandler, *Wordsworth's Second Nature: A Study of the Poetry and Politics* (Chicago: University of Chicago Press, 1984).

16. See *Collected Letters of Samuel Taylor Coleridge,* ed. E. L. Griggs, 6 vols. (Oxford: Clarendon, 1956–71), 2: 1160 (no. 614 to Robert Southey and n), and *The Notebooks of Samuel Taylor Coleridge,* ed. Kathleen Coburn, 4 vols., text and notes (Princeton and London: Princeton University Press and Routledge & Kegan Paul, 1957–), 2: 2342–43, and nn. Coleridge's seal does not contain an eye, but notebook entries indicate a connection with the "heavenly father." Vico scholars comment on the symbolism of the frontispiece, its connection with poetry, prophecy, and a providential eye bestowing wisdom and light.

17. Cited by Blakemore ("Burke and the Fall of Language," 289), though printed with a misplaced quotation mark.

18. In the *Inquiry* Burke recognizes the power of the Hebrew prophets and sees in their language the proof that "Scripture alone can supply ideas answerable to the subject [of God]."

19. See Chapman, "Burke's American Tragedy," 398–99. Blakemore ("Burke and the Fall of Language," 295–96) contends Burke's use of Latin was at times the conscious exercise of a "gentlemanly" class, part of an "insider's" passport used to exclude others and snub their class struggle. But as a full view of Burke's Latin or English quotations this is inadequate.

20. For a full-length study of this issue in Blake, see David V. Erdman, *Blake: Prophet Against Empire, A Poet's Interpretation of the History of His Own Times* (Princeton: Princeton University Press, 1954), esp. 9–10, 169, 191, 201–2, which stresses the differences Blake felt with Burke over the French Revolution; see also William Richey, "*The French Revolution*: Blake's Epic Dialogue with Edmund Burke," *ELH* 59 (1992): 817–37.

21. For Burke on parliamentary reform, see Chapman, *Practical Imagination,* 116–79, esp. 117, 121–31. Burke on slavery and the slave trade presents a complicated set of issues best elucidated in Robert W. Smith, "Edmund Burke's Negro Code," *History Today* 26 (1976): 715–23, an article too rarely cited. For Ireland, see James Conniff, "Edmund Burke's Reflections on the Coming Revolution in Ireland," *JHI* 47 (January–March 1986): 37–59; Louis Cullen, "Burke, Ireland, and Revolution," *ECL* 16 (February 1992): 21–42; and Conniff, *The Useful Cobbler: Edmund Burke and the Politics of Progress* (Albany: State University of New York Press, 1994), esp. 1–51, 251–73. For Burke on religious toleration, see Michael W. McConnell, "Establishment and Toleration in Edmund Burke's 'Constitution of Freedom,' " *The Supreme Court Review 1995,* eds. Dennis J. Hutchinson, David A. Strauss, and Geoffrey R. Stone (Chicago: University of Chicago Press): 393–462, which is an excellent treatment. The best, complete study of Burke on India is now Frederick G. Whelan, *Edmund Burke and India: Political Morality and Empire* (Pittsburgh: University of Pittsburgh Press, 1996). This book acutely recognizes the importance of India in the whole of Burke's political and moral thought.

22. *PH,* 21 (February 20, 1781), 1292–93; Chapman cites Pope's same lines used by Burke seven years earlier to refer to the Intolerable Acts before the War, "Burke's American Tragedy," 409.

23. See *C,* 6: 216 n, which quotes the wife of the British minister at Turin in 1791.

24. *Notes: Printed but Not Published* (British Library), p. 209.

25. For the comparison see Chapman, "Burke's American Tragedy," 394, and Cobban (n. 4 above). Coleridge's view proceeds in *Biographia* 2: 48–49, 58–59, where he discusses surview of mind evidenced through poetic language.

26. The comparison to Priam's daughter struck Graubard in closing his first section of *Burke, Disraeli, and Churchill,* 85.

27. For a sensitive reading of *Reflections* in this light, see James Boyd White, "Making a Public World: The Constitution of Language and Community in Burke's *Reflections,*" in *When Words Lose Their Meaning: Constitutions and Reconstitutions of Language, Character, and Community* (Chicago: University of Chicago Press, 1984), 192–230.

28. *Biographia,* 1: 190 and n.

29. To Sir Gilbert Elliot, September 3, 1788, *C,* 5: 415. For pertinent discussion and quotation, see Chapman, "Burke's American Tragedy," 401, 388 and n, 393, and *Edmund Burke: The Practical Imagination,* 85–86; also Charles Parkin, *The Moral Basis of Burke's Political Thought* (Cambridge: Cambridge University Press, 1956), "The Religious Basis of Burke's Moral Belief," 131–38; and White, *When Words Lose Their Meaning,* 213–16.

30. Sheffield MSS, bk. 27/229, *PH* 18: 233; quoted by Chapman, "Burke's American Tragedy," 409–10.

Notes to Chapter 3: Pope's American Constitution

1. William Ayre, *Memoirs of the Life and Writings of Alexander Pope, Esq.,* 2 vols. (1745), 2: 231. For identification of Ayre as Curll, see Howard D. Weinbrot, "The *Dunciad,* Nursing Mothers, and Isaiah," *PQ* 71 (1992): 479–94, specifically 493.

2. *Edward Gibbon: Memoirs of My Life,* ed. Georges A. Bonnard (London, 1966), 248.

3. For example, *The Reformer* (January 28, 1747–48), 1.

4. Leon Howard, *The Connecticut Wits* (Chicago: University of Chicago Press, 1943), 199, 200, 130. William C. Dowling (*Poetry and Ideology in Revolutionary Connecticut* [Athens: University of Georgia Press, 1990]) briefly mentions *The Anarchiad,* but he discusses it elsewhere (n. 5 below). His argument about "County" ideology and transatlantic connections is interesting.

5. William K. Bottorff cites these sources in his fine introduction to *The Anarchiad* (Gainesville: Scholars' Facsimiles & Reprints, 1967), vii–viii: Charles B. Todd, *Life and Letters of Joel Barlow* (1886); William Bradley Otis, *American Verse, 1625–1807: A History* (1909); Vernon L. Parrington, ed., *The Connecticut Wits* (1926); Marcia E. Bailey, *A Lesser Hartford Wit: Dr. Elihu Hubbard Smith, 1771–1798* (1928); and Theodore A. Zunder, *The Early Days of Joel Barlow* (1934). Dowling cites Bottorff in "Joel Barlow and *The Anarchiad,*" *EAL* 25: 1 (1990): 18–33, but contends that Barlow, despite writing the tenth number of the poem, diverged from the other Wits. Dowling seems cool to Bottorff's evidence regarding the impact of the poem: "So far as the tenth number of *The Anarchiad* contributed to that last reactivation of consensus, and thus to the making of the Constitution, it was Joel Barlow's valedictory gift to the Connecticut friends whose values, at bottom, he had never really shared" (28). How far "so far" is, however, is not clear. J. K. Van Dover, recognizing the connection with *The Dunciad* in "The Design of Anarchy: *The Anarchiad,* 1786–1787," *EAL* 24: 3 (1989): 237–47, is tentative: for him, the poem "represents the most substantial literary response to the forces and events that precipitated the Constitutional Convention in May 1787 . . ." and "*The Anarchiad* was widely read in its time" (237). But, in context, his statement that "It may not have contributed to the shape of the Constitution" (237) implies that it did not. Yet, he says "may" and does not deny that it contributed to the *approval* of the Constitution.

6. John P. Kaminski and Gaspare J. Saladino, eds., *The Documentary History of the Ratification of the Constitution,* vol. 3, ed. Merrill Jensen (1978), 355 n, 325–26.

7. Frederick M. Keener, "Pope, *The Dunciad,* Virgil, and the New Historicism of Le Bossu," *ECL* 15 (November 1991): 35–57; 43, 50–55, mentions the "anti-monarchical or at least anti-Georgian" tendencies of the poem and its critique of aristocracy.

8. *The Correspondence of Jonathan Swift,* ed. Harold Williams, 5 vols. (Oxford: Clarendon Press, 1963–65), 3: 293 (July 16, 1728).

9. Samuel Johnson, review of Joseph Warton's *Essay* (vol. 1) in *The Literary Magazine* (1756), 1: 38.

10. Joseph Warton, *An Essay on the Genius and Writings of Pope,* 2 vols. (London: Thomas Maiden, 1806), 2: 383–84.

11. Theophilus Cibber and Robert Shiels, *Lives of the Poets of Great-Britain and Ireland,* 5 vols. (London: R. Griffith, 1753), 5: 247.

12. Percival Stockdale, *An Inquiry into the Nature, and Genuine Laws of Poetry; including A particular Defence of the Writings, and Genius of Mr. Pope* (London: N. Conant, 1778), 184–85. For Stockdale, a curious figure, see Howard Weinbrot, "Samuel Johnson, Percival Stockdale, and Brick-bats from Grub-street: Some Later Response to the *Lives of the Poets,*" *HLQ* 56 (1993): 105–34.

13. Owen Ruffhead, *The Life of Alexander Pope, Esq. compiled from Original Manuscripts; with a Critical Essay on his Writings and Genius* (London: C. Bathurst, 1769), 347 n, 377.

14. Warton, 2: 319.

15. Michael DePorte, "Avenging Naboth: Swift and Monarchy," *PQ* 69: 4 (1990).

16. Ayre, 2: 154–55.

17. Cibber and Shiels, 5: 235, 247.

18. Ruffhead, 17–18, 29, 335–39.

19. Stockdale, 1–2.

20. Warton, 2: 328, 329, 341–42, 352–53.

21. Howard, 39, 50, 68, 114, 212.

22. Agnes Marie Sibley, *Alexander Pope's Prestige in America, 1725–1835* (New York: King's Crown Press of Columbia University, 1949), 90.

23. Bottorff, viii–ix. He quotes the "surprising switch of Connecticut" from Clinton Rossiter, *1787: The Grand Convention* (New York: Macmillan, 1966), 191.

Notes to Chapter 4: Swift Considers Words, Intelligence, and the Academy

1. *The Correspondence of Jonathan Swift,* ed. Harold Williams, 5 vols. (Oxford: Clarendon Press, 1963–65), 3: 179, 183, 189 (spelling modernized; cited hereafter in the text).

2. See Michael DePorte, "Teaching the Third Voyage," *Approaches to Teaching Swift's* Gulliver's Travels, ed. Edward J. Rielly and Michael DePorte (New York: MLA, 1988), 57–62.

3. S. T. Coleridge, *Lectures 1809–1818 On Literature,* ed. R. A. Foakes, 2 vols. (Princeton and London: Princeton University Press and Routledge & Kegan Paul, 1987), 2: 180–82.

4. See comments connecting Swift and academies in Jay Tribby's review of David S. Lux, *Patronage and Royal Science in Seventeenth-Century France: The Académie de Physique in Caen,* and Alice Stroup, *A Company of Scientists: Botany, Patronage, and Community at the Seventeenth-Century Parisian Royal Academy of Sciences,* in *ECS* 24: 4 (Summer 1991): 519–24, 524.

5. Norman O. Brown, "The Excremental Vision," originally in *Life Against Death: The Psychoanalytical Meaning of History* (Middletown and London: Wesleyan University Press and Routledge & Kegan Paul, 1959), 179–201.

6. For example, John Munro, "Book III of *Gulliver's Travels* Once More," *English Studies* 49

(1968): 429–36; Ila Dawson Traldi, "Gulliver the 'Educated Fool': Unity in the Voyage to Laputa," *PLL* 4 (1968): 35–50; Jenny Mezciems, "The Unity of Swift's 'Voyage to Laputa': Structure as Meaning in Utopian Fiction," *MLR* 72 (1977): 1–21. Douglas Lane Patey, "Swift's Satire on 'Science' and the Structure of *Gulliver's Travels,*" *ELH* 58 (1991): 809–39: "What Swift has in fact done in Laputa is to recreate a special skirmish in the quarrel between Ancients and Moderns, as that quarrel entered the educational philosophy of his time" (821). See also *Gulliver's Travels,* ed. Christopher Fox (New York: Bedford Books, 1995), 8–10.

7. John N. Sutherland, "A Reconsideration of Gulliver's Third Voyage," *SP* 54 (1957): 45–52; Patey (823) touches the issue of intellectual pride; for semiotics, see Martin J. Croghan, "Savage Indignation: An Introduction to the Philosophy of Language and Semiotics in Jonathan Swift," *Swift Studies* 5 (1990): 11–37; Clive T. Probyn, "Swift and Linguistics: The Context behind Lagado and around the Fourth Voyage," *Neophilologus* 58 (1974): 425–39; Brian Tippett ("Into the World of Words," in Gulliver's Travels: *The Critics Debate* [London: Macmillan, 1989], 82–91) suggests much for the third voyage and cites Probyn. Orwell's essay (1946) appears in *Inside the Whole and Other Essays* (London: Penguin, 1957), 121–42; 131, for the quotation. For a recent overview, see Howard Erskine-Hill, *Jonathan Swift: Gulliver's Travels* (Cambridge: Cambridge University Press, 1993).

8. Paul J. Korshin, "Deciphering Swift's Codes," *Proceedings of the First Münster Symposium on Jonathan Swift,* eds. Hermann J. Real and Heinz J. Vienken (1985): 123–34, esp. 131–32. Patey (812) shrewdly links Swift's views on "science" with Pope's on "the theory of proper criticism" in his *Essay on Criticism.*

9. A fascinating account of these and other literary/intelligence connections appears in Eliot Weinberger, *Outside Stories* (New York: New Directions, 1992). Korshin (123–25) uses Graham Greene's *Human Factor* as an entrée for his discussion of Swift. Characters in Greene's novel use copies of Samuel Richardson's *Clarissa* to establish a "book code." William H. Epstein, "Assumed Identities: Gray's Correspondence and the 'Intelligence Communities' of Eighteenth-Century Studies," *EC* 32 (Autumn 1991): 274–88, argues unconvincingly that certain American scholars, including those at Yale, shouldered responsibility for the Cold War.

10. Kathleen Williams, "Gulliver in Laputa," in her *Jonathan Swift and the Age of Compromise* (Lawrence: University of Kansas Press, 1958), 60–63, 66. Griffin ("Interpretation and Power: Swift's *Tale of a Tub,*" *EC* 34: 2 [1993]: 151–68) states that for Swift, "interpretation means power . . . a means of gaining power"; "Interpretation is politics at the verbal level"; and "imposing an interpretation . . . was a matter with direct political consequences." He mentions the third voyage briefly, the project of "abolishing all Words" at the end (152–53, 163, 167).

11. F. P. Lock, *The Politics of* Gulliver's Travels (Oxford: Clarendon Press, 1980), 135.

12. The most thorough, judicious account, not only of the Senate hearings involving Thomas and Hill, but of the politicized nomination process leading to them is Jane Mayer and Jill Abramson, *Strange Justice: The Selling of Clarence Thomas* (Boston: Houghton Mifflin, 1994); see esp. 280–350.

13. *Harvard Scholars in English, 1890–1990,* ed. W. J. Bate, Michael Shinagel, and James Engell (Cambridge: Harvard University Printing Office, 1991), 51. The colleague is Bate.

14. George Campbell, *The Philosophy of Rhetoric,* 2 vols. (London: W. Strahan, 1776), 2: 125–29, 127–29 n; Edgar Mertner, " 'Communication Without Language': A Note on *Gulliver's Travels,* III, v, 21," *Swift Studies* 3 (1988): 124; Brean Hammond, Gulliver's Travels, *Open Guides to Literature* (Philadelphia: Open University Press and Milton Keynes, 1988), 67.

Notes to Chapter 5: Hume's Cultural Critique

1. See Nathan A. Scott, Jr., "The New Trahison des Clercs: Reflections on the Present Crisis in Humanistic Study," *Virginia Quarterly Review* (Summer 1986); and W. Jackson Bate, "The Crisis in English Studies," *Harvard Magazine* (September–October 1982).

2. *A Treatise of Human Nature,* ed. L. A. Selby-Bigge, 2d ed., rev. Peter Nidditch (Oxford: Clarendon Press, 1978), 222–23; *An Inquiry concerning Human Understanding* (Bobbs-Merrill, 1957), 170; *Essays Moral, Political, and Literary* (Indianapolis: Liberty, 1987), 486.

3. *Treatise,* 469–70, 619–20. David Fate Norton makes this case superbly in *David Hume: Common-Sense Moralist, Sceptical Metaphysician* (Princeton: Princeton University Press, 1982), esp. 114–20, 138–40, 150, 237–38, 278–84; while Norton tends to isolate Hume's common sense morality from other parts of his philosophy, I argue that in the analysis of culture this cannot be done, since culture involves both morality and systematic knowledge. Norton is anticipated in part by Terence Penelhum, Wade Robison, Richard H. Popkin, and Páll Ardal—all cited by Norton—and also by T. E. Jessop, "Hume's Limited Scepticism," and E. Griffin-Collart, "Les croyances naturelles de Hume et les principes de sens commun de Reid," in *Revue Internationale de Philosophie* 115–16 (1976): 3–27, 126–42, respectively. See also John P. Wright, *The Sceptical Realism of David Hume* (Minneapolis: University of Minnesota Press, 1983); Nicholas Capaldi, *Hume's Place in Moral Philosophy* (New York: Peter Lang, 1989); and Marie A. Martin, "Hutcheson and Hume on Explaining the Nature of Morality: Why It Is Mistaken to Suppose Hume Ever Raised the 'Is-Ought' Question," *History of Philosophy Quarterly* 8 (July 1991): 277–89. On emotion in Hume's view of morality, a germane supplement is Corliss G. Swain, "Passionate Objectivity," *Noûs* 26: 4 (1992): 465–90.

On aesthetic judgment, see James Engell, "The Source, and End, and Test of Art: Hume's Critique," in *Johnson and His Age,* ed. Engell (Cambridge: Harvard University Press, 1984), 233–53, and *Forming the Critical Mind* (Cambridge: Harvard University Press, 1989), 103–25. In addition, see David Marshall, "Arguing by Analogy: Hume's Standard of Taste," *ECS* 28: 3 (1995): 323–43; however, Hume does not conclude, as Marshall states, that "the standard of taste must be located in an exemplar or authority" (324). Some "very rare critics" are better than others, but the standard—whatever it is—might not be obtained by one critic or group. Marshall is right to stress that, "In Hume's view, all who seek the standard of taste must enter into argument" (338), but Hume bases his own argument on "shared experience," not on "universal agreement" (335); they are not the same.

4. Box, *The Suasive Art of David Hume* (Princeton: Princeton University Press, 1990), 97–99, 255, 4; *Boswell's London Journal, 1762–1763, together with Journal of My Jaunt, Harvest 1762,* ed. Frederick A. Pottle (London: William Heinemann, 1951), 104. Mossner, *The Forgotten Hume: Le Bon David* (New York: Columbia University Press, 1943), 195.

5. For example, Richard H. Schlagel, "A Reasonable Reply to Hume's Scepticism," *British Journal for the Philosophy of Science* 35 (1984): 359–74, and "Meeting Hume's Skeptical Challenge," *Review of Metaphysics* 45 (June 1992): 691–711.

6. *Treatise,* 146, 150; Marie A. Martin, "The Rational Warrant for Hume's General Rules," *Journal of the History of Philosophy* 31 (April 1993): 245–57, esp. 247–51, 256–57. Martin explains the operation of general rules, earlier discussed by Thomas K. Hearn, Jr., and accepted as basic to Hume's thought by, among others, Capaldi and Norton. Hearn ("General Rules in Hume's *Treatise,*" *Journal of the History of Philosophy* 8 [1970]: 405–22) stresses how moral sentiments are corrected by an appeal to general rules; see also Annette C. Baier, *A Progress of Sentiments: Reflections on Hume's "Treatise"* (Cambridge: Harvard University Press, 1991).

7. Richard H. Popkin, "New Views on the Role of Skepticism in the Enlightenment," *MLQ* 53 (September 1992): 279–97; 285, for the direct quotation.

8. Barbara Herrnstein Smith, *Contingencies of Value* (Cambridge: Harvard University Press, 1989).

9. Peter Jones, "Hume and the Beginnings of Modern Aesthetics," *The Science of Man in the Scottish Enlightenment: Hume, Reid, and Their Contemporaries,* ed. Jones (Edinburgh: Edinburgh University Press, 1989), 54–67; 55, for the quotation.

10. For discussion, see M. Jamie Ferreira, *Scepticism and Reasonable Doubt: The British Naturalist Tradition in Wilkins, Hume, Reid, and Newman* (Oxford: Clarendon Press, 1986), 41–58, 237, esp. 41, 52, 58.

11. *Treatise,* 183, 185, emphasis added; *Dialogues,* ed. Henry D. Aiken (New York: Hafner, 1957), 7.

12. Ferreira, 41; Box remarks, "One way to mitigated scepticism is to graduate to it after grappling with Pyrrhonism" (191); it is not merely an act of despair or of pragmatism faced with no better alternative. On skepticism, drawing on Ferreira's work, see Ieuan Williams, "Faith and Scepticism: Newman and the Naturalist Tradition," *Philosophical Investigations* 15 (January 1992): 51–66, esp. 51–52, 54–58; on Pyrrhonism and skepticism see Popkin, "New Views," where he revises his earlier work and remarks that, "the problem of packaging the various types and strands of skepticism in the period is far more complicated than I previously thought" (280), and that Hume "consciously wedded Bayle's total Pyrrhonism with the naturalistic moral science of the Scots" (283), which is akin to Box's remark that Hume graduates out of Pyrrhonism; see also Richard H. Popkin, "Bayle and Hume," *The High Road to Pyrrhonism* (Indianapolis: Hackett, 1989), 149–60. Beverley C. Southgate, " 'Cauterising the Tumour of Pyrrhonism': Blackloism versus Skepticism," *JHI* 53 (October–December 1992): 631–45, discusses the tidal flows of dogmatism and skepticism in England a hundred years before Hume. For Hume's modesty and fear of having been betrayed into dogmatism, see Donald T. Siebert, *The Moral Animus of David Hume* (Newark: University of Delaware Press, 1990), 175; this book is a fine examination of Hume the practical moralist.

13. See Terence Penelhum, *David Hume, An Introduction to His Philosophical System* (West Lafayette: Purdue University Press, 1992), 20; and Adam Potkay, "Classical Eloquence and Polite Style in the Age of Hume," *ECS* 25 (Fall 1991): 31–56; 41, 54, for the quotations.

14. *Essays,* 202; Box, 58. For Hume's historical perspective, see Siebert, 69–104, esp. 92–93, 110–11.

15. Leo Damrosch (*Fictions of Reality in the Age of Hume and Johnson* [Madison: University of Wisconsin Press, 1989]) argues for Hume and Johnson as realists and empiricists with no illusions about the "ultimate truth" of our (or their) constructions of reality; Box, 99; Popkin, "New Views," 281, 289.

16. For analysis of the ACLS booklet, see Tzvetan Todorov, "Crimes Against Humanities," *The New Republic* (July 3, 1989): 26–30; 29, for the quotation.

17. George Levine, Peter Brooks, Jonathan Culler, Marjorie Garber, E. Ann Kaplan, Catharine R. Stimpson, *Speaking for the Humanities,* ACLS Occasional Paper No. 7 (1989), 2, 11, 18, 10, 13, 11, 31, 9, 18, 9, 32, 8, 9, 15, for the quotations. For pertinent discussion of Rorty, relativism, and contingency, see Richard J. Bernstein, *Beyond Objectivism and Relativism: Science, Hermeneutics, and Praxis* (Oxford: Basil Blackwell, 1983), 197–207.

18. John R. Searle, "Is There a Crisis in American Higher Education?" *Stated Meeting Report of the American Philosophical Society* (April 10, 1992): 24–47; for his attack on the ACLS booklet, see 36, 39; *Partisan Review* later published "Is There a Crisis?" Searle is hard on Rorty; Bernstein's view (see n. 17 above) seems more accurate.

19. On the danger of political principles guiding philosophy and education, see Box, 155.

20. *The Philosophical Works,* ed. T. H. Green and T. H. Grose, 4 vols. (Darmstadt: Scientia Verlag Aalen, 1964 [repr. London, 1882]), 3: 252n; see Richard H. Popkin, "Hume's Racism," *The Philosophical Forum: A Quarterly* 9 (1977–78): 211–26.

21. Penelhum, 29–30.

22. Box, 199.

23. John Richetti, *Philosophical Writing: Locke, Berkeley, Hume* (Cambridge: Harvard University Press, 1983), 17; earlier work includes Michael Morrisroe, Jr., "Linguistic Analysis as Rhetorical Pattern in David Hume," *Hume and the Enlightenment: Essays Presented to Ernest Campbell Mossner,* ed. William B. Todd (Edinburgh: Edinburgh University Press, 1974). Paula Wood Brown, *The Unnatural Aspects of Natural Religion Revealed: A Skeptical Reader's Response to Hume's* Dialogues," *SECC* 22 (1992): 269–80; 279, for the quotation; see also, on Hume's style and dialogue, Dennis Rohatyn, "Hume's Dialectical Conceits: The Case of *Dialogue* XII," *Philosophy and Phenomenological Research* 43 (June 1983): 519–32,

esp. 531. For Rorty, see especially *Philosophy and the Mirror of Nature* (Princeton: Princeton University Press, 1979); for dialogue as a rhetorical practice in culture, see Don H. Bialostosky, "Dialogics as an Art of Discourse in Literary Criticism," *PMLA* 101 (October 1986): 788–97. Raymond Williams, "David Hume: Reasoning and Experience," in *The English Mind: Studies in the English Moralists Presented to Basil Willey,* ed. Hugh Sykes Davies and George Watson (Cambridge: Cambridge University Press, 1964), 123–45; 123, for the quotation.

24. Cited by Berlin, *Against the Current: Essays in the History of Ideas,* ed. Henry Hardy (New York: Viking, 1980), 171, 173; Edinburgh University Press published Berlin's essay in 1977.

Notes to Chapter 6: Vico Tells the Story of Stories

1. Vico makes a similar point about the education of the young and the dangers of "analysis" in his letter to Francesco Saverio Estevan, discussed in Michael Mooney, *Vico in the Tradition of Rhetoric* (Princeton: Princeton University Press, 1985), 100–102. References in the text to the *New Science* are by paragraph from *The New Science of Giambattista Vico,* trans. Thomas Goddard Bergin and Max Harold Fisch (Ithaca: Cornell University Press, 1968). Parts of this essay appeared in "Leading Out Into the World: Vico's New Education," *New Vico Studies* 3 (1985): 33–47, and in a review article of Jerome Bruner, *Acts of Meaning, New Vico Studies* 10 (1992).

2. Alain Pons ("L'Invention chez Vico," in *La sexualité: D'où vient l'Orient? Où va l'Occident? Documents du Congrès de Tokyo, "La Deuxième Renaissance"* [Paris: Belfond, 1984], 159–69) provides discussion of invention and ingenuity; see also Mooney, 135–58, esp. 135–36, 150–53.

3. Roger Poole's paper "'Fantasia'—A Name without a Thing, or a Thing without a Name?" presented at the Vico conference in Venice (1978), suggests biographical insights regarding imagination and the formation of character by comparing Bentham and Vico; see also D. P. Verene, "The New Art of Narration: Vico and the Muses," *New Vico Studies,* vol. 1 (Atlantic Highlands, N.J.: Humanities Press, 1983), 23.

4. See, for instance, Mooney, 77, 261–62.

5. See Pons, 162; Verene, "The New Art of Narration," 21–23; Mooney, 132–35.

6. Mooney (106–14) discusses the ideal of the sage committed to public life.

7. Wider context is provided by Hayden White, "Vico and the Radical Wing of Structuralist/ Poststructuralist Thought Today," *New Vico Studies* (1983): 63–68, esp. 66.

8. Joseph Mali, *The Rehabilitation of Myth: Vico's 'New Science,'* (Cambridge: Cambridge University Press, 1992), 3–5, 11, 13, 33, 69, 126–31, 147, 165–67, 180–81, 203, 209. Three books that nicely fit this view without focusing on Vico are Martha C. Nussbaum, *Poetic Justice: The Literary Imagination and Public Life* (Boston: Beacon Press, 1995); Adam Zachary Newton, *Narrative Ethics* (Cambridge: Harvard University Press, 1995); and Mark Turner, *The Literary Mind* (New York: Oxford University Press, 1997). These books treat narrative and myth as an ethical but untraditional teacher also providing a basis for social morality, cognition, and reason.

9. For the relation of history to philosophy and philology, see Mooney, 184–86.

10. Jerome Bruner, *Acts of Meaning* (Cambridge: Harvard University Press, 1990), ix.; references hereafter are parenthetical.

11. See James Engell, *The Creative Imagination: Enlightenment to Romanticism* (Cambridge: Harvard University Press, 1981).

12. Pons, 159.

13. See D. P. Verene, *Vico's Science of Imagination* (Ithaca: Cornell University Press, 1981), 32–35, on imagination and a philosophy of *Leben* or existence; Verene notes (40) that Vico "advocates the value of imagination and memory as the basis of education"; see also Mooney, 116–25, esp. 116: "As in the learning process itself, concern for the aim of education flows quietly through the whole of Vico's

discourse [*De ratione*]." For Vico as a guide for modern liberal pedagogy, see Giorgio Tagliacozzo, "General Education as Unity of Knowledge: A Theory Based on Vichian Principles," *Vico and Contemporary Thought* (Atlantic Highlands, N.J.: Humanities Press, 1979), pt. 2, esp. 136–38.

14. As Verene states, "Vico's science is performative"; see *Vico's Science*, 156; also 99, 107, 125.

15. See Verene, "The New Art of Narration," 35–36. See also "Vico's Philosophy of Imagination," *Vico and Contemporary Thought*, pt. 1, 20–43, subsumed in *Vico's Science of Imagination*, where Verene states, "there are two kinds of *fantasia* in the *New Science*—poetic or mythic *fantasia* and recollective or philosophic *fantasia*" (11; cf. 97, 194).

16. Elizabeth Sewell, "Bacon, Vico, Coleridge, and Poetic Method," *Giambattista Vico: An International Symposium,* eds. Giorgio Tagliacozzo and Hayden V. White (Baltimore: The Johns Hopkins University Press, 1969), 125–36, notes that "hero" is a key word (125–26), and "voyaging and quest" (128) or a "dark journey" (133) represent key concepts for these three thinkers, who "are deeply interested in education" (129).

17. Giambattista Vico, *On the Study Methods of Our Time,* trans. with an introduction and notes by Elio Gianturco, and a preface and translation of "The Academies and the Relation between Philosophy and Eloquence" by Donald Phillip Verene (Ithaca: Cornell University Press, 1990), iii. Page references hereafter are parenthetical. *Study Methods* is the best introduction to Vico. For an earlier pairing of Bruner and Vico, see Maria Goretti, "Vico's Pedagogic Thought and That of Today," *Giambattista Vico: An International Symposium* (1969). Goretti notes that Bruner's *Process of Education* on the stages of education, from early childhood onward, approximates the stages and nature of education Vico envisions. Goretti grasps (574 n) that Bruner and Vico see self and culture bound together in one process of mutual development and becoming. The work of Henry J. Perkinson cited in Giorgio Tagliacozzo, Donald Verene, and Vanessa Rumble, *Bibliography of Vico in English 1884–1984* (Bowling Green: Philosophy Documentation Center, Bowling Green State University, 1986), 29–30, is germane, as is Tagliacozzo's "General Education as Unity of Knowledge: A Theory Based on Vichian Principles," *Vico and Contemporary Thought*, pt. 2.

18. For one attempt, see Verene, *Vico's Science,* 118–26, which emphasizes the imperfect state of human nature and knowledge and identifies the *storia ideale eterna* as "the principle of providence in history" (118).

Notes to Chapter 7: The Politics of Greed

1. While Pope composed *To Bathurst* in 1730–32, *Volpone* reached its greatest popularity on the contemporary stage. See R. G. Noyes, *Ben Jonson on the English Stage 1660–1776* (Cambridge: Harvard University Press, 1935), 69–70. Graham Nicholls notes this and identifies another verbal parallel with the play, in *N&Q* 21 (July 1974): 251–52. The phrase "the use of riches" from the title and others in the poem also echo Isaac Barrow's sermons, which Pope read. See Peter Dixon, *The World of Pope's Satires* (London: Methuen, 1968), 148 and n.

2. Earl R. Wasserman, *Pope's* Epistle to Bathurst: *A Critical Reading with An Edition of the Manuscripts* (Baltimore: The Johns Hopkins University Press, 1960). This is indispensable criticism. Also helpful are Reuben A. Brower, *Alexander Pope: The Poetry of Allusion* (London: Oxford University Press, 1959), 251–60; Maynard Mack, *The Garden and the City: Retirement and Politics in the Later Poetry of Pope 1731–1743* (Toronto: University of Toronto Press, 1969), 86–89, 173–74 n, esp. on Horatian allusion and the figure of Walpole in the poem, and *Alexander Pope: A Life* (New York and New Haven: Norton and Yale University Press, 1986), 513–21; Howard Weinbrot, *Alexander Pope and the Traditions of Formal Verse Satire* (Princeton: Princeton University Press, 1982), 175–79; and David B. Morris, *Alexander Pope: The Genius of Sense* (Cambridge: Harvard University Press, 1984), 182–88, 192, 205.

3. Coleridge, *Biographia Literaria,* eds. James Engell and W. Jackson Bate, 2 vols. (Princeton and

London: Princeton University Press and Routledge & Kegan Paul, 1983), 2: 122 (vol. 7 of *The Collected Works,* general eds. Kathleen Coburn and Bart Winer). The best extended work on the general subject is Marc Shell, *Money, Language, and Thought: Literary and Philosophical Economies from the Medieval to the Modern Era* (Berkeley: University of California Press, 1982). Shell does not discuss Pope. For a broad study, see Patrick Brantlinger, *Fictions of State: Culture and Credit in Britain 1699–1994* (Ithaca: Cornell University Press, 1996).

4. Fernand Braudel, *Capitalism and Material Life 1400–1800,* trans. Miriam Kochan (New York: Harper & Row, 1974 [*Civilisation Matérielle et Capitalisme,* Librairie Armand Colin, 1967]), 359; hereafter *CML.*

5. Quotations from *Bathurst* are cited from *The Twickenham Edition of the Poems of Alexander Pope,* general ed. John Butt, vol. 3 ii, ed. F. W. Bateson, *Epistles to Several Persons (Moral Essays)* (New Haven: Yale University Press, 1951).

6. Weinbrot (see n. 2 above) refers to this "as an emblem of dialectic" (175). Wasserman sees it as the rhetorical figure of *epitrope* and names Aristotle's *Nicomachean Ethics* as a model for the poem's design (21, 36–38).

7. Bateson (89–90 n) elaborates Pope's note.

8. For relevant background discussion, see Howard Erskine-Hill, "Pope and the Financial Revolution," in *Writers and Their Backgrounds: Alexander Pope,* ed. Peter Dixon (Athens: Ohio University Press, 1972), 200–29, and *The Social Milieu of Alexander Pope* (New Haven: Yale University Press, 1975), 103–31, 166–203. Braudel summarizes as follows: "The innovation of the Bank of England was that it added . . . a deliberately organised issuing bank, capable of offering ample credit in notes (whose total amount in fact far exceeded actual deposits)." Thus "It was like no other. . . . Its originality lay in the fact that it put into circulation notes of over twenty pounds sterling to begin with, and of five, ten and fifteen pounds later. Eventually the smallest notes were for ten pounds, the largest for a thousand, all bearing the signatures of the directors of the Bank" (*CML,* 360, 365–66).

9. See the standard work, P. G. M. Dickson, *The Financial Revolution in England: A Study in the Development of Public Credit* (Oxford: Oxford University Press, 1967); also W. R. Scott, *The Constitution and Finance of English, Scottish, and Irish Joint Stock Companies to 1720,* 3 vols. (Cambridge: Cambridge University Press, 1910–12). For developments after Pope, see H. V. Bowen, " 'The Pests of Human Society': Stockbrokers, Jobbers and Speculators in Mid-Eighteenth-Century Britain," *History* 78 (February 1993): 38–53. Bowen points out that while stock scandals exerted little impact on the average businessman, contemporary impression was to the contrary; the government could mount no practical control over stock trading. In the 1760s, some self-regulation began. Braudel gives a swift overview: "There are notes and notes. In the first place governmental orders, prototypes of bank notes, had multiplied in England from 1667 and the use of goldsmiths' notes, later called bankers' notes, was common earlier, in the middle of the century, for the London goldsmiths received silver on deposit against notes. . . . The bank note was born almost spontaneously from commercial usage. It was a matter of urgent necessity" (*CML,* 360).

10. Dixon (136; see n. 1 above) quotes Bolingbroke's "Dissertation upon Parties," first published as *Craftsman* no. 443; *CML,* 358.

11. *Alexander Pope: A Life,* 515. Wasserman (25, 32) sees the Sibylline leaves touching pagan and Christian contexts.

12. *CML,* p. 358, emphasis added.

13. *The Works of Alexander Pope,* vol. 3, ed. Whitwell Elwin and William John Courthope (London, 1871–89), 132, quoting Smith's *Wealth of Nations.*

14. Perhaps following Courthope, Paul J. Alpers ("Pope's *To Bathurst* and the Mandevillian State," in *Essential Articles for the Study of Alexander Pope,* rev. and enl., ed. Maynard Mack [Hamden, Conn.: Archon Books, 1968], 493–94) suggests Pope opposed paper currency. Wasserman corrects Courthope's opinion: "Pope obviously does *not* regard currency 'solely as an instrument of corruption' " (33–34).

There was precedent, however, for widespread paper currency to lapse. Parts of China enjoyed paper money from the ninth through fourteenth centuries, but silver bullion replaced it until paper was reintroduced in the nineteenth century; see John K. Fairbank, Edwin O. Reischauer, and Albert M. Craig, *A History of East Asian Civilization*, 2 vols. (Boston: Houghton Mifflin, 1960–65), 1: 219, 279, 303; 2: 97–98.

15. Fernand Braudel, *The Wheels of Commerce*, trans. Siân Reynolds (New York: Harper & Row, 1982 [Paris: Librairie Armand Colin, 1979]), 426.

16. See Wasserman (25 n), who derives the 50% figure from *A Discourse of Trade, Coyn, and Paper Credit* (1697) by Henry Pollexfen.

17. The view, forwarded by Laura Brown in her *Alexander Pope*, that the poet condoned the South Sea Company in its slave dealings, small and terminated in 1717, has been effectively disproved by Howard Weinbrot, "Recent Studies," *SEL* 25 (1985): 694. Dixon (n. 1 above), 139.

18. *CML*, 358.

19. The lines recall *Rape* 5: 139–40, referring to Partridge the astrologer: "And hence th'Egregious Wizard shall foredoom / The Fate of *Louis*, and the Fall of *Rome*."

20. Wasserman cites *worth* and other puns on lend and affords, where money language and moral language crisscross (29).

21. See Wasserman, 29, 46, 48. An attempt to link *worth* and *word* etymologically refers to Indo-European forms of *wer*. But *worth*, like Old English *weard*, derives from a base meaning "bound up in or involved," while *word* developed from a suffixed form of *wer* akin to Greek *rhetor*.

22. Line 286. Wasserman suggests this reflects the "scribbling on the walls of London houses," a form of graffiti (44).

23. Bateson, 110 n.

24. See Braudel's remarks, n. 8 above. For the sale and corruption of peerages at a later date in British history, see David Cannadine, "The Sale of Honours," and "The Attack on 'Decency'," in *The Decline and Fall of the British Aristocracy* (New Haven: Yale University Press, 1990), 308–25, 325–39, respectively. Cannadine cites one instance of corruption involving shares in the firm McVitie and Price. In 1924, the famous old dictum of Prime Minister Robert Walpole, "Every man has his price," was altered and applied to Prime Minister Ramsay MacDonald. MacDonald received an interest in the firm from Alexander Grant, whom he soon helped make a baronet. The new quip: "But not every man has his McVitie and Price." MacDonald returned his shares (322).

25. For identification of credit as "Lady Credit," see Paula R. Backscheider, "Defoe's Lady Credit," *HLQ* 44 (1981): 89–100; for connections between the feminine, credit, fashion, and the hysteria of stock markets, see Erin Mackie, "Lady Credit and the Strange Case of the Hoop-Petticoat," *CL* 20 (June 1993): 27–43, and Catherine Ingrassia, *Authorship, Commerce, and Gender in Early Eighteenth-Century England: A Culture of Paper Credit* (Cambridge: Cambridge University Press, 1998).

26. See *Essay on Criticism*, lines 315–17, 653–54. Critics note the similarity of the golden mean in *Bathurst* with passages in poems of the "*Opus Magnum*," 1729–44, e.g., *An Essay on Man*, 4: 155–94, 357–60; *CML*, 328.

27. Weinbrot (see n. 2 above), 179; "In the Horatian epistle to Bathurst, Pope made clear that Virtue was not an empty word" (315). Weinbrot compares this with virtue as an "empty boast" in *One Thousand Seven Hundred and Thirty Eight*.

28. Bateson, 96 n; line 372.

29. Wasserman, 54, 64–65, 92–93, 122–23.

30. See Vincent Carretta, "Pope's *Epistle to Bathurst* and the South Sea Bubble," *JEGP* 78 (April 1978): 229. Carretta argues for the poem's immediate political aims connected with the still fresh South Sea scandal and Bathurst's opposition role. Related studies not addressing *To Bathurst* include Christine Gerrard, *The Patriot Opposition to Walpole: Politics, Poetry, and National Myth 1725–1742* (Oxford: Clarendon Press, 1994), esp. chap. 4, "Pope, Politics, and Genre," 68–95; and Howard Erskine-Hill,

Poetry of Opposition and Revolution: Dryden to Wordsworth (Oxford: Clarendon Press, 1996). Despite the drift of Erskine-Hill's argument, I find no direct Jacobite support in *To Bathurst.*

Oliver Wendell Holmes, *One Hundred Days in Europe,* vol. 10, The Riverside Edition of the Writings of Oliver Wendell Holmes (Boston: Houghton Mifflin, 1893 [1887]), 138–39.

31. Elwin and Courthope, 3: 158.

32. From the section (54–55) where Wasserman calls attention to the irony of St. Stephen's name; the saint was the most important deacon in charge of distributing alms to the church's needy "pensioners."

33. Edward Gibbon, *The History of the Decline and Fall of the Roman Empire,* 7 vols., ed. J. B. Bury (London: Methuen, 1909), 1: 76 and n.

34. Wasserman, 102–3.

35. Compare, for instance, Wasserman, 102–3, 130–31.

36. *CML,* 328.

37. Martin Mayer (*The Greatest Ever Bank Robbery: The Collapse of the Savings and Loan Industry* [New York: Scribners, 1990]) makes this case convincingly.

38. See Job 2:9; Balaam echoes Bond, who in line 102 damns the poor.

Notes to Chapter 8: Robert Lowth, Unacknowledged Legislator

1. Robert Lowth, *Lectures on the Sacred Poetry of the Hebrews,* trans. G[eorge]. Gregory, 2 vols. (London: St. Paul's Church Yard: J. Johnson, 1787), 1: 123, 311; hereafter cited in the text.

2. Stephen Prickett, *Words and* The Word: *Language, Poetics, and Biblical Interpretation* (Cambridge: Cambridge University Press, 1986), 41. Prickett's treatment of Lowth is excellent.

3. Howard Weinbrot, *Britannia's Issue: The Rise of British Literature from Dryden to Ossian* (Cambridge: Cambridge University Press, 1993), 407; for discussion of Lowth, see 456–59.

4. James Kugel, *The Idea of Biblical Poetry: Parallelism and Its History* (New Haven: Yale University Press, 1981), 204, 286; Prickett, 106–7; Steven Goldsmith, *Unbuilding Jerusalem: Apocalypse and Romantic Representation* (Ithaca: Cornell University Press, 1993), 108, 110.

5. There is a tie between satire and certain prophetic modes, one recognized in Lowth's day. See Thomas Jemielity, *Satire and the Hebrew Prophets* (Louisville, K.Y.: Westminster/John Knox Press, 1992).

6. Kugel, 2–3 n, 15, 49 n, 57, 73–75, 202; Robert Alter, *The Art of Biblical Poetry* (New York: Basic Books, 1986), 3, 204. See also Kugel, "Poets and Prophecy: An Overview," in *Poetry and Prophecy* (Ithaca: Cornell University Press, 1990), 1–25. For a view differing from both Kugel and Alter, see Michael H. Floyd, "Falling Flat on our ars poetica, or Some Problems in Recent Studies of Biblical Poetry," in *The Psalms and other Studies on the Old Testament* (Nashota, Wis.: Nashota House Seminary, 1990), 118–31. For analysis of Lowth's achievement and Hebrew poetry, see Michael Patrick O'Connor, *Hebrew Verse Structure* (Winona Lake, Ind.: Eisenbrauns, 1980; Dissertation University of Michigan, 1978); from the perspective of religious studies, see Walter L. Reed, "A Poetics of the Bible: Problems and Possibilities," *Literature and Theology* 1 (September 1987): 154–66 (on Frye and Lowth), and Aelred Baker, "Parallelism: England's Contribution to Biblical Studies," *Catholic Biblical Quarterly* 35 (October 1973): 429–40.

7. For background, see Thomas R. Preston, "Biblical Criticism, Literature, and the Eighteenth-Century Reader," in *Books and Their Readers in Eighteenth-Century England,* ed. Isabel Rivers (New York: St. Martin's Press and Leicester University Press, 1982), 97–126.

8. Prickett, 112.

9. This European dimension of Lowth has been explored by Friedrich Meinecke, Isaiah Berlin, Elizabeth Shaffer, and Ina Lipkowitz (Columbia University Dissertation); cf. Prickett, 106, 110.

10. Prickett: "To Lowth we owe the rediscovery of the Bible as a work of literature within the context of ancient Hebrew life" (105).

11. Kugel, 274–86

12. Weinbrot, 459.

13. Prickett, 116, in his chapter "The Language of the Great Code"; derived, it seems, from Prickett's work is John C. Villalobos, "A Possible Source for William Blake's 'The Great Code of Art,' " *English Language Notes* 26 (September 1988): 36–40. For Lowth's impact, pertinent scholarship includes Prickett, 105–23; Murray Roston, *Poet and Prophet: The Bible and the Growth of Romanticism* (London: Faber & Faber, 1965); Rolf Lessenich, *Dichtungsgeschmack und althebräische Bibelpoesie im 18. Jahrhundert* (Köln und Graz: Böhlau, 1967), and *Aspects of English Preromanticism* (Cologne and Graz: Böhlau, 1989), 150; and Vincent Freimarck, introduction to Lowth's *Lectures* (Hildesheim: Georg Olms, 1969 [rpt. of trans. by G[eorge]. Gregory, 2 vols. (St. Paul's Church Yard: J. Johnson, 1787)]), "The Bible and Neo-Classical Views of Style," *JEGP* 51 (1952): 507–26, and "The Bible in Eighteenth-Century Criticism" (Cornell University Dissertation, 1950). See also, these dissertations: Robert Paul Fitzgerald, "The Place of Robert Lowth's *De Sacra Poesi . . .* in Eighteenth-Century Criticism" (State University of Iowa Dissertation, 1964); Ina Lipkowitz, "Romanticism and Biblical Poetics" (Columbia University Dissertation, 1991), Chapter 1, "A Romantic Bible: Robert Lowth and Johann Gottfried Herder," contains useful points; Patricia Anne Collaton Downs, "Praise and Prophecy: Christopher Smart and the Visionary Sublime" (York University Dissertation, 1992), yokes Lowth and Smart. The high ratio of excellent dissertation work to actual publications indicates the difficulty of interesting a wider secular audience in Lowth. That these dissertations are not oriented to religious doctrine but are themselves secular, aesthetic, and critical supports this conjecture.

14. Gay Wilson Allen, "Biblical Analogies for Walt Whitman's Prosody," *Revue Anglo-Americaine* 10 (August 1933): 490–507. See also his chapter on Whitman's prosody in *American Prosody* (New York: American Book Co., 1935), 217–43; and *The New Walt Whitman Handbook* (New York: New York University Press, 1975), 215–24, 347. In a note unpublished in his lifetime, Whitman counted the number of words in the Bible, the works of William Cowper, and his own. James Perrin Warren, " 'The Free Growth of Metrical Laws': Syntactic Parallelism in 'Song of Myself,' " *Style* 18 (1984): 27–41; *Walt Whitman's Language Experiment* (University Park: Pennsylvania State University Press, 1990), 72–73. Allen, *New Handbook*, viii.

15. Calvin E. Stowe, ed., *Lectures on the Sacred Poetry of the Hebrews* (Andover: Flagg and Gould, 1829). Prickett, 42, 109, 114; Richard Gravil, " 'The Discharged Soldier' and 'the Runaway Slave': Wordsworth and the Definition of Walt Whitman," *Symbiosis* 1 (April 1997): 48–66; Prickett discusses Lowth and *The Prelude* in *Words* and in " 'Types and Symbols of Eternity': The Poet as Prophet," *Working Papers of the Minnesota Center for Advanced Studies in Language, Style, and Literary Theory* 1 (Spring 1981): 19–35; Robert D. Weisbuch, *Atlantic Double Cross: American Literature and British Influence in the Age of Emerson* (Chicago: University of Chicago Press, 1986), and Gravil link Wordsworth, Whitman, and Blair (though not Lowth). A case exists for links between Lowth, Whitman, and poets familiar to Whitman—Macpherson, Cowper, Blake, and Coleridge. For Emerson, see Robert D. Richardson, Jr., *Emerson: The Mind on Fire* (Berkeley: University of California Press, 1995), 11–14.

16. Prickett, 41,119, 110.

17. Gibbon, *Miscellaneous Works*, vol. 3 (1815), 579.

18. Kugel, 210; Preston, 112; Kugel, 274–86.

19. See James Engell, "The New Rhetoricians" and "What is Poetry?" in *Forming the Critical Mind: Dryden to Coleridge* (Cambridge: Harvard University Press, 1989), 194–249; for comparative treatment, with an eye to ongoing practice, see Claudio Guillén, "On the Uses of Monistic Theories: Parallelism in Poetry," *NLH* 18 (1986–87): 497–516, 500.

20. Sailendra Kumar Sen, "The First Imagery Critic, Robert Lowth," *N&Q* 30 (228) (February 1983): 1, 55–58.

21. Scott Harshbarger, "Robert Lowth's *Sacred Hebrew Poetry* and the Oral Dimension of Romantic Rhetoric," in *Rhetorical Traditions and British Romantic Literature,* eds. Don H. Bialostosky and Lawrence D. Needham (Bloomington: Indiana University Press, 1995), 199–214. Harshbarger comments helpfully on relations between Lowth's and Blair's *Lectures* and Romantic writers who read them (208–9). John Engell provided the observation about Cooper's interest in oral culture.

22. Lowth on the sublime is mentioned by some earlier scholars: Samuel Holt Monk, *The Sublime: A Study of Critical Theories in Eighteenth-Century England* (Ann Arbor: University of Michigan Press, 1935 [repr. 1960]), 77–83; Vincent Freimarck (see n. 13 above); Martin Price, *To the Palace of Wisdom: Studies in Order and Energy from Dryden to Blake* (Garden City: Doubleday, 1964 [Carbondale: University of Southern Illinois, 1970]), 370; and briefly Prickett, 108–9.

23. Kugel, 278–81, 279.

24. Hans-Georg Gadamer, *Truth and Method* (New York: Seabury Press, 1975), 67, emphasis added.

25. Coleridge, *The Statesman's Manual,* in *Lay Sermons,* ed. R. J. White in *The Collected Works of . . . Coleridge* (London and Princeton: Routledge & Kegan Paul and Princeton University Press, 1972), 28–30; see also 79 and n.

26. Anthony John Harding (*Coleridge and the Inspired Word* [Kingston and Montreal: McGill-Queens University Press, 1985]), argues that "The distinctively biblical quality of Coleridge's idea of the Imagination"—and by extension of the symbol—"derives from this understanding of the Old Testament as true history" (77–78); Prickett (43–44, 117–18) recognizes the context of Coleridge's discussion; for Coleridge and Lowth, see Engell, *Forming the Critical Mind,* 95. Ina Lipkowitz ("Inspiration and the Poetic Imagination: Samuel Taylor Coleridge," *SiR* 30 [Winter 1991]: 605–27) ties Coleridge's remarks on symbol and allegory, and his general avoidance of typology, to his interest in biblical interpretation; see also J. Robert Barth, S.J., *The Symbolic Imagination: Coleridge and the Romantic Tradition* (Princeton: Princeton University Press, 1977).

27. Paul de Man, "The Rhetoric of Temporality," in *Interpretation: Theory and Practice,* ed. Charles Singleton (Baltimore: Johns Hopkins University Press, 1969); for a detailed comparative overview, see Tzvetan Todorov, *Theories of the Symbol,* trans. Catherine Porter (Ithaca: Cornell University Press, 1982). A strong reply to de Man is Thomas McFarland, "Involute and Symbol in the Romantic Imagination" in *Coleridge, Keats, and the Imagination: Romanticism and Adam's Dream,* eds. J. Robert Barth, S.J., and John L. Mahoney (Columbia: University of Missouri Press, 1990), 29–57, esp. 29–37. Like Barth and Harding, McFarland pinpoints the context: "Coleridge . . . in the famous distinction between symbol and allegory . . . is referring not to literary theory, as a noncontextual reading might suggest, but to religious faith" (41). He is referring also to history. Another riposte to de Man that recognizes the context of Coleridge's definition is Denis Donohue, *The Practice of Reading* (New Haven: Yale University Press, 1998), 124–27.

28. Nicholas Halmi, "From Hierarchy to Opposition: Allegory and the Sublime," *Comparative Literature* 44 (Fall 1992): 337–60, 346 n; Prickett, 105.

29. *The Collected Letters of Samuel Taylor Coleridge,* ed. Earl Leslie Griggs, 6 vols. (Oxford: Clarendon Press, 1956–71), 2: 866.

30. Preston, 98, 123 n. 4; see also 97, 99–102, 121–22.

Notes to Chapter 9: Lincoln's Language, and Ours

1. Parenthetical references are to *Abraham Lincoln, Speeches and Writings,* ed. Don E. Fehrenbacher, 2 vols., *1832–1858* and *1859–1865* (New York: Literary Classics of the United States, The Library of America, 1989). The standard edition remains *The Collected Works of Abraham Lincoln,* ed. Roy P. Basler, 9 vols. (Springfield, Ill., and New Brunswick, N.J.: The Abraham Lincoln Association and Rutgers

University Press, 1953–55), with supp. vol. (Westport, Conn.: Greenwood Press, 1974), and supp. vol. with Christian O. Basler (New Brunswick: Rutgers University Press, 1990).

2. Quoted in Andrew Delbanco ed., *The Portable Abraham Lincoln* (New York: Viking, 1992), xv; his excellent one-volume selection contains a perceptive introduction.

3. James M. McPherson ("How Lincoln Won the War with Metaphors," *Abraham Lincoln and the Second American Revolution* [New York: Oxford University Press, 1990], 93–112) treats Lincoln's "skill in the use of figurative language" (95) and for it gives the usual explanation: rural life and lack of schooling rather than attention to texts and precepts. But, as McPherson points out in a subsequent chapter, quoting Lincoln's law partner William Herndon, Lincoln "thought slowly and acted slowly"; he worked "exhaustively" (114). I stress that Lincoln composes prose this way. The title of McPherson's book implies the process outlined at the start of the present essay; Edmund Wilson, "Abraham Lincoln: The Union as Religious Mysticism" in *Eight Essays* (Garden City: Doubleday, 1954), 181–202; 182, for the quotation. Wilson's two phrases later quoted are from this essay (188).

While tending to separate Lincoln the public, often extemporaneous orator from Lincoln the literary stylist—the two are complementary—Waldo W. Braden's *Abraham Lincoln, Public Speaker* (Baton Rouge: Louisiana State University Press, 1988) provides valuable information; Herbert Joseph Edwards and John Erskine Hankins ("Lincoln the Writer: The Development of His Literary Style," *University of Maine Bulletin* 64 [April 10, 1962], in the University of Maine Series, 2d ser., no. 76 [Orono]) offer sound comments. Paul M. Angle, "Lincoln's Power with Words," *Abraham Lincoln Association Papers* (Springfield, 1935): 59–87, while appreciative, relies on "hidden laws" of genius and underestimates Lincoln's study, reading, and conscious application.

4. Jerry Sanders of the operations department of the Lincoln Boyhood National Memorial, Lincoln City, Indiana, provided information for this section. David C. Mearns, "Mr. Lincoln and the Books He Read," in *Three Presidents and Their Books: Jefferson, Lincoln, Franklin D. Roosevelt* (University of Illinois Press, 1955). For general discussion, see David Herbert Donald, *Lincoln* (New York: Simon & Schuster, 1995), 28–32, 46–49.

5. Harry S. Truman, "On Reading," Post-Presidential Files, Desk File, Box 3; see *The Autobiography of Harry S. Truman*, ed. Robert H. Ferrell (Niwot: University of Colorado Press, 1980), 115.

6. For the Scottish New Rhetoricians and their importance in creating a new, less-ornate style, see James Engell, "The New Rhetoricians," in *Forming the Critical Mind* (Cambridge: Harvard University Press, 1989), 194–219. First published in *Psychology and Literature in the Eighteenth Century*, ed. Christopher Fox (New York: AMS Press, 1987), 277–302; revised in *Rhetorical Traditions and British Romantic Literature*, eds. Don H. Bialostosky and Lawrence D. Needham (Bloomington: Indiana University Press, 1994), 217–32.

7. Chauncey M. Depew, *My Memories of Eighty Years* (New York: C. Scribner's Sons, 1922), 57–58.

8. Lindley Murray (1745–1816?), *The English Reader,* enjoyed numerous editions, many held at the Gutman Library American textbook collection, School of Education, Harvard University. I concentrated on the 1811 Poughkeepsie and 1815 Burlington, Vt., editions.

9. Mearns (see n. 4 above), 51.

10. Douglas L. Wilson, "What Jefferson and Lincoln Read," *The Atlantic Monthly* (January 1991): 51–62. Wilson, *Honor's Voice: The Transformation of Abraham Lincoln* (New York: Knopf, 1998), 61, 57, 106. Chapter 2, "Self-Education," is especially germane. "Honor's Voice" is a phrase from Gray's "Elegy," one of Lincoln's favorite poems.

11. Mearns, 58–59.

12. See Don E. Fehrenbacher, *The Dred Scott Case: Its Significance in American Law and Politics* (New York: Oxford University Press, 1978).

13. *DAB*. The Trumbull family, originally "Trumble," emigrated to Roxbury, Mass., in 1639, and it is possible that this reminded Lincoln of his ancestors arriving in Massachusetts near that time. For the Hallecks, see Nelson Frederick Adkins, *Fitz-Greene Halleck, An Early Knickerbocker Wit and Poet* (New

Haven: Yale University Press, 1930), and E. A. Duyckinck, ed., *Memoirs of Fitz-Greene Halleck* (1877). Wilson's study, *The Life and Letters of Fitz-Greene Halleck* (New York: D. Appleton), cites a letter of Halleck's in which the poet mentions Lincoln's reading habits. Wilson notes how closely Halleck associated himself with Byron, Scott, Southey, Irving, and Cooper—and that he met Coleridge. Wilson quotes Johnson's phrase about the "well of English undefiled" with regard to *"English"* and specifically not *"American Literature"*: As did many Americans then, Wilson thought the two literatures should be regarded as one (251, 263, 264). Despite his cross-cultural importance—or perhaps because of it, given the rise of exclusively American studies since the 1940s—Halleck has silently slipped from the American canon.

    14. David Herbert Donald, "The Making of the President, 1860," *Harvard Magazine* (November/December 1995): 55–57; 57, for the quotation; Douglas L. Wilson, "What Jefferson and Lincoln Read," 57.

    15. Garry Wills, *Lincoln at Gettysburg: The Words That Remade America* (New York: Simon & Schuster, 1992), 160. Giving the place and date of Blair's *Lectures* (Edinburgh, 1783), only Wills's reference note (288 n. 9) implies a British origin; Lord Curzon is cited by Angle (n. 3 above, 60 n) from William Barton's *Lincoln at Gettysburg* (1930).

Notes to Chapter 10: Recommitment

    1. Jay Fliegelman, *Declaring Independence: Jefferson, Natural Language, and the Culture of Performance* (Stanford: Stanford University Press, 1993), 2–3, 6–7, 26–27, 96–97, 119. Morgan Library, New York City, GLC 5302.

    2. Warren Guthrie, "The Development of Rhetorical Theory in America, 1635–1850," *Speech Monographs* 15: 1 (1948): 61–71; 16: 1 (1949): 98–113; 18: 1 (1951): 17–30. Guthrie's detailed study also addresses at length British rhetoric, necessary because of its overlap with and influence on American rhetoric.

    3. Edmund Wilson, "Abraham Lincoln: The Union as Religious Mysticism," in *Eight Essays* (Garden City: Doubleday, 1954), 187.

    4. Jay Heinrichs, "How Harvard Destroyed Rhetoric," *Harvard Magazine* (July/August 1995): 37–42.

    5. Alison Schneider, "Bad Blood in the English Department: The Rift Between Composition and Literature," *Chronicle of Higher Education* (February 13, 1998): A14–15.

    6. Lincoln, *Speeches and Writings* (see chap. 9), 2: 3–11.

    7. Edward P. J. Corbett, Maureen Dowd, Richard Lanham, Walter Nash, Robert Reich, William Safire, Robert Scholes, and Garry Wills constitute a limited list.

    8. Reported in *Vogue* (August 1990): 209.

    9. Quoted by Maureen Dowd, "The Language Thing," *The New York Times Magazine* (July 29, 1990): 32.

Index

Adams, John, 160
Adams, John Quincy, 8, 164
Addison, Joseph, 6, 43, 126, 135, 143, 146–47, 158
Adorno, Theodor, 64
Aesop, 147
Akenside, Mark, 146
Alcibiades, 45
Alexander the Great, 95
Alexander, Lamar, 171
Allen, Gay Wilson, 124
Alter, Robert, 121, 125–26
Amin, Idi, 19
Angleton, James Jesus, 56
Arbuthnot, John, 51
Aristotle, 3, 22, 93
Arnold, Matthew, 30, 90, 120, 125, 127, 170
Atterbury, Francis, 58, 61
Augustus, 41, 45, 47, 115–16
Auld, Hugh and Sophia, 10
Austen, Jane, 92, 168
Ayre, William, 33, 43–44

Barbauld, Anna Laetitia, 168
Bacon, Sir Francis, 60, 73, 82, 84, 88, 90, 92
Barlow, Joel, 35, 38, 47, 179
Barthes, Roland, 100
Basler, Roy, 142–43, 166
Bate, W. J., 143
Bathurst, Allen, first Earl of, 44, 102, 106, 112
Beattie, James, 8, 128–29, 145
Bedford, Francis Russell, fifth Duke of, 27

Belsey, Catherine, 89
Benjamin, Walter, 138
Berkeley, Bishop George, 64
Berlin, Sir Isaiah, 79, 126
Berry, Phyllis, 59
Bingham, Caleb, 164
Bismarck, Prince Otto von, 21
Bixby, Lydia, 154–55
Blackstone, Sir William, 148, 149, 165
Blackwell, Anthony, 128
Blair, Hugh, 6, 8, 124, 125, 128, 130, 132, 137, 145, 160, 164
Blake, William, 6, 18, 21, 25, 27–28, 48, 121, 123–24, 133, 137
Blakemore, Stephen, 177
Bloom, Allan, 52
Blunt, Sir John, 106, 107, 116
Boccage, Madame du, 58
Bolingbroke, Henry St. John, first Viscount, 42–43, 104
Bond, Denis, 107–8, 113
Boniface, Saint, 28
Boone, Daniel, 52
Booth, Wayne, 172
Borgia family, 58
Boswell, Alexander, Lord Auchinleck, 66
Boswell, James, 66, 143
Bottorff, William K., 38–40, 49, 179
Bouhours, Dominique, 67
Bowen, Elizabeth, 56
Bowen, H. V., 186
Bowers, Fredson, 56

Bowles, William Lisle, 157
Box, Mark, 66, 78, 183
Bradbury, Malcolm, 62
Braudel, Fernand, 102, 104–7, 112, 116, 186
Brennan, William, 7
Brockman, J. M., 148
Brooks, Cleanth, 130
Brown, Norman O., 53
Brown, Paula, 78
Browning, Reed, 177–78
Bruner, Jerome, 5, 83, 86–89, 91–92
Buckingham, George Villiers, fifth Duke of, 44
Burke, Edmund, 2, 4–7, 15–32, 33–36, 48, 63, 66, 69, 94, 121, 133–34, 139, 143, 145, 148, 150, 154, 165, 168
Burney, Frances, 168
Burns, Robert, 140, 145, 147, 152
Burr, Aaron, 19
Bush, George, 171–72
Butler, Samuel, 128
Buxtorf, Johannes II, 128
Byatt, A. S., 62
Byron, George Gordon Noel, sixth Baron, 61, 152, 192

Cagney, James, 57
Campbell, George, 8, 61, 64, 128, 164
Campbell, Joseph, 91
Campbell, Thomas, 152
Carlyle, Thomas, 156
Carson, Rachel, 5
Carter, Elizabeth, 168
Ceauşescu, Nicolae, 19
Chamberlain, Joshua Lawrence, 169
Chambers, Robert, 148, 169
Chandos, James Brydges, first Duke of, 44
Channing, Edward T., 164–65
Chapman, Gerald, 29
Charles II, 47
Chase, Cynthia, 132
Chateaubriand, F. R., 124
Cheney, J. V., 165
Cheney, Lynne, 73–74
Chesterfield, Philip Dormer Stanhope, fourth Earl of, 58
Cheyne, George, 34
Churchill, Winston, 7, 22, 94, 164
Cibber, Theophilus 42–43
Cincinnatus, 28, 47
Clap, Thomas, 47

Clifford, James, 143
Cobban, Alfred, 26
Coleridge, Samuel Taylor, 2, 6, 9, 16, 18, 22–23, 26, 28, 52, 64, 87, 89–90, 102, 121, 124, 132–33, 135–39, 145, 167, 172, 178, 192
Connecticut Wits, The, 5, 38, 40, 46–49, 151, 165, 179
Cooper, Reverend Mr., 146
Cooper, James Fenimore, 130, 192
Corneille, Pierre, 68
Courthope, W. J., 105
Cowper, William, 123, 146–47
Crane, R. S., 9
Croghan, Martin, 53
Culler, Jonathan, 100
Curll, Edmund. *See* Ayre, William
Curzon, George Nathaniel, first Baron and first Marquis, 160

Daggett, David, 39
Damrosch, Leo (Leopold, Jr.), 183
Dana, Richard Henry, 165
Dante, Alighieri, 34, 94
D'Auberteul, Michel René Hilliard, 46
David, 123, 136
Davies, Robertson, 62
Day, Henry N., 164
Defoe, Daniel, 6
de Man, Paul, 100, 137–38, 190
Dennis, John, 126
Depew, Chauncey, 145
DeQuincey, Thomas, 16
Derrida, Jacques, 65, 71, 100
Descartes, René, 95
Dickinson, Emily, 92
Dickinson, John, 151
Dilthey, Wilhelm, 88
Dilworth, Thomas, 146
Dilworth, W. H., 44
Dixon, Peter, 107
Dior, Christian, 172
Domitian, 58
Donald, David H., 143
Doolittle, Hilda (H. D.), 56
Douglas, Stephen A., 4, 142, 149, 154, 160
Douglas, Stephen H., 151
Douglass, Frederick, 7, 10, 13, 141, 143, 151, 164
Dowling, William C., 38, 179
Dryden, John, 43, 47–48, 105, 122
Dwight, Timothy, 48

Eco, Umberto, 101
Eddy, William, 53
Edgeworth, Maria, 168
Edwards, John, 128
Edwards, Jonathan, 9
Eichhorn, Johann Gottfried, 122, 128, 137
Eliade, Mircea, 140
Eliot, T. S., 56, 97, 125
Ellmann, Richard, 56
Elwin, Whitwell, 105
Emerson, Ralph Waldo, 86, 88, 102, 124–26, 165–66
Empson, William, 56, 88, 139
Engell, John, 190
Evans, Gwynne Blakemore, 56
Everett, Edward, 9, 125
Ezekiel, 17, 136

Faulkner, John, 176
Fichte, Johann Gottlieb, 140
Fletcher, John, 126
Fontenelle, Bernard Le Bovier de, 67
Foote, Shelby, 142
Forster, E. M., 56
Foucault, Michel, 92
Fox, Charles James, 35, 143
Franklin, Benjamin, 17, 143
Freud, Sigmund, 53, 172
Frye, Northrop, 88, 91, 140

Gadamer, Hans-Georg, 88, 122, 136
Galileo, 95
Gassendi, Pierre, 67
Gay, John, 40, 51, 53, 58, 146
George I, 58, 109
George II, 4, 44, 58, 110, 115–16
George III, 16
Gibbon, Edward, 6, 34, 115, 126
Gibbons, Thomas, 133
Gillray, James, 28
Goldsmith, Oliver, 66, 146
Goldsmith, Steven, 125
Goethe, Johann Wolfgang von, 105
Grant, Alexander, 187
Grant, Ulysses, 169
Graubard, Stephen, 16
Gray, Thomas, 24, 146–47
Greene, Graham, 56
Greene, Nathaniel, 36
Gregory, George, 120

Grey, Sir Edward, 26
Griffin, Dustin, 57
Grotius, Hugo, 95, 128
Guillén, Claudio, 129
Guthrie, Warren, 192
Gyllenborg, Count Carl, 58

Habermas, Jürgen, 74, 167
Hackett, James H., 9
Halleck, Fitz-Greene, 152, 192
Halleck, Henry W., 152
Halleck, Peter, 152
Halmi, Nicholas, 138
Hamann, Johann Georg, 79, 128
Hammond, Brean, 61
Hand, Learned, 7
Hanks, Dennis, 147
Hardt, Hermann van der, 131
Hardy, Thomas, 125
Harris, James, 145
Hartford Wits, The, 151. *See also* Connecticut Wits
Hartman, Geoffrey, 132
Hastings, Warren, 27, 31–32
Hathaway, Henry, 56
Havel, Vaclav, 171–72
Hazlitt, William, 16, 26, 60, 167
H. D. *See* Doolittle, Hilda
Hegel, G. W. F., 89, 133, 138
Henry VIII, 43
Henry, Alexander, 150
Henry, Patrick, 150, 156, 164
Herder, Johann Gottfried, 121–22, 128
Herndon, William, 147
Heron, Robert, 26
Herrick, Robert, 151
Hill, Anita, 59
Hobbes, Thomas, 66, 89, 167
Hogarth, William, 9
Holmes, Oliver Wendell, 114, 165
Home, Henry. *See* Kames
Homer, 123, 126
Hood, Thomas the elder, 147
Hopkins, Gerard Manley, 124
Hopkins, John, 108, 114
Hopkins, Dr. Lemuel, 35
Horace, 44–46, 100–101, 122, 165
Horkheimer, Max, 64
Howard, Leon, 38, 39, 40, 47
Howells, William Dean, 165

Hume, David, 4–6, 21, 43, 63–80, 81, 104, 140, 146
Humphreys, David, 35–36, 38–39
Hutcheson, Francis, 66
Huxley, Aldous, 16, 173

Irving, Washington, 192
Isaiah, 17, 24, 26

Jackson, Andrew, 8–9
Jacobi, Friedrich Heinrich, 79
Jakobson, Roman, 129, 139
James, Henry, 92
James, William, 86, 88, 139
Jefferson, Thomas, 7, 63, 70, 143, 147–48, 150–53, 156, 160, 164–65
Jensen, Merrill, 39–40
Job, 137
Johnson, Barbara, 132
Johnson, Joseph, 124
Johnson, Samuel, 6, 9, 16, 22, 34, 41, 52, 63–64, 66, 68, 77–78, 94, 109, 113, 120, 126, 143, 145–48, 150, 152, 166, 168–69
Jones, Peter, 68
Joyce, James, 97
Juvenal, 24, 46, 109, 113–15

Kames, Henry Home, Lord, 164, 168
Kant, Immanuel, 6, 68, 70, 74, 78–79, 89, 121, 133–35, 139–40
Keats, John, 25, 79
Kennedy, John F., 141
Kierkegaard, Soren, 93
King, Martin Luther, Jr., 7, 94, 141, 156, 164
Kircher, Athanasius, 61
Kirkham, Samuel, 146
Kissinger, Henry, 56
Klein, Jürgen, 176
Knox, Vicesimus, 45
Knox, William, 147, 152
Koppel, Ted, 170, 173
Korshin, Paul, 54
Kristeva, Julia, 100
Krutch, Joseph Wood, 143
Kugel, James, 125–26, 134–35
Kyrle, John, 97, 109, 112, 114

Lamon, Ward, 9
Lamartine, Alphonse de, 124
Landor, Walter Savage, 165

Lauderdale, James Maitland, eighth Earl of, 27
Law, John, 116
Leavis, Queenie, 9
Lee, Robert E., 158
Lee, Sophia, 168
Leibniz, Baron Gottfried Wilhelm von, 89
Lennox, Charlotte, 168
Lessing, G. E., 90
Lévi-Strauss, Claude, 85, 88
Lincoln, Abraham, 2–4, 6–9, 13, 26, 29, 94, 109, 141–61, 164–70, 172, 174
Lipkowitz, Ina, 126
Llandaff, Richard Watson, Bishop of, 21
Lock, F. P., 58
Locke, John, 64, 67, 87–88, 101, 116
Lodge, David, 62, 170
Longinus, 76, 133–34, 139
Lowes, John Livingston, 131
Lowth, Robert, 4, 6, 8, 21, 24, 116, 119–40, 160, 164–65, 169
Lowth, William, 128
Lukin, Henry, 128
Lully, Raimund, 61

McCarthy, Joseph, 59
Macaulay, Thomas Babington, 2
McConnell, Mitch, 99
MacDonald, James Ramsay, 187
McHenry, Henry, 147
Macpherson, James, 123–24, 164
McPherson, James M., 191
McWherter, Ned R., 171
Mack, Maynard, 43, 104, 111
Madison, James, 148, 160
Mali, Joseph, 85
Manley, John Mathews, 57
Mansfield, Harvey, Jr., 176
Marlowe, Christopher, 89
Marshall, David, 182
Martin, Marie, 67
Marx, Karl, 86
Massinger, Philip, 104
Meade, George Gordon, 158
Mearns, David C., 146
Meibomius, Marc, 128
Meyer, Johann Friedrich von, 128
Michaelis, Johann David, 121–22, 128
Michelangelo, 172–73
Milton, John, 3, 5, 7, 24–28, 34, 43, 70, 165
Monroe, James, 160

Moore, Tom, 2
More, Hannah, 168
Mossner, Ernest Campbell, 66
Murray, Lindley, 6, 145–47, 151–52, 160

Napoleon, 20
Nero, 58
Nevins, Allan, 141
New Rhetoricians, The, 132–33, 145, 148, 160, 164
Nietzsche, Friedrich, 93
Norris, Christopher, 89
Norton, David Fate, 182

O'Brien, Conor Cruise, 176
Octavian. *See* Augustus
Orwell, George, 7, 16, 53
Owen, Wilfred, 7

Paine, Thomas, 150, 165–66
Parker, Theodore, 153
Parkman, Francis, 165
Pascal, Blaise, 67
Patey, Douglas Lane, 53
Paul, Saint, 24, 104
Pearson, Norman Holmes, 56
Pease, Thomas H., 49
Percival, James, 157
Persius (Aulus Persius Flaccus), 46
Philby, Kim, 56
Phillips, Charles, 152
Pindar, 123
Plato, 17, 94
Pol Pot, 19
Pons, Alain, 89
Pope, Alexander, 2, 4–6, 8–9, 24, 32–49, 51, 58–60, 68, 93, 97, 99–116, 122, 146–47, 151, 165, 174
Popkin, Richard, 67, 183
Potkay, Adam, 70–71
Pound, Ezra, 56
Preston, Thomas, 140
Prickett, Stephen, 120–21, 125–26, 138
Priestley, Joseph, 4, 128, 167
Prior, Matthew, 146
Probyn, Clive, 53
Purcell, Edward, 90

Quintana, Ricardo, 53

Radcliffe, Ann, 154
Ramsay, Allan, 72
Ramsay, David, 143
Rawson, Claude, 61, 177
Reagan, Ronald, 16, 156
Reischauer, Edwin, 56
Rembrandt, 172
Reynolds, Sir Joshua, 90, 168
Richards, I. A., 67, 69, 88, 130
Richardson, Samuel, 34
Richardson, William, 168
Richetti, John, 78–79
Rickert, Edith, 57
Richmond, Charles Lennox, third Duke of, 17
Ricoeur, Paul, 88
Riffaterre, Michael, 100
Riggs, Luther, 49
Robertson, William, 6, 146
Roosevelt, Eleanor, 7
Roosevelt, Franklin D., 156, 164
Roosevelt, Theodore, 164
Rorty, Richard, 74, 87
Roscommon, Wentworth Dillon, fourth Earl of, 101
Rosenmueller, Ernst Friedrich Karl, 128
Ross, Man of. *See* Kyrle, John
Roston, Murray, 125–26
Rousseau, Jean-Jacques, 86
Rowlandson, Thomas, 9
Ruffhead, Owen, 42, 44
Ruskin, John, 132, 165
Rymer, Thomas, 68

Sainte-Beuve, Charles Augustin, 76
Sandburg, Carl, 143
Sartre, Jean-Paul, 4
Saussure, Ferdinand de, 101
Schleiermacher, Friedrich, 139
Schoettgen, Christian, 128
Scott, Dred (Supreme Court decision), 150
Scott, Sir Walter, 152, 192
Scott, William, 143, 145–47, 152
Searle, John, 75–76
Sen, Sailendra Kumar, 130
Shaffer, Elizabeth, 126
Shaftesbury, Anthony Ashley Cooper, third Earl of, 66, 139
Shakespeare, William, 3, 6, 9, 24, 26, 78, 92, 132, 143, 148–49, 151, 165, 168
Shelley, Percy Bysshe, 83, 88, 92, 124

Sheridan, Frances, 143
Sheridan, Richard Brinsley, 9, 13, 35, 143, 164
Sheridan, Thomas, 13, 143, 145, 152, 164
Sherburn, George, 60
Sherman, Roger, 39–40, 49
Shiels, Robert, 42–43
Sibley, Agnes, 48
Sidney, Sir Philip, 123, 170
Sinclair, Upton, 5
Sisera, 28
Smart, Christopher, 123–24
Smith, Adam, 4, 8, 89, 105–6, 128–29, 145, 167
Smith, Wilfred Cantwell, 87
Smollett, Tobias, 40–41, 43
Socrates, 45
Solomon, 136
Solon, 165
Somerville, Thomas, 19
Sotheby, William, 138
Sophocles, 26
Southey, Robert, 152, 167
Specter, Arlen, 59
Spence, Joseph, 120
Stanton, Edwin, 141
Steele, Sir Richard, 6, 143, 158
Stevens, Wallace, 91
Stockdale, Percival, 44–45, 180
Stowe, Calvin E., 124, 169
Stowe, Harriet Beecher, 124, 169
Swift, Jonathan, 2, 4–5, 22, 34, 36, 40–43, 49,
    51–62, 174

Taney, Roger B., 150
Temple, Sir William, 44
Thomas, Clarence, 59
Thomson, James, 146
Thoreau, Henry David, 165
Thrale, Hester Lynch, 147
Tillotson, Geoffrey, 146
Tippett, Brian, 53
Todorov, Tzvetan, 74
Tonson, Jacob, 109
Truman, Harry S., 143
Trumbull, John, 35, 47, 151–52
Trumbull, Lyman, 151
Tutu, Desmond, 31
Twain, Mark, 142, 145

Van Gogh, Vincent, 172
Verene, Donald P., 92, 184–85
Vico, Giambattista, 4–5, 8, 23, 29, 81–97, 165
Virgil, 24, 34, 47, 94, 104
Voltaire, 63

Wadsworth, James, 36
Wain, John, 143
Walmesley, Gilbert, 166
Walpole, Robert, 44, 46, 105, 107, 113–15, 187
Ward, John, 107
Ward, Seth, 61
Warren, James Perrin, 124
Warton, Joseph, 3, 34, 41–46, 48
Washington, George, 22, 29, 35–36, 39, 47, 94,
    142–43, 148, 150–51
Wasserman, Earl, 100, 105, 114–15
Waters, Peter, 107–8
Watson, Richard. *See* Llandaff
Watts, Isaac, 147
Webster, Daniel, 148, 153, 160
Weems, Mason Locke, 142–43
Weinbrot, Howard, 76, 113, 120, 123
Wesley, John, 9, 147
Whately, Thomas, 164, 168
Whitehead, Alfred North, 85
Whitman, Walt, 6, 26, 123–24
Wilberforce, William, 25, 164
Wilde, Oscar, 172
Wilkins, John, 57
William III, 103
Williams, Kathleen, 57
Williams, Raymond, 3, 79
Williams, William, 36
Wills, Garry, 160
Wilson, Douglas L., 143, 158
Wilson, Edmund, 142, 149, 155, 166
Wilson, James Grant, 152, 192
Witherspoon, John, 164
Wollstonecraft, Mary, 4, 22, 63, 168
Woolf, Virginia, 9, 140
Wordsworth, William, 2, 23, 25–26, 67, 82, 90,
    95, 124, 131–33, 137, 178
Wren, Sir Christopher, 114

Young, Edward, 25, 34